The History of the English Toy Theatre

Here Captain Clarence arrives with the Theatre Royal Drury Lane in miniature, and the Miller and his Men in a forward state of preparation.

THE HISTORY OF THE ENGLISH TOY THEATRE

GEORGE SPEAIGHT

Publishers PLAYS, INC. *Boston*

For Mary

Acknowledgments

Plates 2 and 9 and all the text illustrations are from sheets in the author's collection with the exception of those on pages 36 and 42 which are from the British Museum, on page 99 which is from the Enthoven Collection in the Victoria and Albert Museum and on pages 33 and 180 which are from the collection of Mr William Hobbs. The following plates were photographed by Stan Bult (plate 20); Violet Phelan (plates 14 and 15); M. Pic, Paris (plate 3); Edwin Smith (plate 16). Plates 21 and 22 were supplied by courtesy of Benjamin Pollock Ltd. All colour plates were photographed by Tony Barthorpe.

The frontispiece is from *Young Troublesome, or Master Jacky's Holidays* by John Leech, 1845

By the same author:

The History of the English Puppet Theatre

Professional and Literary Memoirs of Charles Dibdin the Younger (edited by)

© George Speaight 1946, 1969
First published under the title *Juvenile Drama: the History of the English Toy Theatre*. 1946
Revised edition 1969
First American edition published 1969 by Plays, Inc.
8 Arlington Street, Boston, Massachusetts
Library of Congress Catalog Card Number 69–13124
Published in Great Britain by Studio Vista Ltd
Blue Star House, Highgate Hill, London N 19
Printed and bound in Great Britain by
Richard Clay (The Chaucer Press) Ltd
Bungay, Suffolk

Contents

Preface

The greater part of this book was written during the last months of the Second World War while I was stationed in Ceylon waiting to be discharged from the Navy. (Let me here express my gratitude to the Senior Officer who understandingly gave permission for an 'author' to live ashore in civilian quarters during this time.) In those circumstances memories of England sprang fondly into the mind and evocations of winter firesides seemed particularly sweet; hence, no doubt, the elegiac note in which some of the text is couched. The book was published in 1946 and went out of print within a few months; in those days of paper rationing no reprint was possible, and the book has become very scarce, with second-hand copies commanding a high price. After twenty-three years a new edition will, I hope, be welcomed.

For this edition I have revised the text wherever it was necessary to correct mistakes, included new information that has subsequently come to light, and added fresh material to bring the story up to date. All the illustrations are new, as with such a rich field to choose from it seemed a pity to duplicate pictures that had already been reproduced once. But with these exceptions the book remains as I first wrote it. I might write it differently now, but that would make it a different, and not necessarily a better, book.

Many people have helped to provide corrections and additions for this new edition, to whom I extend my grateful thanks. I would particularly mention Mr Gerald Morice for his constantly watchful eye which first drew my attention to William West's hidden publications; Mrs Dodie Masterman for opening my eyes to many subtleties of draughtsmanship and engraving; Miss Sybil Rosenfeld for some valuable comparisons between scenic designs and Toy Theatre scenery; Mr D. Seaton Reid for generously sharing with me the fruits of his own careful research; Mr Louis W. Bondy for information about theatrical 'turn ups'; Mr Ifan Kyrle Fletcher for ever generous assistance; Mr Hayward Marks for his notes on Mr Pollock's printing press; Mr Gosta M. Bergman for new light on possible French origins; Mr Herbert Hinkins for opening his collection so readily to my requests; Mr Martin Holmes for his assistance at the London Museum; and Mrs Marguerite Fawdry for prodding my enthusiasm for the toy theatre whenever it showed signs of flagging. Kew Gardens 1968

6

Author's note to the first edition

'The story of an obsession' might be a suitable sub-title for this book, the preparation of which has occupied a disproportionate amount of my time and money for as long as I can remember. The active collecting of material has been going on for something like fourteen years, but I must readily acknowledge that without the help of many friends and fellow enthusiasts the result now offered to the public could have never been so complete.

First and foremost I must acknowledge the assistance I have received from Mr M. W. Stone. Mr Stone has not only given me full access to his magnificent collection of Juvenile Drama prints, and allowed me to make copious use of his own MS. notes on the history of the toy theatre, but he has also undertaken on my behalf a great deal of research in clearing up obscure points during my absence from England on active service. This book does not claim to be the last word on the Juvenile Drama, but every attempt has been made to render it a complete and definitive history of the subject, so far as the material available today will allow, and whatever merit it may possess in that respect is entirely due to Mr Stone's patient study and generous cooperation.

Next I must salute my predecessors in the field, the many journalists and writers, enthusiasts of the theatre or amateurs of the curious, who have helped to lay the foundations of a history of the toy theatre. One must especially mention Ralph Thomas, the first authority for any student of the Juvenile Drama; John Ashton, the first actual historian of the subject; C. D. Williams, for his recent studies of the later toy theatre publishers; and, most of all, A. E. Wilson, the first person to write a complete book on the subject. Although a certain duplication is unavoidable I have tried to approach the subject along quite independent lines, and I hope that readers who are already familiar with Mr Wilson's pioneer work will find enough new light on the subject here to justify another publication.

And finally I must express my thanks to a great many friends who have illuminated many an obscure point with their discoveries and their pens. To Mr Gerald Morice, for unfailing enthusiasm and encouragement, and for two fascinating 'Juvenile Drama Bulletins' prepared by him for the British Puppet Guild; to the Secretary of the British Puppet and Model Theatre Guild for permission to quote from them; to Miss Margaret Lane, and Messrs D. L.

Murray, Stanley Bult, and H. Medcraft for allowing me to reproduce extracts from what they wrote. To the collectors of the Juvenile Drama who have laid their treasures open before me, or supplemented the findings of Mr Stone, especially Mr Herbert Hinkins, Mr C. H. Green, Mr W. W. Nops, Mr J. Brady, Dr Francis Eagle, and Mr Walter Dunlo. To Mr Paul McPharlin for notes from America; to Mr Malcolm Morley for unearthing the American toy theatre; and to all the American libraries and museums which have sent me details of their collections. To Mr Edward Kersley for his fascinating discovery of Cole's *Poetical Present*; to Miss Phyllis Hartnoll for research in Birmingham; to Miss Mabel Hartley for a host of Victorian references; to Miss M. H. Dodds for tracing children at the Regency theatre; and to Mr Roland Knaster for advice on the by-ways of juvenilia. To the staff at the British Museum Print Room and Reading Room, at the Richmond Public Library, and at the Colombo Public Library. To the booksellers who have assisted me in the quests, notably Mr P. H. Muir of Elkin Mathews, Mr Lyon of the Court Book Shop, Mr David Low, Mr Kyrle Fletcher, and Messrs Sotheby & Co. To Mr Alan Keen, the first in a new line of toy theatre makers, and to Miss Louisa Pollock and Mr H. J. Webb, the last in the old.

And to all those who have assisted in the search and are not acknowledged by name, my apologies and thanks.

London—Glasgow—Bombay—Colombo   1945

Sprite

1 Origins

The pedestrian who made his way along the pavements of London at the end of the eighteenth century can have paused before no more inviting a shop window than that of the printseller. At Humphrey's in St James's, at Matthew Darly's, at Tegg's, the windows, bellying across the pavestones like a square-rigged ship under canvas, were cut into numerous small panes, behind which gesticulated and grimaced the colourful figures of the latest caricatures. It was the golden age of English popular art. The naturalistic engravings of Hogarth had given way to the expressionism of Gillray and Rowlandson, Newton and Roberts. A fantastic world peopled their prints: clergymen as thin as rakes and as fat as barrels; women's breasts and buttocks swelling beneath a neo-classical fashionable négligé; John Bull slowly stirring his old bones to indignation and anger at the menace of Boney across the Channel; purple noses, choleric faces, warts; the gross, genuine, dramatic world of English caricature.

The appeal of this essentially popular art is so immediate that one tends to ignore the means by which it has been achieved. There are, however, certain characteristics that may be said, rightly, to distinguish the genre. In the first place, every picture tells a story; the conversation piece has always been, indeed, a typically English form, and these caricatures simply carry on the tradition from Hogarth. We like to look at a picture like a scene in a play, with all the characters in position. But the caricaturists of the late eighteenth and early nineteenth centuries went a step further in this direction than Hogarth, by throwing their characters into self-evident *dramatic* postures. They stood with arms akimbo, they shook their fists, they stamped; nature had given way to the world of the theatre. And the impression of actors upon a stage is further reinforced by the layout of the prints themselves; the characters seem to be placed in one plane, and there is even a tendency to see them in profile. But above all, it was the gift of colour, in rich, vivid, flat tones that set the print shop windows on fire, and caught the eyes of all the passers-by, and held them peering through the panes at the treasures within.

These prints are intrinsically dramatic in feeling, they are even up to a point theatrical in design; but they do not portray or reflect the contemporary theatre. There are portraits of actors and actresses in plenty during the eighteenth century; delicately mezzotinted, elegantly costumed, elaborately bewigged, these head and shoulder portraits are everything except theatrical; they might as well portray a Whig statesman or a City worthy as an actor. The stage was no longer a vehicle for popular art, and popular art did not include the stage in its survey of society.

The time was soon coming, however, when the contemporary stage and the popular print were to effect a marriage, and this book is entirely concerned with the most interesting fruit of that union. Already, in 1800, there were indications of what was to come. In the windows of the printsellers, in that year, there might be seen an altogether new type of theatrical engraving; alone upon a large sheet, a woman with strange robes falling to her feet stands sideways to the imagined audience and, with a heavy gesture that one can almost see, raises a minatory and accusing arm; beneath is written the first lines of a speech, 'Hold Pizarro—hear me . . .'; all is coloured by hand, in hues richer than life. The actress is Mrs Siddons, and the play is *Pizarro*, adapted from the German of Kotzebue by Richard Brinsley Sheridan, and performed at Drury Lane in 1799. This print was drawn, etched, and published by Robert Dighton, who appears to have been the originator of the full-length coloured theatrical portrait.

Robert Dighton was born in about 1752, and in his life he united the two worlds of art and the theatre, as he studied drawing and worked as an actor. His first engravings were issued in about 1790, and by 1800 he had specialized in an individual form of full-length portrait profile; as time went on these tended to become more and more caricatures. The drawing was sometimes clumsy, and the colouring crude, but the characterization was effective. He found his subjects from among the characters and eccentrics of London, Brighton, Oxford, Cambridge, and the stage. He died in 1814.

He only published six full-length theatrical portraits: in 1794 Stephen Kemble as Hamlet, in 1799 John Kemble and Mrs Siddons in *Pizarro*, in 1800 Mr Cooke, in 1802 Mr Braham as Orlando, and in 1806 Madame Catalani in *Semiramide*. They are all in the same style, large rather sprawling figures, dramatic gestures in profile, highly coloured, essentially theatrical rather than naturalistic; they are, in fact, forerunners of a style that was to be known years later as 'twopence coloured'.

Robert Dighton had two sons, both of whom became artists. Denis Dighton, the elder, published one theatrical portrait in 1811 of Mrs H. Johnston in

Timour the Tartar; he became known as a painter of battle scenes. Richard Dighton followed closely his father's style, but his portraits, which began as caricatures, ended as profiles; he lived until 1880. There are seven theatrical portraits recorded: Mr W. Farren as Sir Peter Teazle (no date), Mr Kean as Lucius Junius (1818), Mr Liston in *Love, Law and Physic* (1819), Mr C. Kemble as Charles Surface (1821), Miss M. Tree (1821), Miss Wilson in *Arta-xerxes* (1821), and Mr Mathews at Home (1822). Richard followed his father's tradition, but by this time other influences were at work, and popular theatrical prints had found new fields to conquer and a new format to embellish.

While Robert Dighton was undoubtedly the first popular artist to produce inexpensive full-length coloured portraits of actors and actresses in their favourite rôles, there were other minor artists who began to fulfil the same need at the same time. The popularity of the theatre was growing, and there must have seemed an increasing market and a bright future for theatrical portraits. If they could be produced cheaply, and while a play was still fresh in every theatregoer's mind, they were assured of a good sale. But there were difficulties in the quick production of high-class engraved portraits, and besides, in every popular success there were perhaps three or four actors or actresses whom the public would like to see displayed in the costumes and attitudes proper to the piece; and it would take time and money to prepare portraits of them all.

There is really no mystery about what happened now; it was only a logical development. Some time round about the year 1810 somebody had the idea of printing four small theatrical portraits on a sheet, instead of one large one; to give the sheet a common interest, they were all portraits of characters from one play. The sheet would be headed, 'Characters in such-and-such a play as performed at such-and-such a theatre', and beneath each figure would be written the name of the actor and the part he was playing. No examples of these first tentative *single* sheets have survived, but their existence can, I think, safely be deduced from what preceded and what followed them; within two or three years their scope had been widened, and of the next stage there is ample documentation. It must have been soon obvious that to do a play justice, and to provide an adequate souvenir of the performance, more than four characters would have to be represented. This difficulty was overcome by sometimes printing six slightly smaller characters on a sheet, and by issuing two or three or even more sheets for each play. For instance, to quote an early example, we have two sheets inscribed 'Principal Characters in the Popular Pantomime of *The Fairy of the Oak, or Harlequin's Regatta.* As performed with unbounded applause at Astley's Amphitheatre.' The first sheet contains four small characters: Pantaloon played by Mr Usher, Servant by Mr Redishaw, Harlequin, and Clown. These sheets are described as 'Published as the Act directs. By permission of J. Astley Esq. by W. West, 13 Exeter Street, Strand, Sept. 10th, 1811.'

11

Annette in *The Maid and the Magpie*   Annette with handkerchief   Annette with basket

And why only the principal characters? Why not *all* the characters? In fact why not a complete reproduction in miniature, as it were, of the production? This would show, not only every character, but the important characters in every different costume — with and without cloak, in battle or hunting dress, and so on. It was an easy step from this to show the important characters in the different attitudes they assumed during the action of the play, kneeling, fighting, on horseback, at table, angry, or in tears.

And after the characters, why not the scenes? And so, alongside the plates of characters there also appeared plates of scenes, usually with a wing attached, all copied from and based upon the original production. The sheets were sold, normally, for a penny plain, to be coloured up at home, or for twopence already hand-coloured at the shop.

Here, then, was a complete drama in miniature. The characters could be pasted on cardboard and cut out; the scenes could be mounted and placed in a small model theatre, faced with a tasteful reproduction of the proscenium at Drury Lane; and the play could be performed all over again. What an idea for boys!

The only thing lacking was a book of words; the theatre playbook would do if necessary, but in due course special books of the play began to appear. *West's Original Juvenile Drama*, the early ones are headed, 'written and adapted to West's Theatre, Scenery and Characters, with Songs, Duets, etc., adapted to popular Airs'.

Annette with letter

Annette fainted

The Juvenile Drama was born.

Very soon the interest in the play seems to have proved greater than the interest in the actors, and the publishers no longer bothered to print the names of the actors beneath each character; but the small figures remained genuine theatrical portraits; with or without the name as a guide the faces of such popular actors as Kean, Farren, Liston, and so on, may be distinguished time and again among the plates of figures. At the same time, to meet the original demand for theatrical portraits, the publishers reverted to large single portrait plates of eminent performers.

Thus we have traced the genealogy of the toy theatre from popular theatrical portraits to what was really a form of theatrical souvenir, which, in its turn, was adapted to form an entertaining occupation for 'juveniles'; later the high quality of the early sheets declined, and, as we shall see, they became more and more a rough-and-ready toy for children. An alternative line of development, however, would trace its origin to foreign originals. A. E. Wilson suggests that the first plays were copied from German toy theatre plays. The earliest German toy theatre publishers, however, such as Gustav Kühn of Neuruppin and Winkelmann of Berlin, did not start before the 1830s and could not have influenced the English publishers. Although some of the crib sheets published at Augsburg in the eighteenth century involved figures for cutting out, I do not think that there was ever any theatrical association; the peep-shows published by Engelbrecht in the eighteenth century did have a theatrical quality, but there was never any question of cutting out or actual performances. All in all, I do not think these German publications, interesting though they are, bear any real resemblance to the purely English Regency drawings of the early Juvenile Drama sheets.

There is, however, one kind of foreign publication that may have markedly influenced the English Juvenile Drama. At the very beginning of the nineteenth century there were a number of theatrical agencies in Paris which specialized in providing, for the benefit of provincial and foreign managers, all the information needed for the production of the latest plays in the Parisian theatres. This information sometimes took the form of engraved sheets of the characters and scenery. In 1806 there were four such agencies. Agence générale des Théâtres, founded by M. Bonnet-Bonneville; Correspondance générale des Théâtres, founded by M. Larvalle-Lécouver; Café des Comédiens, directed by M. Touchard; and Correspondance des Spectacles, founded by M. Perlet. Only a handful of the sheets published by these agencies have survived, all from the house of Perlet, but even these few — as, for example, a sheet of characters and a scene for the opera *Irato* by Méhul, first performed in Paris in 1801 — show a marked similarity to the English sheets of ten years later. If these sheets did, indeed, influence the Juvenile Drama, it is, however, even more certain that the English toy theatre never began as a child's toy at all.

I am not, of course, suggesting that there is anything degrading or belittling in the fact of toy theatres in the hands of children; on the contrary, it is the crowning glory of the Juvenile Drama that it so completely conquered and occupied the nurseries. But it is important to get the sequence right and the origins clear, and it is the particular and fascinating progress of the Juvenile Drama from the theatre to the home that makes its history so intriguing and its appeal so wide. The Juvenile Drama grew out of the Adult Drama, the toy theatre was just exactly the big theatre in miniature; actors, costumes, scenery, were all faithfully copied from actual productions on the London stage, and reproduced for their miniature performance. The origin of every toy theatre play is to be found upon the living stage, and so, before considering the history of the Juvenile Drama further, it is necessary to see what that stage was like, and what kind of plays were being performed upon it.

2 The Regency and Early Victorian Theatre

The first years of the nineteenth century witnessed a profound social change sweeping across the face of England. The industrial revolution, with everything that that implies in factories and workshops, in prosperous manufacturers and teeming city slums, was reorientating the foundations of British society; the drift from the country had begun, and London was soon to be cursed as the 'great wen'. Into the towns of England there came flooding the dispossessed peasant and the hungry immigrant; the smoke that now began to issue from tall factory chimneys did not dim their quickened wits, nor did long hours at a loom or at a work-bench sap their gregarious vitality; when at last the gates opened and the workers were spilled out, at the end of a long day, upon the city pavements, they asked for, and they found, release from drudgery and an escape from monotony and grime.

There was one easy escape in drink. 'Dead drunk for a penny' was the inscription outside taverns, and the 'blue ruin' of gin was an insidious but easy path to the Nirvana of forgetfulness. Nevertheless, we must not see the life of this period in too lurid colours because it lacks the pampered amenities of our own age; these new industrial men and women were not uncouth besotted animals, but human beings, lusty with life and tingling with the sharp intelligence of the cockney. In the villages from which they had come an occasional travelling theatre or puppet show had brought long-remembered entertainment, and now they turned naturally to the theatres for recreation and respite.

London itself escaped revolutionary change; here were no factories, mills, or mines. But even in London, the centre of commerce, government, and the court, the new age was stirring; the fortunes of the English theatre were inextricably dependent upon the London stage; and the London stage was inextricably dependent upon the new and ever-growing audiences swarming

15

each dusk from workshop, warehouse, and shop. The entertainment that this new popular audience demanded was frankly escapist; they did not want philosophical debate, or smart witty dialogue; they did not want plays about the problems of contemporary life; they wanted richness, where their lives were poor; they wanted colour, where their lives were grey; they wanted excitement, where their lives were dull. The Restoration theatre had been almost entirely a court entertainment, and the galleries had been largely filled by the footmen of the gentlemen in the boxes; during the eighteenth century the London theatre had become certainly less exclusively fashionable, city merchants and their wives increasingly made up the audiences, and there were complaints of the rough elements who filled the cheaper seats, but on the whole the theatre had remained a predominantly genteel entertainment. Now the flood-gates were open, and the stage was to become for over fifty years — until in fact the music hall took its place — the undisputed popular entertainment of the day. Theatres were not, of course, abandoned by the rich or the fashionable, who, indeed, often shared the intellectual tastes of the populace, but upper-class standards of intelligence and wit (so far as any existed) were henceforth to be abandoned in favour of the popular standards of the masses.

Before we consider the drama of the period, we can with advantage place it in its setting by a short survey of the theatres and theatrical conditions of the time.

The situation in London, which was mirrored in the provinces, was over-shadowed by the dominant position of the two royal patent theatres of Covent Garden and Drury Lane; these two theatres claimed that, by a grant issued by Charles II, they were the only theatres at which plays could be performed. This claim was upheld by the courts, who allowed, however, non-dramatic entertainments to be given in other theatres — which were known as the minor theatres. This monopoly of the patent theatres was eventually abolished in 1843, and the whole history of nineteenth-century drama is bound up with the struggle of the minor theatres for the right to perform plays. In 1800 there were nine theatres regularly open in London — the two Theatres Royal, the Opera House in the Haymarket, and six minor theatres, as follows: the Theatre Royal, originally the Little Theatre as built by Samuel Foote, in the Haymarket, which had a modified licence to perform farces and light pieces; the Sans Souci, a sort of variety theatre in Leicester Square; Sadler's Wells Theatre, specializing in water spectacles; the Royal Amphitheatre, across Westminster Bridge, founded by Astley, where spectacular shows were given in a circus arena; the Royal Circus, later renamed the Surrey, in Blackfriars, which was a rival concern to Astley's Amphitheatre; and the Royalty Theatre, in Wellclose Square, which was used by Astley as a winter home for his spectacular entertainments.

By 1840 these six minor theatres had grown to about sixty. How was it that they could show such vitality, despite a law forbidding them to perform the drama? In the first place, many of the entertainments at Astley's, the Royal Circus, and Sadler's Wells could be classified as spectacles and not plays; when the law was rigidly enforced they were forbidden to have any dialogue at all in these entertainments, and changes of scene and the main outlines of the plot were conveyed by appropriately worded placards carried on to the stage, or round the arena; later the law was more or less openly flouted, but even then the spectacle was what the audience had come to see, and whatever dialogue was introduced was just enough to link together the various episodes; it was at a rehearsal of *Hamlet* at Astley's that Ducrow, who succeeded to the house, is said to have complained 'Cut the dialect and come to the 'osses.' But by no means all the entertainments given at the minor theatres were spectacles, and, indeed, if we read their playbills we find that they were constantly performing what appears to be the regular drama. This was made possible by the convenient device of the 'burletta'; the principle that opera and musical plays came outside the patent theatre's monopoly was readily admitted, and this gave a loophole through which the minor theatres could smuggle almost any play into their repertoire; provided they could play appropriate music at intervals and insert a few songs, any play could be classified as a musical piece, or burletta, and be performed unhindered. At first, in the early years of the century, it was considered necessary to rewrite the play in rhyme, and have a more or less constant musical accompaniment; but later, for some years before the patent was finally abolished, the entire prohibitive system was breaking down, and it was considered good enough to insert five songs into a play to sanction its performance at the minor theatres. This, of course, admitted anything, and even Shakespeare was played on these unhallowed stages; but in the main the minor theatres were the home of a type of entertainment that was certainly dramatic and certainly theatrical, but in which the emphasis was placed rather upon scenery, spectacular effects, and music than upon the unadulterated appeal of dramatic dialogue.

But during this time, while such shifts were being employed at the minors, what was happening at the patent theatres, the Theatre Royal of Covent Garden and Drury Lane? Here surely the drama could flourish unhindered?

The history of the patent theatres had not been a happy one. In their endeavours to confine all within their net, they had been rebuilt far too large in the 1790s; and then, after the enormous cost of building, they were always getting burnt down before they could pay for themselves. Covent Garden was burnt to the ground in 1808 and 1856; Drury Lane in 1809. Their size was enormous—Covent Garden seated over 3,000 in the audience, and any intimate style of acting was impossible; if the galleries couldn't hear what was being said on the stage they, very sensibly, threw things at the actors and shouted so that no one else could hear anything either. Under these conditions the actors were forced to adopt very broad effects, and the managers to devise spectacular shows, fine scenery, and music to carry to the extremities of the auditorium; in fact, the fare at the patent theatres became almost indistinguishable from the fare at the minor theatres! And at neither could it be said that the play was the thing.

Going to the theatre was not an idle evening's diversion, it was an expedition; performances started at 6.30 or 7 and reserved seats were only gradually introduced about the middle of the century. The programme consisted of a full-length drama, a short farce, and a pantomime; or perhaps a tragedy by one of the old authors, a burlesque, and a melodrama—always at least three items. If there were seats available spectators would come in for half price at about nine, in time for the concluding piece; the entire show seldom finished before midnight.

The most fashionable and comfortable seats were in the boxes, which extended all the way round the circles; these cost about five shillings at the best theatres. If you were an enthusiast of the drama, and went to see and not to show yourself off, you sat in the pit, which was everything on the ground floor (there were no stalls); you paid up to three shillings to sit on an unbacked bench. Above the circles were the galleries, to which you could climb for a shilling or less, and from which issued forth the low-throated rumble of applause or damnation upon which the fate of the play ultimately depended. Long runs were unknown; if a new play was well received, the management would announce it for a further performance, but these seldom extended for more than a few weeks; if the play was a success it would go into the occasional repertoire; if not—and generally—it disappeared almost overnight into the dark limbo of forgotten drama.

The stages upon which these plays were enacted had not entirely lost all marks of their Elizabethan origin. An apron stage jutted well forward of the curtain into the pit, on either side of which the line of the boxes continued right up to the proscenium opening; in place of the lowest of these boxes on either side of the stage there were two doors, leading directly upon the apron stage and in front of the proscenium curtain; the actors used these doors when necessary during the action of the play, and invariably for taking calls after it was over. Thus, the down-stage and most important part of the acting area was bound by an invariable setting of giltwork and imitation marble, no matter what the scenery of the play might be; naturalism had not yet driven convention from the British stage.

Along the front of the apron stage ran a line of footlights; at the beginning of the century these were invariably of oil, but within a few decades this was generally replaced by gas; occasionally a dancer, slipping and falling upon their unshielded flames, was seriously burnt.

Beneath this new and more brilliant illuminant, scenery was painted more brightly and made more splendid. But the old technique of the eighteenth century was at first unchanged; scenes were painted on flats—that is, canvas stretched across a light framework of wood, which were held by grooves in positions that ranged every few yards from the curtain to the extreme up-stage. These flats were built in two halves, dividing in the centre, which were slid into place from either side; 'the scene closes in' was a frequent stage direction of the period. An alternative method, which was increasingly coming into use at this time, was to paint the backcloth on a single piece of canvas, which could be rolled around a wooden spar when not required; these are known as 'bottom tumblers'. In front of the backcloth, pairs of wings were arranged, placed in grooves between it and the proscenium, to conceal the entrances and exits of the actors; normally the wings would be painted to represent the same scene as the backcloth, but there was a convention that the first wings, immediately behind the curtain, should carry on the effect of the proscenium doors and boxes by invariably representing stage pillars or curtains. The use of gas made floods, or top-lights feasible, and to shield these from the audience's view 'top-pieces' were evolved, which stretched from the top of one wing to the other, and were accordingly painted to match. Again the front top-piece represented a curtain.

Obviously, in these conditions, true realism was not obtainable. There was, however, a certain movement towards architectural realism in scene-painting, and at Covent Garden William Capon painted for John Kemble a series of vast architectural canvases, carefully studied from actual remains; but even these ambitious examples of the scene painter's art were never more than paintings; built-up scenery was almost unknown; a cottage interior would have grandfather clocks, guns, strings of onions, pictures, windows, and doors blandly painted upon the flat backcloth; only if a table, a chair, or a gun was actually used in the action of the play would it be allowed upon the scene, as it were, in the round.

As the century progressed a far more convenient way of getting unwanted scenery off the stage was perfected; the flats were 'flown' by ropes and pulleys to a vast upper region above the stage, there to hang suspended until required again. Cut-out scenes, through which vistas of receding perspectives were disclosed, could be raised or lowered in a few seconds. Later came built-up scenery and the box set, but these lie outside our period.

A special form of scene that deserves passing mention is the drop scene or act drop; this was used instead of the front curtain between the acts, and was always a highly decorated *chef d'œuvre* of the local scene painter. As its name implies, it was dropped from above—not pushed in from the sides—and before flying was introduced it would be wound around a big roller; it was sometimes of enormous weight—the drop scene and apparatus at Drury Lane weighed 800 lb.

The most elaborate form of scenic display used in the early nineteenth century was the panorama or diorama. This consisted of a view painted upon a long strip of canvas that was slowly wound across the stage; contemporary critics have left glowing accounts of Clarkson Stanfield's dioramas at Drury

PARK'S SCENES IN THE RED ROVER.   *1st Panorama.*   N°5

1 to join

London. Pub by A.PARK.17 Leonard St Finsbury.

Part of a moving panorama

Lane of such subjects as a voyage from Spithead to Gibraltar, the Niagara Falls, or a journey through Egypt.

Two types of scenic effect which could only be obtained at specially equipped theatres call for individual mention. The first is the water spectacle. Sadler's Wells Theatre, lying beside the New River, was assured of a plentiful water supply, and used it to the full in producing a series of most elaborate aquatic dramas; a receptacle for water, measuring 100 feet by 40 feet, was installed on the stage, in which mimic naval engagements of every kind were freely represented. A whole series of dramatic aquatic spectacles can be traced to this stage and to other theatres which copied its example.

The second individual effect was the equine or wild beast spectacle designed for the circus theatres at Astley's Royal Amphitheatre or the Royal Circus. These had begun by being plain circus rings, in which more or less dramatic displays were given; later, theatres grew up around them. The arrangement was that the building resembled an ordinary theatre, except that a sawdust arena took the place of the pit, and it was in this arena that the main performance on horses and animals took place; the stage proper, however, continued in use, and for the second half of the programme the arena was sometimes filled by the half-price spectators and a play was presented on the stage alone.

These 'illegitimate' dramatic spectacles met with such success, and so suited the spirit of the age, that the other theatres, both patent and minor, went to the greatest pains to emulate them and out-vied each other in introducing real live animals and such like effects upon their stages.

The costumes of the period reflect the same tendencies as the scenery. There was a desire for more magnificence and more colour, and a romantic, but not yet scientific, feeling towards period correctness. The eighteenth century had, on the whole, tended to perform all plays, whatever age or country they represented, in what was little more than a variant of the contemporary costume of the time; most of us are familiar with the bewigged Hamlets and the conventional dresses of the women in eighteenth-century theatrical prints. Now there was a general feeling that period plays should be played in period costumes, but there was as yet very little research or knowledge of the subject. The result was a field day for the imaginative costumier, who could indulge his fancy as he wished without the restrictive hand of the accurate historian on his shoulder. Costumes have probably never been so truly theatrical as they were at this time. Both Kemble and Macready, however, went to some pains in search of accuracy, and by the middle of the century Charles Kean at the Princess's Theatre was presenting Shakespeare in what were more archaeological reconstructions than dramatic productions.

And so, within these theatres, before these painted scenes, and in these imaginative costumes, what was the part the actor had to play? We have already shown that dramatic dialogue and character drawing were handicapped by the vast size of the patent theatres and by the semi-dramatic repertoire at the minor; the actor was compelled to resort to broad effects, to unmistakable displays of passion or grief or joy; he had to mouth his sentences, and drive every point home; in short, to over-act. I do not think it is for the twentieth-century critic, who attends a theatre from which every broad and 'theatrical' effect has been driven by a delicacy of character study, and in which the actors are often inaudible at the back of the circle, to criticize too harshly the heavy and bombastic style of these early nineteenth-century actors. A modern smart audience might find something amusing in their grimaces and their wide sawing gestures, but there is plenty of evidence that the audiences of their own time were thrilled and entranced by their performances. The boos and hisses that greeted the villain as he stalked across the stage were not only a commentary on the simple minds of the audience, but a tribute to the actor who so held them in his spell.

It was an age of great actors. We cannot do more than glance at the names of a few of the more famous. At the beginning of the century the legitimate stage was dominated by the Kemble family, of whom John Philip Kemble was

A horse combat from *Timour the Tartar*

the most able; he was at various times manager of both Covent Garden and
Drury Lane. He must have been a fine actor, and a producer with a real feeling
for the drama; he was a man of education and taste; but somehow he seems
to have missed the spark of genius, and there was a certain coldness and reserve in his character that would have better suited the previous century;
one of his greatest rôles was Shakespeare's Coriolanus. Undoubtedly the
greatest actor of the period was Edmund Kean; within the few years of his
tragic life he electrified the theatrical world with acting whose intensity and
fire have never been equalled before or since. To see him play, a contemporary
critic wrote, was like reading Shakespeare by flashes of lightning; but between
the peaks of emotional achievement he would mouth and strut like a fairground stroller. A later actor-manager of both Covent Garden and Drury
Lane was William Macready, who inherited the mantle of Kemble; also a fine
actor, of some taste and intelligence, he seems to have lacked both the classical austerity of Kemble and the romantic fire of Kean; his acting was more
colloquial in manner, heavier, but perhaps a little dull. About the middle of
the century Samuel Phelps, a fine, unintellectual, and essentially popular
actor, spurned the patent theatres, and produced a remarkable series of
Shakespearean and other legitimate productions at Sadler's Wells. And then
come Sir Henry Irving and the great actor-managers of the close of the century, with whom we are not concerned here.

It is really the actors of the second rank who do more to determine the
dramatic history of the age than a few supreme stars; in these the early nineteenth century is rich. We can only mention Liston, a fine comedian who was

blessed with one of those innocently humorous faces that compel laughter; Grimaldi, who developed the character of the Clown in the Harlequinade into its chief attraction, and who must have been a mimer of genius; Elliston, who managed Drury Lane for a time but abandoned it for the Surrey, which he made famous for melodramas—not really conspicuous as an actor, but a brilliant manager; and T. P. Cooke, O. Smith, Farley, Yates, and so many others, who night after night sustained melodrama after melodrama with their good and capable talents.

The actresses of the period are less remarkable. At the beginning of the century the stage was graced by Mrs Siddons, another member of the Kemble family, who was probably the finest tragic actress in the history of the British theatre; her style, however, belonged rather to the eighteenth century, and there was no one to take her place until the days of Ellen Terry. One popular performer of the early nineteenth century, however, does call for special mention: Madame Vestris was a clever actress, a charming singer, and a successful manager; in partnership with her husband, Charles Mathews, and with the assistance of the brilliant librettist J. R. Planché, she was responsible for a series of delightful extravaganzas, first at her own Olympic Theatre and later at Covent Garden and elsewhere. Their light amusing nonsense was an agreeable setting to her own 'piquante' and diverting performance. Madame Vestris was particularly fond of 'breeches parts', that is of dressing up as a man or a boy, and anyone who has studied her theatrical portraits can easily understand why she was so eager to display her shapely legs and thighs before the footlights. One may be surprised—and grateful—that the censor, who throughout all this period was extremely sensible of the least hint of impropriety, should have countenanced these delightful exhibitions without demur.

Among the other leading actresses of the period were Fanny Kemble, an exquisite and intelligent elocutionist with an instinctive aversion to the life of the theatre; Fanny Kelly, an actess of great vivacity and charm in both sentimental and comic rôles; Miss O'Neill, whose classical beauty and fine presence made her a not unworthy successor to Siddons; Madame Malibran, a fine actress as well as a great singer in both Italian and English opera; and Madame Celeste, whose versatile talents and business acumen at the Adelphi put her in the same class as Vestris.

What, then, were the plays that were performed in these settings and by these actors? The Romantic Movement, initiated by Horace Walpole and exploited by 'Monk Lewis', William Beckford and Mrs Radclyffe had already burst upon a correct and highly civilized society before the close of the eighteenth century. It left its mark upon architecture in the amusing Gothickism of Strawberry Hill and Fonthill, in the orientalism of the Chinese Pagoda at Kew Gardens and the Brighton Pavilion, and eventually in the more sober Gothic Revival of Pugin and the new House of Commons. It left its mark upon literature in the numerous 'horrific' romances of the early nineteenth century, and eventually, in the historical reconstructions of Sir Walter Scott. Upon the theatre too, romanticism ran unchecked, like one of its own many-headed dragons, giving life to every country and epoch that it touched. This was just the escapist stuff that the people wanted: colour, mystery, romance, impossible happenings in strange places—that was the recipe that every theatre manager laid before his patrons.

The original impetus of the Romantic Revival was in the direction of medievalism: spectres stalked frequently beneath the frowning battlements of ruined castles; innocent daughters of worthy yeomen were abducted by sinister barons, to pine away in gloomy dungeons till they were rescued by re-turned sweethearts; chivalrous figures from English history performed noble actions before an admiring populace. Romanticism next looked overseas, and in Germany found fertile soil; the works of Kotzebue were feverishly translated, and Rhineland castles were almost as popular as Gothick ones; picturesque robbers were displayed in their secret lairs, and supernatural happenings on the Eifel gave employment to numerous property makers. From Germany the rage swept all across Europe, lighting wherever the picturesque promised enchantment, and finding an especially congenial home in Italy, where *banditti* were to be observed sunning themselves upon the slopes of volcanoes, and crossing themselves piously at frequent intervals. From France came a constant stream of adaptations, many from Guilbert de Pixérécourt who may be regarded as the founder of this school of melodrama. Ranging further afield, the Romantic playwrights seized upon the mysterious Orient, and here, without any very strict regard to geography, noble Moors and treacherous Arabs were seen to engage upon crafty designs in the desert, while Persians, Siamese, Tartars, and Aethiopians appeared inscrutable or dignified or villainous as the circumstances required.

Turning to more recent history at home, the romantic drama touched even eighteenth-century crime with its magic wand, and produced a fine crop of highwaymen, galloping gaily across turnpikes, kissing the ladies, and eventu-ally betrayed by a jealous member of the gang; whatever the attractions of vice, it was a law that virtue should triumph in the end. Closely akin to these were the desperate pirates and the salty smugglers, the mutineers, the honest tars, and the noble but humourless naval officers, whose exploits in many an aquatic drama maintained Britannia as mistress of the seas.

These romantic settings were displayed in a type of drama that came to be known as melodrama. Its seeds had been sown in the eighteenth century by George Lillo, whose drama of contemporary life, *The London Merchant, or George Barnwell*, held the stage well into the nineteenth century; but the movement away from the high-flown poetic tragedies, which Elizabethan precedent still inflicted upon the stage, towards prose dramas of contemporary life was twisted and reorientated by the Romantic Movement, which we have just considered. The audiences of the Regency and early Victorian periods did not

Massaroni   *Maria Grazie*

Skelt's characters in *The Brigand*

want to see the problems of their own time displayed in the theatre. As we have already stressed, their mood was escapist; and so a prose drama grew up whose interest lies rather in its setting and properties than in its plot. This melodramatic movement was valuably aided, but not really originated, by the French and German influences of Pixérécourt and Scribe, Kotzebue and Schiller. The plots themselves, and even the characters became standardized to a degree that recalls the stock *personaggi* of the Commedia dell 'Arte; the juvenile hero and heroine, the 'heavy man' or villain, the old father, the comic servants, all reappear time after time in the melodramas of the period; by whatever stratagems or accidents the plot may be diverted it is always certain that the good and the bad will be painted in unmistakable whites and blacks, and that in the end, after no matter what deadly trials and dangers, all will come right, evil will be vanquished, and the good will live happily ever after.

There is a great deal to be said for stock plots and characters, and because today it is the fashion for every play to pose a new question in a new set of circumstances, that is no reason to disparage the nineteenth century for unoriginality of plot and character. The many hack dramatists of the theatres frankly wrote to a pattern, and a very good theatrical pattern it was. And how they wrote! Charles and Thomas Dibdin both had over 200 plays performed; Planché, Fitzball, and Pitt well over 100; Stirling, Buckstone, and Douglas Jerrold over 60; Pocock, Reynolds, Dimond, and many others 30 or more.

As the century went on the contemporary melodrama, as opposed to the romantic melodrama, did begin to find its way on to the stage, and the many adaptations of Dickens's novels must have had a considerable influence. It is now that we begin to get our Maria Martens, our Sweeny Todds, as well as our Oliver Twists; and following these the more explicitly social anti-drink melodramas, in which the temperance reformers stole a rather effective page

25

Smugglers Carousing

Nautical melodrama

from what many of them must have regarded as the devil's copy-book. But this movement really belongs to the middle and later half of the century, and is a little outside the scope of this book.

In this list of dramatic forms we must again mention the spectacle. This was normally an extended and more magnificent melodrama, but there were occasions when contemporary events, such as the coronation of George IV or the battle of Waterloo, were represented as pageants in the theatre. Spectacle was a quality that ran through every stage production, but at times it also must be considered to stand alone as an independent type of drama.

To follow the melodrama the audience liked a farce. The farces and comedies of the period defy analysis; their material was simple and homely — cantankerous old men, lovers' quarrels and reconciliations, disguises and mistaken identities, Irish servants, all helped out with liberal doses of puns and hearty bustling action. The humour was unsophisticated, and largely relied upon the broad comic acting of stalwart well-tried comedians; the plots were sentimental and extremely proper; the settings were very often contemporary, but neither asked, nor answered, any social questions. These farces and comic operas were almost all slight one-act affairs, specially written to fit in among the more substantial fare of the evening's programme.

There ran through the spirit of the age a taste for the fantastic, the ludicrous, and the absurd. When a critic of our own time, whose name I refrain from pillorying, describes it as the 'day of unabashed realism', he is either thinking of the end of the century instead of the beginning, or he has never really studied the period at all. This taste for the impossible for the sake of the impossible is already evident in the popularity of melodrama, but reaches its height in the extraordinary run of burlesques and extravaganzas that swept the stage during the first half of the century. Nothing was safe, nothing was too sacred for the burlesque writers to fasten upon, and turn into a grotesque mockery of the original. Every popular success was burlesqued before it was many months old: *Black Eyed Susan* became *Black Eyed Sukey*, *The Sorrows*

26

of Werther was guyed as *The Sorrows of Water, or Love, Liquor and Lunacy.* Even, or rather, especially Shakespeare was exposed to the indignity of *King Lear and His Daughters Queer* or Romeo and Juliet dressed up as costermongers. However contemptible some of these pieces may be in themselves, only an age that was dramatically vibrant with life could have thrown up such froth and bubble.

Even more remote from realism, even more extravagant, was the extravaganza proper. This consisted, so far as it consisted of anything tangible, of a well-known story from classical mythology or from the popular fairy tales retold in a topical manner. J. R. Planché was the king of extravagandists, and it was with his *Olympic Revels* that Madame Vestris launched her management at the Olympic Theatre. The story was the life of the gods on Olympus; the rhymed text sparkled with puns, colloquialisms, absurdities, and topical allusions; the costumes were exquisite and gay; the scenery was artistic, amusing and sumptuous. This was followed by *Olympic Devils*, and a long line of nonsensical, delightful, ridiculous, and witty absurdities. The extravaganza proper perhaps appealed to a more sophisticated section of the playgoing public than did melodrama or farce, but the elements of extravagance were everywhere; and nowhere did it touch more fantastic heights than in the pantomime.

Pantomime had been well launched in England early in the eighteenth century. It was a strange entertainment even then, a mixture of ballet and fantasy; the 'opening' as it was called, retold some classical legend of antiquity, some well-known historical incident, or some popular tale; scenic effects were elaborate and costly; music played throughout; and the familiar story was, for the greater part, expressed in dumb show. Interwoven with this, a dance-drama in mime was enacted, with Harlequin seeking Columbine through the impediments and difficulties raised by her dotard father and his foolish servant.

The nineteenth century brought two influences to bear upon this entertainment. Firstly the scope of the opening was immensely broadened to admit a farcical and extravagant treatment of almost any subject under the sun; classical mythology was still treated as in *Harlequin's Court of Apollo* or *Harlequin, Vulcan and Venus*; old plays were rehashed as in *Harlequin and Georgey Barnwell* or *Harlequin and Friar Bacon*; English history gave a *Harlequin and Wat Tyler* or *Harlequin Guy Fawkes*; English legend supplied *Harlequin and the Witch of Edmonton* or *Harlequin and St George and the Dragon*; nursery and folk-tales led to *Harlequin and Cinderella* or *Harlequin and Jack the Giant Killer*; and pure mad extravagance provided *Pope Joan, or Harlequin on Card Island, Harlequin Crotchet and Quaver,* or *Harlequin Poonoowingkeewanglibeedeeflobeedeeluskeebang.* The treatment of all these themes was in crude rhymed couplets, full of puns and topical jokes. They were, in fact, the extravaganzas of the million.

Pantomime tricks. Boxes and sacks are transformed into appropriate people: a barrel of Russian stores into a Russian hussar, and so on. The dotted lines indicate where the trick figures should be folded.

The nineteenth century, however, also altered the whole emphasis of the Harlequinade; mainly under the influence of Grimaldi the character of the Clown became pre-eminent, and a vast amount of funny business was introduced of which the Clown and Pantaloon were the instigators. Most of this was played before streets of everyday shops or scenes of well-known public places —an anchor that held these fantastic adventures close to earth. Harlequin and Columbine continued to dance gracefully, but his main function now was to wield a magic bat, which changed everything he struck into something else; some of these 'tricks,' as they were called, embodied clever puns and all were amusing—a sentry box would be transformed into a file of soldiers, a gardener into a wheelbarrow, a barrel of grease into a polar bear, and so on. The actual effect was carried out by dropping or raising painted wooden flats.

Pantomime was not originally a children's entertainment at all, nor was it in any way connected with Christmas; but by the middle of the nineteenth century it had come to acquire both these associations. The more extraordinary and unsuitable subjects for the openings dropped out, and they came

28

Nº 5.

More transformations from Harlequin's bat: a chimney-pot into a chimney-sweep, a coal-basket into a coalman, a chest of Turkey rhubarb into a Turk, and a bottle of blacking into a Negress.

to deal almost exclusively with nursery stories; the transformation scene grew in importance and became a very elaborate affair indeed; and although the Harlequinade remained at least half the entertainment and very popular for many years, its importance gradually declined, until in the twentieth century it disappeared entirely. The Principal Boy, a girl all thighs and ostrich feathers, and the Dame, a male impersonator, belong to the latter half of the century and are outside our period.

Some of the best pantomimes were written by the Dibdins and by Planché; many are anonymous. At their best the extravaganza and the pantomime represent the nineteenth century's most original contribution to English dramatic art; they inspired the most ambitious scenic effects of the age; and they deserve a more sympathetic and less patronizing study than they have generally received.

Some of the most famous actors and dancers to perform in pantomime were Ellar and Bologna as Harlequin, Blanchard and Barnes as Pantaloon, Grimaldi and Kirby as Clown, and Mrs Parker as Columbine.

29

3 The Juvenile Drama

In this necessarily brief and incomplete survey of the early nineteenth-century theatre I hope that what has often been dismissed as a barren and decadent period will be seen to be full of life and interest. Dramatically the age may have produced little of serious value, but theatrically it was a very exciting time indeed. Unfortunately, of all the arts, that of the theatre is the most transitory; plays can be re-read and re-produced, but the atmosphere of an original production, the spell of the acting, the effect of the scenery, and the reaction of the audience have already faded by the following morning. What would we not give to recapture the theatre of Shakespeare, of Congreve, or of Garrick? What, indeed! What would we not give to sit in the pit at Drury Lane and see (even if we could not hear) Kean as Richard the Hunchback? Or in the boxes at the Olympic see Vestris rogueing with the Olympian gods? Or in the gallery at Astley's, behold the proudly caparisoned Oriental potentate direct his dark court in imperial procession? Gaze horror-struck at pale ghosts haunting the moon-washed tower? Or watch the elegant grace of Harlequin and the antics of Clown before the Chinese Pagoda at Hyde Park Corner?

What would we not give? A few shillings were enough. All this is preserved in the sheets of the Juvenile Drama.

If we catalogue the features of the theatre that we would wish to recapture, there is little indeed that the Juvenile Drama cannot supply. The exteriors of a few theatres are preserved in odd scenes, but for these we have other and more accurate sources. Once inside the theatre, the prosceniums sold to front the model stages are often copied from actual theatres, and are always typical of theatrical architecture and convention. Here we can see the gilded wood-work and the chandeliers; the proscenium doors, the apron stage, the promi-nent footlights, and the boxes with ladies and gentlemen in evening dress gazing out fixedly towards the audience; and above all this, the Arts, perhaps, fancifully painted, charioteering towards the Sun. Here is the orchestra, with thickly whiskered musicians displaying a majestic disregard for the conductor. Now, too, may descend the resplendent drop scene, in which a lady in a Victorian crinoline waits expectantly upon a jetty to which an Elizabethan gallant is dexterously being conveyed in a Venetian gondola.

Of the play itself we have the scenery, wings, and top drops complete. Time quickly erases the masterpieces of the scenic artist not only from memory but from the canvases on which they are depicted; there is not much storage room, the public wants new scenery every season, and so last year's exhibition piece is painted over to make a clean canvas for this year's novelty. The art of scene painting was at its zenith at this period; built-up scenes and tricks with lighting had not yet driven the painted backcloth from the fashionable stage, and the cult of realism had not yet sobered the vivid theatricality of the painted flats; scenes were well-painted, vivid, exaggerated, unrealistic, and theatrically effective. It was the last ecstasy of imagination and illusion before the cold light of realism. But they were good craftsmen, too, these scene-painters, as many a careful architectural perspective can show. Their names have all been forgotten; here, as a tribute to these maestros of an all too permeable art, let their blazon stand! Greenwood, Capon, Marinari, Stanton, Andrews, Scruton, Stanfield, Roberts, Grieve, Marshall, Tomkins, Wilson. But the works of these artists and of their many unknown comrades have not entirely perished; there in the toy theatre, smaller, but intrinsically the same, they are preserved.

There, too, we can see the crude but hearty 'effects' of the stage. The flaps of the Harlequinade tricks; the flying ballets and floating fairies on their substantial clouds; the little boats and coaches that lent the effect of distance to the delineation of perspective; the stage trapdoors, the 'practicable' windows, bridges, tables, chairs, and crockery.

A stage-coach all set for a highwayman to hold up

Of the actors and actresses we have the costumes: the high waists and long straight skirts of the Regency, the low necks, the nubial emphasis, the hair in ringlets; the tight pantaloons, and knee breeches, the elaborate waistcoats, the swallow-tailed jackets; and all the apparatus of Romanticism, the cloaks, the tights, the russet boots, the broad-brimmed hats with feathers nodding; the monks' habits, the peasants' smocks, the oriental robes; the sashes, the straw flop hats, the sparkling jewellery; the armour, swords, dirks, cutlasses, muskets, and pistols. And all the clothing of extravagance: the multi-coloured patchwork of Harlequin; the red and white circles and triangles, the flappy breeches, the grotesque make-up of Clown; here we can trace fashion through half a century, as Columbine's Regency skirt grows shorter and is splayed out with steel ribs, her waistline sinks to somewhere near normal and contracts alarmingly, and her sleeves first puff like balloons upon her shoulders and then entirely disappear. Here too are the grotesqueries of pantomime—the sprites and goblins, the gigantic masks, the fairy wings, and all the classical-mythological-historical nightmare of the imaginative costumier.

Restrained by no historical sanctions or archaeological pedantries, costumes were designed solely for theatrical effect; the moth has long since eaten into the gorgeous velvets, the satins, the gauze frills, the jaconet muslin, the tulle, the sarsnet; the armour has gaped wide long since, and the swords rusted in their scabbards; but in miniature, like the scenes before which they proudly paraded, they still carry their effect across the footlights of a century to the audience of today.

Of the actors, too, we sometimes have the faces; but long after all faces had become merged into a common mould, we still have the attitudes and gestures, the histrionic carriage; we can *see* these figures act. There were only two basic positions: the first in profile, the body twisted slightly away from the footlights, one foot thrown forward, and the arm raised; sometimes it grasped a cup, sometimes a dagger, sometimes it pointed an accusing finger, sometimes it warded off an impending blow, but whatever the circumstance, it was a golden rule that the arm must be up. The second position was facing the audience, with feet well apart, and both arms thrown wide above the shoulders; if you were wearing a cloak this was especially good; it expressed amazement, rage, exultation, or grief. In the profile position the angle of the arm can be varied; if it is above the shoulder the mood is noble, regal, or arrogant; if it is below the shoulder the mood is submissive, questioning, or crafty; and of course all this can be done facing left or right. Already we can see the stock gestures with which the same actors, night after night, expressed the same emotions in a succession of different, but very much the same sort of plays. What an excellent system of character drawing! We cannot hear these actors speak—that alone is denied to us, but we can see them strike their habitual pose for every emotion that the play demands.

And so, as we look, through these scenes and characters of the Juvenile

Drama, everything is there except the words. And they, too, are provided for us in the special books of the play that accompanied the sheets. A little imagination, or better still a histrionic manipulator, will complete the charm and re-create before us, tiny but perfect, the theatre of the years between 1810 and about 1850.

I do not recommend anyone who feels excited about the theatre of this period to start his investigations by reading a lot of the plays; they have their charms, but a little, as they say, goes a long way, and too much of their hollow bombast and mechanical construction tends to produce an effect of fatigue in the printed page. I have at home a romantic chest crammed full of printed texts of nineteenth-century dramas, but I must confess that I have never done more than dip into it; if they are read at all, they should really be read at one sitting, for the matter will hardly stay in the mind long enough to bear an interruption.

The plays themselves are, I suggest, the least important things about the early nineteenth-century drama; the subject becomes a fascinating one if it is approached from the opposite direction—from the viewpoint of the audience, and as a vehicle for the magnificent impressionism of scene painters and costumiers. If you want to study and really enjoy this period of the theatre you cannot do better than start by buying the plays as Juvenile Dramas—if you are lucky enough to find any.

The finale of a harlequinade

4 The Publishers

Who started the Juvenile Drama? That is the question that one asks almost
as soon as one learns that it exists. I hope that I have succeeded in showing
that it was something that evolved gradually rather than appeared suddenly;
but one can still wonder who was the first person actually to print several
small theatrical characters on one sheet.

The earliest sheets that have been preserved are dated 1811. In that year
sheets of characters were being published by the following people: William
West at his Circulating Library in Exeter Street; Mrs Hebberd at her Circulating Library in Upper Charlton Street; J. H. Jameson in Duke Court; and
I. K. Green who published some sheets under his own name at West's Circulating Library. The next year, 1812, we have prints published by H. Burtenshaw at his Theatrical, Military, Historical and Comic Print Warehouse in
St Martin's Lane; by this time West, too, was describing his premises as a
'Theatrical Print Warehouse'.

Of all these publishers, William West was by far the most active, and the
earliest surviving dated sheets of all, in February 1811, bear his name. During
this year he seems to have published sheets for about a dozen plays; his first
prints are a little hesitant in style, but improve quickly. Failing other evidence one would assume that he must have been the originator of the idea
and that the other publishers were copying his example. After West the most
enterprising publisher seems to have been Jameson; he was responsible this
year for issuing about half a dozen sets of character sheets, drawn extremely
crudely. Mrs Hebberd put her name to a couple of plays; Green only issued
a few odd sheets, and those at West's address.

That is all the evidence there is. The fact that there were four publishers at
work by 1811 certainly suggests that something must have been started a

little earlier, but these prints were considered of no value at the time and it is not surprising that the earliest examples have disappeared. On the other hand, all these 1811 sheets are a little crude and uncertain in technique, one can almost see the idea taking shape as one looks through them, and by 1812 a regular style is becoming apparent; so it seems that the technique could not have been very long growing before 1811. One would probably assume that some time in, or a little before 1810, the idea began to take shape; and for want of further evidence it would be reasonable to think that West, who shows the greatest mastery and clearest style from the first, was the actual originator.

But all these attractive theories are rudely shaken in the year 1834 when J. K. Green, who was starting off in a big way as a toy theatre publisher, proudly announces himself on the cover of his books of words as 'the Original Inventor and Publisher of Juvenile Theatrical Prints, Established 1808'. This, presumably, was the insignificant I. K. Green who got West to put out three sheets of combats for him in 1811! (The eighteenth-century 'Latin' practice of not recognizing a capital 'J' in the English alphabet lingered on into the first decades of the nineteenth century.) What else can we discover, then, about him? In the year 1812 he was more active: in January he published a stage front, in March some sheets of Harlequins, Clowns, and Columbines, in April three theatrical portraits, in May a few sheets of the principal characters in *The Secret Mine* and in *Valentine and Orson*, in July the principal characters in *The Seven Wonders of the World, or Harlequin Colossus*. All these sheets were engraved as being published by I. K. Green and sold by H. Burtenshaw, St Martin's Lane, and B. Perkins, Carnaby Market. In 1814 a very crude edition of *The Tiger Horde* was published by Green and Slee, at a theatrical print warehouse in Bishopsgate. After this there is nothing for nearly twenty years, when J. K. Green begins to issue a long list of cheap toy theatre plays, and announces himself as 'the original inventor'.

On the face of it it hardly seems likely that this obscure figure who disappears after four years, and who never even had premises of his own but had to get other publishers to act for him, should have been responsible for originating all the glories of the Juvenile Drama. However, no one else has ever claimed to be 'the inventor' (though probably no one would have thought it worth the trouble at the time), and no one seems to have disputed his claim when he made it (though all the original publishers were then out of business, and West, though still alive, was probably past caring), so we are left with no alternative but to try to square Green's claim with the obvious insignificance of his early work.

I think the clue must lie in the close connection between Green and West that is indicated by the fact that Green was able to publish some sheets in 1811 from West's address; is it not possible that Green, who must have been a young man at the time, was a partner of West's, or worked for him? Perhaps

The Secret Mine plate 1. Detail from the artist's sketch.

The same detail from West's sheet

The same detail from Green's sheet

it was while he was a bright youth working with West in 1808 that he had the idea of engraving several small theatrical portraits on one sheet—the idea that led to the Juvenile Drama; West, as the employer, took the idea up and benefited from it, but all the time the young Mr Green was priding himself on the idea that *he* had been the actual originator. Or perhaps young Green, a theatre fan and an amateur artist, had had the idea on his own, but had lacked a printing press or the capital to launch out as a publisher himself; so he was reduced to hawking his drawings round the print publishers, and getting one of them to act as his agent. How galling it must have been for him to see these publishers taking up and exploiting *his* idea, while he was ignored and his work disregarded. It must be admitted that his crude engravings do not merit much attention, but his mind may have become embittered by this experience, and he may have determined to get something back from the man who had battened on his idea. That may explain his actions now.

By 1812 we find that Green is publishing through the firm of Burtenshaw, so it appears that West had refused to act as his agent any longer; West was now a busy publisher, issuing new plays every month, and there was no reason on earth why he should clutter up his stock with the prentice efforts of young Green. One would assume that Green no longer had any connection with him, but for an extremely curious incident that has never before been appreciated in its true light.

Green's first proper play was *The Secret Mine*; now this play was also published in the same year by West, and there exist in the British Museum what appear to be the original artist's sketches for the plates, together with both West's and Green's versions, which are almost identical. Either West was copying Green, or Green was copying West, or they both worked from the same artist's original. A schematic arrangement, based on certain distinctions between the drawings and the plates, will make the problem clear and suggest its solution:

	Plate 1	*Plate 2*
Drawing	Small figures in the background	No swords on characters
West	Small figures in the background	Characters have swords
Green	No small figures	Characters have swords

The evidence of Plate 1 indicates that West was not copying Green. Therefore Green was copying either the drawing or West's plate. The evidence of Plate 2 indicates that Green was not copying the drawing. Therefore Green was copying West's plates. So one would assume that West commissioned the drawing, engraved and published the play, and that then the poor struggling hack Green copied the engravings and put out his own version in rivalry. Pirating like this was common among publishers of all kinds at this period. *But* Green's edition of the play is dated May 1st, 1812, and West's edition May 7th, 1812, so Green was apparently the first to publish. To make the matter clear, I place the relevant events in a timetable as follows:

April 24th, 1812, *The Secret Mine* first performed at Covent Garden.
April 25th (?) An artist sketches the characters and costumes for a Juvenile Drama edition, commissioned by West.
May 1st. Green publishes a 'pirated' edition, copied from West's engravings.
May 7th. West publishes the authentic edition, from the artist's sketch.

There are only two possible explanations of these events. Green may have copied West's printed play, and predated his sheets to make them look like the first edition (which we should indeed have assumed, if there were not the artist's sketch to show that West was the originator); West then would have appeared to be the copyist, and the copyright would have belonged to Green. The other possibility is that Green was able to see the engraved plate before the sheets were actually printed and published. In other words, Green was still employed round about West's printing place, and used his position to copy the proof engravings or take them away, and put out an edition of his own before West's was ready. In either case young Mr Green appears to have been a bit of a rogue, even if he was 'the Original Inventor and Publisher of Juvenile Theatrical Prints'.

I do not think that the actual copying of another publisher's sheets can be regarded as a very serious crime, for that sort of thing was rife and the copyright laws a very poor protection to the author, artist, or publisher; but by his false dating of his sheets, or his quick work with the drawing, Green shows that he was quite exceptionally sharp. And if he was capable of smart work of this kind, what regard can we place on his honesty at all, and can we believe him when he claims to have been the original publisher?

I should, perhaps, mention that Mr A. E. Wilson, noticing the discrepancy in dates in these sheets of *The Secret Mine*, suggests that West's date is that of a reprint. These publishers certainly did change the dates when they reprinted their stock, but West could hardly have got through an entire edition between the end of April and the first week in May—there is normally a difference of several years between the reprints, and of course the play could not have been published before the first performance on April 24th.

A similar incident took place in July of the same year. This centres round a couple of portraits of Mr Kirby as Clown in *Jack and Jill, or the Clown's Disasters*; this pantomime was first performed at the Lyceum on July 30th, 1812. Green's sheets are, to all appearances, identical with West's—with the exception, of course, of the publisher's imprint, which in this case only gives B. Perkins as agent. The idea that a busy and successful publisher like West would stoop to copying from an itinerant hack like Green is unthinkable, but once again Green's plate is dated July 31st and West's August 1st; once again Green appears to be first in the field with a production that is shared with

West. In this case it almost seems as if Green was using the same copper plate as West; how then did he get hold of it? I cannot believe that West would have given permission for this sort of competition. One is forced to the conclusion that Green stole the plate and faked the date!

As I have shown, Green published two more plays in 1812. Both of these were also published, in the same month, by West! When we examine the sheets we find what we expected: with *Harlequin Colossus*, first performed on June 22nd, Green's sheets are dated July 2nd, and West's sheets July 4th, and once again there is a decided similarity. This edition was also published by Mrs Hebberd, and it is not quite clear how the succession ran, but it seems a reasonable deduction that Green was up to the same game again, by faking the date on his pirated sheets. Two years later he makes a momentary appearance upon the scene with a new partner, and, of course, may have been responsible for many plays in the interval that have completely vanished, but then he disappears in silence and mystery for eighteen years until 1832.

What is the explanation of this disappearance? One can only guess. One ingenious theory is that he was transported for infringement of copyright! Perhaps he enlisted in the army. No one can tell, and there we must leave him till we come to consider his later career in a different period. However amateurish his engravings may have been, and however doubtful his business ethics, the young Green remains an enigmatic and an important figure in our history. He was certainly not the original publisher to popularize the Juvenile Drama by good and numerous prints, but he may have been — so far as there was one — its inventor. He was born in 1790; it was the eyes of a young man of eighteen, the fresh romantic vision of a boy, that first saw the possibilities of 'Juvenile Theatrical Prints', and perhaps glimpsed something of the future that was in store for these first hesitant sheets of theatrical characters.

Of the other early contemporaries of West there is little that can be said, because nothing is known; when we speak of these 'publishers' of theatrical prints we must not imagine gentlemen like Mr Macmillan or Mr Murray, respectable purveyors of art and culture. The men and women who issued these cheap little engravings to catch the theatrical fancy of the day were indigent stationers and jobbing printers, grubbing a miserable livelihood from the fashion of the moment; in the wretched slums round Drury Lane, along with all the hangers-on and riff-raff of the stage, the expensive Cyprians and the cheap whores, these modest publishers displayed their gaudy stock of cheap booklets, valentines, penny numbers, paper games, and under the counter some grubby pamphlets of erotica, within their dim low-ceilinged circulating libraries. It was to swell this kind of ephemeral stock that the first sheets of theatrical characters were engraved, and printed on small hand-presses in unventilated basements. The history of the Juvenile Drama is lost in the unchronicled lives and unrecorded deaths of a few poor printers and stationers, whose hands shaped something more magical than they knew.

J. H. Jameson, near Bow Street, was issuing Theatrical Character Sheets by May in 1811, and went on to have an apparently successful career as a Juvenile Theatrical publisher; during the next fifteen or so years he issued over fifty plays; his first sheets are extremely crude, but soon he was employing good artists, and his work is very interesting; unfortunately his sheets are extremely scarce. The majority of these plays only consist of two or three sheets of principal characters, without any scenes, and it is obvious that they were designed as theatrical souvenirs; he described his premises as a 'theatrical print warehouse'.

And now we must consider the great William West, 'the aristocrat among theatrical stationers' as he has been called. He was baptized in the parish of St Paul's, Covent Garden, in 1783. By February 1811, at the age of twenty-seven, he was publishing sheets of theatrical characters from what he described as a circulating library in Exeter Street, off the Strand. He must have had a devouring passion for the stage, for from that time there was hardly a successful play performed on any London theatre for the next twenty-odd years of which Willy West did not issue a Juvenile Dramatic version. He must have possessed a genuine artistic flair too, for he got good artists and engravers to draw for him, used excellent printing paper, and produced in his sheets what will really, I think, come to be recognized as the most delightful decorative engravings of the Regency period. His industry must have been considerable, for he published about 140 plays at an average rate of one every other month throughout his publishing career. Many of these plays, of course, were not full acting editions; all the plays issued in the first year were merely sheets of principal characters, but by 1812 he was beginning to issue sheets of scenes as well; *Timour the Tartar*, which was completed in April 1812, appears to have been the first real Juvenile Drama play, as the characters were accompanied by several large scenes, each having a wing at the side of the plate. Whether the plays were yet really intended to be performed one can hardly say, but they had obviously passed the stage of being just pretty pictures. Prosceniums of the Theatre Royal were being published in this year too, and no doubt the scenes were set up on many a model stage and the characters cut out and displayed in their familiar attitudes. Real toy theatre performances must have started about now as bright boys and youths began to get the idea, but it must be emphasized that for a long time, and certainly as long as West published, the plays continued to be excellent reproductions of the actual stage performances.

How little we know about this man whose name entered thousands of English homes, and whom we now salute as one of the great figures of the Regency theatrical world! Evidence of the prosperous condition that he enjoyed at this time is provided by a delightful trade card, of which I possess, I believe, the only copy that has survived, and also a magnificent catalogue sheet, of which the only known copy is in the British Museum: 'West's Catalogue of

Original Tragic, Fancy, and Comic Characters. As performed at the Theatres Royal, Covent Garden, Drury Lane, Lyceum, Surrey, Astleys, Sadlers Wells, etc., etc.' The boldly flourished lettering proclaims, 'The Whole of the Characters are Finely Engraved, from Original Drawings, in their Exact Costume, and Printed on Fine Drawing Paper, purposely for Colouring. And Published by Permission of the Proprietors of the Different Theatres.'

But West was not really a man of business; he began plays and never finished them, he fell in love with others and issued more sheets than he had announced. When he printed the first character plate of *Malvina* in 1826 he stated that it would be complete in six plates of characters, but he went on to publish eight, and then two double plates of processions. This sort of thing was always happening; at other times months would elapse before he got all the sheets out for a play everyone was waiting for, or there would be delays of years between the characters and the scenes. 'He was a very dilatory man,' George Cruikshank, who worked for him, once said, 'the boys used to go into his shop and abuse him like anything for his frequent delays in publishing continuations of his plays.' What a picture! The London street boys jeering and swearing at the old man behind his own counter!

He has left an engraving of his shop in Exeter Street as it was in 1813, in a pantomime trick scene; it is a two-storied brick building, with an attic; in bold letters across the facia 'Exeter House' is painted; on the ground floor is the shop, with two many-paned windows on either side of a glass door; at the side a door on the street gives admittance to the living-quarters upstairs. Above the shop front is neatly written 'Circulating Library, Haberdashery etc.'; above the door is the name 'West', and on either side of the house, as if added afterwards, is the inscription 'West's Theatrical Print Warehouse'. Through the windows we can dimly see theatre proscenium fronts, sheets of characters and scenes, single portraits, and wrapped-up parcels. This is where his first plays were published, and there seems little doubt that he can only have been a stationer in a small way of business when he started; even when he was established as a juvenile theatrical publisher his catalogue indicates that he also sold 'Superfine Water Colours, and Camel Hair Pencils, Wholesale and Retail'.

William West did not confine his publishing activities to toy theatre plays. This district was the centre of London's pornographic book trade at that time, and West contributed to this with a large number of little 32mo booklets, illustrated with folding coloured frontispieces, containing saucy songs from the repertory of singers at the vulgar tavern concerts at such resorts as the Coal Hole, the Cider Cellars, and the Shades, which were then springing up on either side of the Strand. These booklets carry such titles as *The Randy Songster* or *The Cuckold's Nest of Choice, Flash, Smutty and Delicious Songs,* and the titles of the songs—like 'Cupid's Battering Ram', 'The Brass Founder's Cock', 'Lord Bateman's long Jock', 'The Ladies' Arses, O', and 'The

Beauties of the C'—sufficiently indicate the nature of their contents. To the modern eye these vulgarities seem harmless enough, but their existence throws a revealing light upon Regency and early Victorian society, and it is amusing and ironical that these little booklets were under the counter while the boys were buying their toy theatres above it.

Later in his life he gave up the shop in Exeter Street, and retired to Wych

West's shop in Exeter Street

Street; here his last plays, *Olympic Revels* and *The Brigand*, were issued in 1831; they are as good as the best he ever did. A portrait of him at about this time, discovered in the Harvard College Theatre Collection, shows him peering through his spectacles, with a square 'carpenter's' paper hat on his head—the very picture of a cockney craftsman. He continued to live on in Wych Street for many years, and his shop remained open, but no more new plays were published and the business sank into ruin and decay. We have some memories of him at this time; J. F. Wilson describes his premises at the end of the 1830s as 'a very melancholy looking shop' next door to Valentine's, an old curiosity shop kept by a Jew, in which journalists were fond of foregathering; he goes on to describe West and his wife as 'a couple of shrivelled-up creatures, having the appearance of octogenarian misers. They were always shabbily clad, although reputed to be well off, and seldom indulged in the luxury of a clean face. Their counters and shelves in the shop were crowded with old stock, covered with dust, and their only pleasure seemed to consist in petting a tame fox which was always with them, and drinking of Mother Trimby's best.' 'Mother Trimby' was a buxom widow who kept the Duke of Wellington tavern in Drury Lane, at which the poor hack writers, artists, and printers of the district were wont to congregate.

So the great West goes down to darkness and the grave, tippling his liquor and fondling a pet fox! It was an age of eccentrics. There is one last glimpse. 'It is now many years,' Edward Draper writes in 1868, 'since poor Willy West—the great publisher, if not the originator, of characters and scenes, finally closed his little dark shop, whence had emanated so much salutary amusement to the boys of a former age. A short time before his death, he commenced selling off his stock at ridiculously low prices. The poor old man could be heard gasping behind a simple screen which divided his death-bed from the public portion of the shop. There might then be had, capitally drawn, and, when coloured, gorgeous as summer flowers, engraved character portraits of all the dramatic celebrities of a past generation; . . . the bright colouring of such a series as *Blue Beard, The Elephant of Siam,* and the other oriental plays was specially wonderful. The scenery was unrivalled in its picturesqueness.'

West died on November 28th, 1854. No other publisher obtained possession of his plates, and there seems to be a legend that he had them broken up rather than allow sacrilegious hands to lay hold of them; but there is no reference to any such injunction in his will, which I have succeeded in tracing at Somerset House. In it he leaves five pounds to his nephew, William Lloyd, and everything else to his friend, James Johnston, a butcher of Clare Street; his estate was valued at three hundred pounds. This will was made in 1850, probably after the death of his wife; behind the legal phrases one glimpses the picture of a lonely old man, childless and widowed, turning to a neighbouring tradesman as his only friend in the evening of his life.

I cannot do more, here, than mention a few of the most prominent publishers who followed West, in order to indicate the general history of the subject; I have grouped the full particulars of every publisher of whom I know in the Appendix.

At about the time when West was still at the height of his career, in 1822, a new and powerful rival appears upon the scene under the name of Hodgson and Co. in Newgate Street; there is some doubt as to exactly what the 'and Co.' consisted of, but it might suggest that the Juvenile Drama was being taken up by business men and made respectable. Hodgson and Co., however, also published a number of cheap story books and topical pamphlets, and there is nothing very respectable or 'educational' about them; they were just the usual run of gaily printed and highly coloured ephemera to which the Juvenile Drama so intrinsically belonged. Hodgson and Co. remained in business for about ten years, and during that time published nearly seventy plays; they are all excellent examples of the Juvenile Drama at its best; good artists were employed, the printing is excellent, and the colouring superb. There is a distinct tendency, however, to make the plays more complete and more capable of being performed than were West's and Jameson's; for all their charm many of these early plays were very incomplete and rather slap-dash affairs, and practical performances must have severely tried the ingenuity of any youthful producer; now with Hodgson and Co., there are enough sheets for every character to appear in all the positions required in the action, and every play is provided with all the scenes and wings necessary. Exceptionally large-sized scenes were also printed which look splendid when coloured and set up; now, too, each play has a special book of words—West did publish some books, but not by any means for all his plays. There is also a slight shift of emphasis in the choice of plays: West's only criterion seems to have been what was a success on the London stage; Hodgson continued to make careful reproductions and adaptations of contemporary successes, but they obviously have a boy audience in mind, and concentrate on exciting melodramas and spectacles; they did not do a single pantomime, perhaps because they considered their juvenile public was neither young enough to enjoy them as children, nor old enough to appreciate them as parents.

The Hodgson and Co. plays are so good that one wonders what made them give up in about 1830; the sheets and plates were scattered and many taken over by smaller publishers. Something, however, seems to have been saved from the wreck, for in 1832 we find Orlando Hodgson publishing plays on his own. There is no definite evidence that Orlando is the same Hodgson who formed Hodgson and Co., but personally I am inclined to think he was; the evidence of the various plates and addresses is a little tedious, and I have detailed it in the Appendix. One may perhaps assume that Hodgson's partners, who may have been William Cole, S. Maunder, Howes, or H. Kenilworth, came to some disagreement as to whether the business should continue, and that eventually it was disbanded. Mr Hodgson himself set up a new business under the name of Orlando Hodgson in Cloth Fair, and began issuing a completely new set of plays; he only seems to have carried on for four years, during which he published six plays. These plays are quite different in style to the Hodgson and Co. publications, but they are extremely good and, in their theatrical way, are my favourites among all the Juvenile Dramas; little or no attempt has been made to draw the faces of the actors with any accuracy, but the figures themselves are most spirited, the costumes excellent, and the colouring quite magnificent. There is a splendid exuberance in these plays of Orlando Hodgson that exactly fits their subjects; compared with them the earlier publishers seem a little insipid. Orlando Hodgson's plays may lack the careful accuracy of his predecessors, and carry the germ of decadence within them, but what a grand, what a histrionic final tableau they make for the original Juvenile Drama!

We have now come to a turning point in our history; West published his

44

The exuberance of Orlando Hodgson

last play in 1831, Hodgson and Co. about the same year, and Orlando Hodgson in 1834; there was now a swarm of smaller publishers dealing in these prints, but these were the greatest figures, and by the time the young Queen Victoria ascended to the throne they were all out of business; it cannot be emphasized too strongly that what is so often referred to as a Victorian pastime was in its origins and in its heyday entirely pre-Victorian and mainly Regency in character.

What was happening? We have seen how the first souvenir sheets of theatrical characters came to be accompanied by scenes and wings, and mounted up and cut out for display; we have seen how these display figures were used by boys to perform the dramas upon model stages; and we have seen how the plays came to be designed especially and primarily for performance. By 1830 there is no doubt at all that the Juvenile Drama was designed solely as a pastime for the home; it had, in fact become the toy theatre.

Now, the price at which these sheets had been sold, ever since the very beginning, had been normally a penny plain and twopence coloured for the small-size plate; this price was amazingly cheap for the fine engravings and exquisite colouring of West and Hodgson, quite apart from their value as theatrical souvenirs, but when plays began to get more and more complete, and longer and longer, the pennies and twopences began to mount up; Hodgson's *Magna Charta* had as many as eighteen sheets of characters, and his *Zoroaster* twenty-nine large scenes; so we find that in Cole's price list of 1829 the cheapest play, *The Temple of Death*, cost three shillings uncoloured in the small size, complete with the book, and for the coloured versions in the extra large size no less than fifteen plays cost over a pound; *The Vision of the Sun* was priced at 26*s*. 10*d*., and *Zoroaster* at 29*s*. 6*d*.! This was far more than the average boy could afford, and so there was every inducement for someone to put out a cheaper type of play in competition. After all, the boys didn't really care now whether their plays were accurate copies from the theatres, and from now on the toy theatre technique becomes standardized, the printing less careful, the paper cheaper, and the colouring much cruder. The resultant sheets were sold at a halfpenny plain and a penny coloured.

The names principally associated with this popularization of the toy theatre are Green, whom we have already met, and Skelt. Martin Skelt is said to have been a shoemaker in the Minories, and he may have displayed Juvenile Drama sheets in his window, as an agent of the various publishers; some time early in the 1830s he began to buy up the stocks and copper plates of publishers who were closing down, substituting his own name, and reissuing them. In this way he got hold of some of Hodgson's plates, and among others, almost the entire stock of R. Lloyd, who had had a nice little publishing business opposite the Coburg Theatre; for these plays he maintained the original price of a penny. Then he seems to have started publishing on his own account, and did a few plays of his own, also at a penny a sheet, but he very soon turned to a cheaper type of halfpenny sheet and published a terrific run of about fifty plays in this style. The capital for these purchases is said to have been provided by a grant he received as compensation when his original premises were demolished to make way for the Blackwall Railway.

Skelt's was really a family business; there were Martin, Matthew, Benjamin, and Ebenezer all in partnership at various times, but it is difficult to disentangle the complexities of who succeeded whom. They were terrific mono-

SKELT'S CHARACTERS IN PIZARRO. Plate 6

Soldiers Firing Rolla Pizarro Spanish Soldiers

Pizarro asleep

Elvira Davillo Ataliba Almagro Rolla wounded

A halfpenny plate of characters by Skelt

polists, and did their best to buy out every other publisher and get all the plays into their own hands; the industry and enthusiasm of this obscure and apparently Jewish family is really phenomenal; they issued no less than five different versions of that popular toy theatre favourite *The Miller and his Men,* and two versions of nearly a dozen other plays. But where they seem to have excelled was in the distributing system; thousands upon thousands of sheets must have been printed, many of them coloured by hand, and they were sold at newsagents and stationers not only all over London, but all over Great Britain. They must have employed quite a number of toy theatre 'bagmen' to travel the provinces in search of trade. The plays themselves are said to have been published at the rate of one large sheet each week; this contained four small quarto plates, and had to be cut up by the retailer. A generation of boys grew up to whom the toy theatre meant Skelt, and the words became almost synonymous; in far off Edinburgh, in 1860, at a small stationer's shop in Leith Walk, a boy named Robert Louis Stevenson used to gaze with wonder and delight at Skelt's sheets of 'gesticulating villains, epileptic combats, bosky forests, palaces and warships, frowning fortresses and prison vaults'; years later, in 1884, he wrote in an essay which has given a phrase to the language, 'Penny Plain and Twopence Coloured', that 'the name of Skelt itself has always seemed a part and parcel of the charm of his productions . . . Indeed, this name . . . appears so stagy and piratic, that I will adopt it boldly to design these qualities.'

As a publisher, the Skelts cannot compare with West and the Hodgsons. Their plays are mostly old favourites and little different to those of their contemporaries in style; by the fact that they republished a great many sheets from older smaller firms, they act as a link with an earlier period, and the volume of their work entitles them to a major place in any toy theatre history; but, as publishers, that is all one would say. They should, however, be given pride of place as popularizers of the toy theatre; it was due to their energy and business skill that toy theatre plays went into almost every middle-class home in the kingdom, that innumerable Theatres Royal front drawing-rooms witnessed innumerable thrilling dramas and bloody combats, that red fire was burnt and crackers pulled in innumerable grand explosions. 'Skeltery' was enshrined in the homes of England.

They made no fortune from this enterprise; I think their voracious appetite for buying up old stock outran the financial rewards of halfpenny sheets. The 1840s seem to have been their heyday, but the business lingered on into the 'sixties. I have been told that they drank heavily, and that there were times when they lay helpless in the upstairs room while the children ransacked the shop below; plates that were avidly bought were never published, and then found their way to the pawnbroker. At the end, Benjamin Skelt died in Stepney workhouse. But their reward was to come: Robert Louis Stevenson's delightful essay on the toy theatre has preserved their name in English literature, and given it a publicity wider perhaps than it really deserves; every literary dabbler has read of Skelt, and the absurd statement that he 'invented' the toy theatre has even been made in *Modern English Biography* by a gentleman named Frederic Boase. Any serious historian of the Juvenile Drama feels obliged to depose Skelt from the high place to which a literary allusion has thrust him, but we must not fall into the opposite error of disparaging his work; he was not the first or the greatest publisher, but his plays are amazingly good for the price at which they were sold, and his influence was enormous; we need not grudge him his niche of glory.

J. K. Green, the mysterious 'original inventor', reappears in 1832 with a few theatrical portraits, and in this second appearance was a contemporary of the Skelts. He would now be a man of about forty-two; perhaps he saw that the original style of Juvenile Drama needed to be replaced by something cheaper designed more explicitly for the use of children; and decided to return to his first interest. His first two plays, issued in 1834, were in penny sheets, but after that he reduced the size of the sheets and published a steady stream of over fifty halfpenny plays during the next twenty-three

GREEN'S SCENE IN The Red Rover Sc. 6 Trick. N.º 10.

THE DART

Sold by J.REDINGTON, 208, Hoxton Old Town.

London, Pub. April, 4 1836, by J.K.GREEN, 3, George S.t Walworth New Town. Price Halfpenny.

A halfpenny scene by Green

years. He published from a variety of addresses in Walworth, south of the river, and disposed of his stock through a number of London agents, but it is doubtful if his plays ever obtained the wide distribution or became so well known as those of the Skelts.

He does not seem to have taken over any plates from previous publishers, but some of his plays are copies—this seems to have been an old habit of Green's; his *The Waterman* is copied from Skelt, *Douglas* from Dyer, and *Aladdin* from Orlando Hodgson. However, the great bulk of his stock were new original productions; he went in for highwaymen dramas and panto-mimes in a big way, and one can say, as one said of Skelt, that they were excellent value for the money; the engravings are a little stereotyped but very charming in themselves, but they were rather spoilt by the cheap paper on which they were printed and the crude colouring. The later Green, as we must call him, is entitled to rank equal to the Skelts as a splendid publisher of children's toy theatre plays, which still retained intrinsically the style and manner of the original Juvenile Drama.

Green published his last play in 1857; he had first been connected with the trade, according to his own account, in 1808; it is an astonishing record of nearly fifty years. There is a story that he drank himself to death in 1860. This grand old man of the Juvenile Drama described himself in his census return, grandiloquently, as a 'historical engraver', but found no honour in his own lifetime; he deserves all the recognition we can pay him now.

One of Green's agents was J. Redington, a small jobbing printer and stationer in Hoxton Street, who had published a few crude plays of his own; after Green's death Redington took over the business, bought all Green's plates, and republished nineteen of the plays under his own name. He was eventually succeeded by Pollock.

When the Skelt business was finally given up a number of their plates passed to a publisher named W. G. Webb in Old Street, who had already issued a few excellent plays; but most of these plates were broken up or entirely destroyed by rust.

And there for the moment we must leave our chronicle of toy theatre publishers; by about the year 1870 the fashion had changed, boys were getting other kinds of amusement, and already these sheets of characters and scenes depicting long-forgotten actors in long-outdated plays seemed slow and old-fashioned; in that year only these two genuine publishers of the old Juvenile Drama remained, Redington and Webb, in an obscure corner of London, north of the City.

There is a tendency for purists to despise the cheap popular prints published by Skelt, Green, and the later publishers. I am sure this is a mistake; the Juvenile Drama fulfilled itself in these halfpenny plays, and was never so vibrantly alive as when the shops were full of their gesticulating actors and the Victorian baroque of their scenery. They have not the distinction nor the artistry of their Regency predecessors, but they have a tremendously real, crude, and often amusing charm, and have not only preserved but improved the format of their original production. These toy theatre plays really were actable, the movement initiated by Hodgson was carried further still, all the snags of representation were foreseen, and every play provided a wide choice of attitudes for every character in every situation; the book of words for the first time gave full directions for executing a successful performance.

It is a little difficult to say how far these later plays are based on actual, contemporary stage productions; a handful of plays had established themselves as toy theatre favourites, and these were issued in version after version by rival publishers. These revivals were certainly not normally based upon any distinct performances at any distinct theatre, but their general manner and style was undoubtedly true to the general manner and style of the stage. But Green, Skelt, and their contemporaries issued a large number of original toy theatre plays, that were inspired by current stage successes; can we rely on these sheets to reproduce the theatre of the 'forties and 'fifties in the same way that West and Hodgson have preserved the theatre of the 'twenties?

Perhaps less accurately and exactly, but in a general way they undoubtedly do. Every character passed through the levelling process of being engraved in the same style as every other character, and there was certainly no longer any attempt made to copy the actor's features, but the costumes show in their wealth of detail every sign of careful observation, and I am sure can be relied on as accurate reproductions of what was being worn on the stage. The scenery, too, especially the topical London views in the pantomimes, was still well copied from the actual backcloths in the theatres. Even when the plays were intended for no other purpose than to be cut up by children they still remained excellent reproductions of the contemporary theatre. As late as 1860 Webb's *Harlequin Jack and the Beanstalk* was a splendid version of that year's Drury Lane pantomime, and his *Miller and his Men* was very well copied from the last production of this play in London at the Haymarket Theatre in 1861.

But the toy theatre was a very conservative theatre, and it refused to move with the times; it was born in an age of melodrama and pantomime, of painted flats and side wings, and it would have nothing to do with any modern movements on the stage; such new plays as were published after 1850 all belonged in spirit to the previous century. No less than ten plays from Sir Walter Scott were adapted to the toy theatre, but only one play from Dickens; that is a measure of the narrow boundaries of its period. By 1830 the Juvenile Drama had perfected a technique: the characters stood so, with arms thus, facing left, right, or centre; their costumes were Gothick, Bohemian, or Oriental; so was the scenery; there was the cottage scene, and the palace scene, both exterior and interior, the landscape, the sea calm and the sea angry, the forest, the cave. The toy theatre had acquired a repertoire of its own. This repertoire was in fact identical with the repertoire of any minor theatre in the year 1830; but though the theatre changed the toy theatre never did; it went on for years, drawing upon the old plays and the old scenes, leavened at first with new productions, but never fundamentally changed.

In these later sheets we find all the distilled quintessence of romanticism that Stevenson described as 'Skeltery'; his description is so perfect that I shall not attempt to emulate it, and can only implore everyone who cares for these things to buy and read for themselves the little book of essays called *Memories and Portraits* in which it is reprinted. To the lover of the toy theatre these later sheets bring a delightful crudity that is lacking in the earlier, more pretentious publishers; because they aim at a complete reproduction, their necessary failures and the stratagems they employ to put the characters through their parts raise many a smile. We may indeed treasure the Juvenile Drama for its historical reconstructions; but it is the toy theatre with all its crudeness and quaintness, its bandit kings transfixed in the moment of dying, its family parties at table, its stiff and unalluring heroines, it bolster clouds, its geometrical sunsets, that we love.

5 Publishing the Play

Let us imagine that we are the owners of a small stationer's shop in London some time between, say, 1815 and 1830. In our windows we display the latest weekly or monthly numbers of the current serial romances, almanacks, little books interpreting dreams, little books of puns, jokes, and riddles, nursery tales in penny chap-books, topical pamphlets about the latest murders or scandals in high society, paper games, play books and sheets of the Juvenile Drama. We have noticed that these last seem to have quite caught on and are selling very well, so we decide to set up and start publishing some plays for ourselves. What are the problems before us, and how were they overcome by the other publishers?

First of all we have to decide on a play. Shall we issue a new play that has never been done before, or shall we reissue a play that has already proved popular? If we want to play safe, we should take the second course. And even now we have three alternatives. We can have a new version of a favourite play specially drawn; we can copy some other publisher's version; or, simplest of all, we can buy the engraved plates from a publisher who is going out of business, substitute our own names, and publish the play like that.

All these methods were frequently used. Quite a handful of plays established themselves as toy theatre classics, and these were published again and again. The most popular of all was *The Miller and his Men*; this belongs to the German romantic school; it describes a prosperous miller in some rugged Bohemian valley, who grows so wealthy that he can buy up all the farms for miles round, and who is paying court to the daughter of one of his tenants. In reality, however, the miller is the leader of a band of robbers who are terrorizing the district. The poor young lover of the tenant's daughter gains admission to the band and discovers all; the local count with a squad of

52

soldiery arrives to impose justice; and the miller's jealous mistress consigns him and his band to perdition in a terrific explosion. It is a very jolly play, full of disguises and rather complicated fights.

Next to the miller there was a crop of oriental pieces that were immensely popular; *Aladdin*, *Blue Beard*, and *The Forty Thieves* were not pantomimes or even children's stories but straight exciting Eastern spectacles; so too was *Timour the Tartar*, one of Astley's equine melodramas. Another very popular horse piece was *The Battle of Waterloo*, which outlived the more contemporary interest of several other battle plays.

Among the many nautical pieces the most popular were *The Red Rover*, adapted from Fenimore Cooper's novel, and *Black Eyed Susan*, a domestic piece that attained terrific success at the Surrey with T. P. Cooke in the leading part as William. In this play William returns home from the sea to find a stranger kissing his wife; he outs with his cutlass and strikes him, only to find that it is his own captain! At the court-martial he is condemned to death for striking a superior officer, but a last-minute twist of the play pardons him and all ends happily. Also very popular was *The Flying Dutchman*; this combines the tang of salt water with the mystery of the supernatural; the story is how a beautiful girl is carried off by Vanderdecken to be his spectral bride; they are heroically pursued by her lover through blue fire, lightning, thunder, and tempest, and at the end she is successfully rescued. Another popular play that used up plenty of red and blue fire, and ran through the whole gamut of ghostly sensationalism, was *Der Freischutz*. There are ghosts and spectres in plenty, too, in 'Monk' Lewis's *One o'clock, or the Knight and the Wood Daemon*, but this time in a Gothick setting.

Among more sentimental pieces the great favourite was *The Maid and the Magpie*; this tells how a friendless girl is accused of stealing a spoon; circumstantial evidence looks very black against her, but it is discovered just in time that a magpie is to blame. This makes a pleasant toy theatre play, with less ranting and roaring than is usually required, though the stage business with the magpie and the spoon is on rather a small scale to carry effectively to the audience. Another romantic sentimental piece was *The Blind Boy*, who was born, sightless, the heir to the throne of Poland, and hidden away in the country, but was at last discovered and restored to his inheritance.

All these plays, as can be seen in the Appendix, were issued by at least half a dozen different publishers; other melodramas that bear the same marks of popularity were *The Old Oak Chest*, which introduces both robbers and smugglers, *The Woodman's Hut*, a cottage and castle drama, which is concluded with a fine forest fire, *The Forest of Bondy*, in which the chief actor is an intelligent dog with an unerring nose for the scent of villainy, and *Pizarro*, which displays the noble and primitive Peruvians to great advantage compared with their Spanish invaders.

Having, then, decided on republishing an old play, we may be able to buy suitable plates from another publisher. This was done time and again, and we can sometimes trace the same sheets through two or three different hands. Having acquired the plates the easiest thing to do is just to add our own name in front of the old publisher; thus we find numerous sheets marked 'Skelt late Lloyd', the 'Skelt late' being added in a totally different and cruder style. It is, however, very little extra trouble to erase the old name and address from the plates, and engrave our own in its place; we can see that this has been done, for instance, in the well-known plays published by Pollock, most of

Engagement between the Life Guards and Cuirassiers. Death of Shaw the Lifeguardsman.
London, Published by B. Pollock, 73, Hoxton Street, Hoxton.

An engagement from Pollock's *The Battle of Waterloo*, previously published by both Green and Redington

which can be found first with Green's and then with Redington's imprint, or in Skelt's *Aladdin* which came out again under Webb's name. If we examine the original copper plates we often find that quite a groove has been worn along the publisher's imprint with the constant changes and erasures.

If we cannot use somebody else's plates it will still save a lot of trouble if we can just copy their sheets. As we have already seen, literary piracy was rife, and there was, in practice, very little protection for the original publisher; West's and Dyer's *The Brigand* were combined to make a new version for Green; Webb's *Blue Beard* seems to be copied from Skelt, who probably got it from someone else. It is a fascinating but exhausting pursuit to try and trace the progress of these sheets from publisher to publisher; research on these lines can hardly be said to have started yet, and we cannot at present do more than glimpse the full story.

Piracy might consist in simply making a freehand copy, or in trying to transfer the original sheet on to a copper plate. Green's *Rob Roy*, for instance, seems to be based on West's version as far as the incidents are concerned, but it differs in the details; while his *Aladdin* is apparently traced from Orlando Hodgson—the characters are the same but arranged in a different order on the sheets to disguise their origin, and most of the scenes are identical but in *reverse*. This would, of course, be the case if a tracing from the original sheets was cut direct on to the plates.

It cannot be expected that the good publishers liked having their sheets copied without any fee and then sold in competition, and they certainly made some efforts to prevent it; many of the early sheets carried the phrase 'published as the Act directs' followed by the date. The Act referred to is the Engraving Copyright Act ('Hogarth's Act') of 1735, amended in 1776 and 1777; under this, copyright was secured to the designer or publisher of a print for a period of twenty-eight years from its date of first publication; this date, with the name of the owner of the copyright, had to be engraved on every print. The penalty for illegal copying was the forfeiture of the plate and all prints, with a fine of five shillings for every pirated print. The date on the print was the only security for the original artist or publisher; there was no other kind of registration. This will explain young Green's eagerness to get the earlier date on to his sheets every time. Sometimes, too, the portraits have a printed warning against copying at the bottom of the sheet, and the books of words carry the phrase 'Entered at Stationer's Hall' or, occasionally, 'at the Stamp Office', which was apparently considered an additional safeguard. At Stationer's Hall a registry was kept for the registration of copyright; unless a book was registered here the proprietor could not bring any action for infringement of copyright. This procedure was only applicable to the books of words, as the prints themselves were not eligible for registration. The Stamp Office administered the act known as 60 George III cap. 9, under which every pamphlet was required to pay a Stamp Duty of three shillings per sheet (in a single copy, and covering the entire edition). This would normally have involved a tax of six shillings on every title published. This act was always more or less a dead letter, and I doubt if many Juvenile Drama publishers paid any duty at all on their play-books; it was, anyhow, repealed by 3 and 4 William IV cap. 23, in 1833. Despite all this, however, there is no doubt that piracy raged very nearly unhindered; these cheap prints were, more or less, anybody's property.

The most determined attempt to prevent piracy was launched in 1831 by a combination of three publishers—Lloyd, Dyer, and Marks—who issued the following 'Caution to Print Sellers, etc.' in that year: 'Whereas several spurious and piratical prints have lately been sold and hawked for sale, this is to give notice that the undersigned publishers most respectfully solicit the trade, that should anything of the kind be again offered from this date, they will have the goodness to reject them, as it is their intention to take **LEGAL PROCEED-INGS** against any person or persons who sell the same, they being vile copies of some of the plates of the undersigned, published and sold at one half the price of the original, with a malicious intent of defrauding the same.'

This blast stirred somebody's guilty conscience, for less than three weeks later the partnership of Park and Golding issued a breathless notice to the trade, beginning 'As the above **CAUTION** no doubt **AS** (*sic*) been widely circulated in the true spirit of malice, and for the express purpose of intimidating and compelling the trade to refuse all such publications as may be offered to them, through any other hands than those employed by the above named, of whose Notorious Piracies **WE** the undersigned beg to call not only their attention but that of the trade also . . .', and going on to guarantee to reimburse the costs of any action that a trader was involved in as a result of purchasing any of the prints published by Park and Golding. (The full text is preserved in the Jonathan King collection at the London Museum.)

The most curious feature of this acrimonious exchange is that the witness to Park and Golding's reply was none other than William West, the Grand Old Man of the Juvenile Drama, who had just published his last play. Perhaps he was retiring in dudgeon at the appearance of so many competitors, among whom Lloyd and his friends had been prominent.

Perhaps, however, we scorn any copying, and decide to publish a really new original Juvenile Drama. We shall find that this is a vastly more complicated undertaking. Probably the first thing to do was to stand a round of drinks to the actors from one of the theatres, and get to know in advance of what was coming on. A new drama by Fitzball, Pitt, or Moncrieff, or a new pantomime by Dibdin or Planché might sound attractive; back-stage gossip would indicate the number of characters and scenes, which would affect the number of sheets that would be required; and on the first night an artist, specially commissioned by us, would occupy a good seat with pencil and note-book ready in his hands. Sometimes the permission of the proprietor of the theatre would be obtained, and the fact proudly stated on the sheets; one can imagine that any theatre proprietor would be only too glad to have his productions advertised free of charge in this way, and doubtless there were free passes for the Juvenile Drama publishers.

Plays at almost all the London theatres were adapted as Juvenile Dramas; the Theatres Royal of Covent Garden and Drury Lane provided a great many, but the repertoire was by no means confined to them, and all the larger minor theatres were drawn upon. There is direct evidence that West made adaptations from productions at Sadler's Wells, Astley's, the Surrey, the Lyceum, the Coburg, the Regency, the Adelphi, and the Olympic, as well as from the Theatres Royal.

So we have decided on the theatre and the play, and our artist is comfortably established in what we hope will be a free seat on the opening night.

During the play it will be his duty to make a quick rough sketch of every character in his or her costume, and of every scene. In 1822 Hodgson published a sheet illustrating how an artist should sketch the characters. The technique was to go to the theatre with a selection of *undressed* characters, in conventional theatrical poses, already sketched in one's note book. During the performance all the artist had to do was to 'dress' the characters in their stage costumes, noting the colours of each article of clothing at the same time. In the conditions of an actual performance one obviously cannot expect the accuracy of a specially posed portrait, but it is worth remembering that the lights in the auditorium normally stayed alight throughout the performance, so the artist was capable of a good deal more than a hurried scribble in the dark.

In very few cases has it been possible to actually compare the scenic design for a theatre production with the toy theatre sheet, but some designs in a Sadler's Wells scene book preserved in the Garrick Club library are for plays that were published as Juvenile Dramas, and in the two cases for which it has been possible to make comparison the resemblance is close, though not exact.

Later that night or the next morning the artist will draw the characters and scenes out in detail, supplementing his notes and sketches with his memory and doubtless a general knowledge of stage technique. If we are one of the early publishers all that we shall expect is one drawing of each principal character, with perhaps an extra one if there is a change of costume; there should be six, or perhaps only four characters on a sheet of paper, measuring about six and a half by eight and a half inches; this makes each figure about two and a half to three inches high. Some of the early publishers—and as late even as Hodgson and Co.—had their figures drawn standing, as it were, upon a stage parallel with the shorter side of the paper; but it was soon found that by turning the paper round so that the longer side was at the top and bottom, two rows of three, four, or five characters each could be squeezed in, making eight or ten on a sheet. Skelt, Green, and the publishers who followed them with halfpenny sheets, cut down the size slightly to about six by eight inches, and the characters to about two inches. Sometimes in the background, behind the figures, little sketches of the scenery or incidents in the play would be indicated, but with competition and cheapness these were omitted, except on the first sheet, which always had a decorative title around a miniature scene.

So much for the lay-out of the character plates. The scenes were often drawn in two sizes—the same size as the characters', and another larger, about twelve inches by nine and a quarter; Hodgson and Co. issued an especially large size of scene, measuring fifteen inches by twelve. The first scenes were issued with one wing on the sheet, thus reducing the actual size of the backcloth; later, all the wings were drawn together on separate sheets. The halfpenny publishers reduced the small scenes to the same size as the character sheets, and issued a number of larger scenes for selected plays, measuring about twelve inches by eight. There is no doubt that the larger size is much more satisfactory for practical toy theatre performance.

The characters were almost always drawn in the one standard size, which seems to have been accepted as normal from the very beginning, and there is a difference of no more than an inch between the earliest and the latest publishers. West did, however, issue a few sheets of very small characters for *The Battle of Waterloo* and *The Miller and his Men*; these only measured about an inch and a half in height. The size of paper was probably stabilized as the normal quarto engraving paper—i.e. one large sheet of paper folded twice and cut to make four sheets; but occasionally double plates were issued, to contain long processions and such like, for which twice the usual price was asked.

The number of sheets for any play varied considerably. As we have seen, the earliest plays issued by West and Jameson only consisted of two or three sheets of principal characters; when scenes were added this would have brought the total up to perhaps an average of six or eight sheets for a play. With Hodgson we find that the number of sheets rises enormously, because almost every character is drawn in two or three different attitudes, and it was quite common to have twenty or thirty sheets to a play. Skelt and Green carried this completeness further still, and Green's *Jack Sheppard* needed no less than sixty-four sheets to complete it; this was the longest play ever done for the toy theatre and must have required, as Theo Arthur once wrote, 'a rich uncle (after dinner) or a godfather in good humour' to finance its purchase.

These then were the drawings prepared by the artist. Our next procedure must be to have them engraved. It was far more upon the engraver and the printer than upon the original artist that the final effect depended, and these men were, of course, not mechanical hacks but equally entitled to be described as artists themselves. The gulf between the prints of, say, West and Green, lies far more in the inferior printing than in the inferior design, and the plates of Green when well printed on good paper, as I have recently seen them done, produce quite astonishingly good prints.

The technique of hand engraving is so largely forgotten today that it will, perhaps, be worth while to describe in some detail exactly what was involved. All these processes had to be undergone before a single toy theatre sheet appeared for sale in a single shop.

The plate to be used might be either of steel, zinc, or copper; steel requires a rather different technique and was never, I think, used; zinc was used occasionally, but does not keep well for many years, and copper was undoubtedly the normal material. This plate had to be highly polished to make it perfectly smooth, and this alone entailed a great deal of work; some of the materials used for polishing were sandstone, pumicestone, snake stone, charcoal with oil or water, and polishing felt. The plate now must be covered with a thin coating of a wax-like substance called the 'ground', to protect it from the acid which will eventually be applied; these grounds were generally composed of some combination of beeswax, asphaltum, Burgundy pitch, and gummastic, and could be applied directly while hot, or cold, in the form of a paste, dissolved with oil of lavender. If hot, the ground is spread over the plate by a 'dabber', made of horsehair covered with cotton-wool and finally with kid or silk; if cold, the soft paste ground is rolled over the plate by a leather-covered roller; the plate must now be heated until the surface shines, to drive off the oil of lavender and render the ground hard. At this stage the ground, however applied, is smoked by placing the plate, ground downwards, in a hand-vice, and burning a bundle of wax tapers below it; the smoke is incorporated in the ground, and enables the lines cut in it to be more easily seen. As soon as the ground has cooled, we are ready for the engraving proper to begin.

The engraver may or may not be the original artist; in more pretentious prints it was usual to write at the bottom 'so and so del., so and so sculp. or fecit' to indicate the artist and engraver respectively. Engravers varied from creative artists of great ability to literal interpreters of whatever drawing was placed before them; the engravers of the Juvenile Drama probably belonged to both schools, but the uniform appearance, the 'house style' which distinguishes a West, a Hodgson, a Green, or a Redington, so that the expert hardly needs to look at the name at the bottom of the sheet, is undoubtedly due to the characteristics of the engraver who was attached to that particular firm. It was upon the engraver that the appearance of the print really depended, and at times he seems to have been allowed a great deal of latitude. There are a few original drawings for early West sheets in the British Museum, and if one compares these with the ultimate prints one can see that a great deal of embroidery and detail was left to the discretion of the engraver; I have also in my possession a number of original drawings for the plays of Skelt and Webb, and some of these are extremely rough, merely indicating the characters and the attitudes they should occupy on the sheet. On the other hand, I also have a few drawings finished down to the finest detail, and Mr G. Skelt, who claimed to be a descendant of the famous family, stated that the designer drew in every detail, which was merely copied exactly by the engraver. The truth would appear to be that when the engraver was known and trusted, he was allowed a great deal of licence, but if he was only a copyist, which is what many of them prided themselves on being, he had everything set before him. Of course, if the designer was also the engraver, he would not bother to make a detailed drawing, and this may explain the rough sketches in my collection, as it is believed that Webb drew and engraved all his sheets himself.

We have then the problem of transferring a pencil sketch or drawing on to the prepared copper plate. It could, of course, be engraved directly in free hand, but the engraver would normally like to have some clearer indication of where and how the cuts were to be made. This can be obtained if the drawing is made in lead pencil on thin paper, by damping the paper and laying it, face downwards, on the grounded plate, which is then rolled through the press with a little less than ordinary printing pressure. Something of the pencil lines will be impressed upon the ground, and the result will be a drawing in grey lines on the black ground. If the original drawing is not suitable, it will be necessary to trace it upon thin paper first. This method has the advantage that the impression is the reverse of the drawing, so the final print will once again reproduce the drawing the 'right way round'.

An alternative method is to coat the plate with a soft ground, which is obtained by mixing with the ordinary components about half their weight of lard or tallow. If a drawing is placed on top of this and traced over, the impression of a hard, sharp pencil will be picked up in the soft ground underneath; I suggest that this, or some similar procedure, would explain the 'reversed' copies of Green's *Aladdin* scenes, to which we have already referred.

The engraver now takes a needle set in a holder and draws through the ground with it, exposing the copper plate beneath; wherever he makes a scratch a line will appear in the print. To obtain different thicknesses of line, he may use needles of different degrees of fineness. Shading can be represented by an effect known as stipple, which consists of making a large number of small dots, and was often used to represent the shadows around the face and neck. But on the whole these Juvenile Drama prints are line engravings only, and make little attempt to give body or depth to their characters or scenes.

When all the required design has been cut through the ground, the plate is ready for 'biting'. An acid solution, known as the 'mordant', is prepared, normally consisting of nitric acid with rather more than an equal amount of water; this is placed in a dish; the back of the plate is protected with a coating of Brunswick Black, and then the plate is immersed in the bath. The copper is protected by the ground except where lines have been scratched in it; here the acid comes into contact with the metal, and etches or bites a furrow wherever the needle has gone. The time necessary for this action to take place may vary considerably with conditions from a minute to a couple of hours. At the end the bath will be stained green with dissolved copper.

This process is technically known as etching, and permits almost as great a freedom of line as in an ordinary pencil drawing; engraving, strictly speaking, consists of cutting grooves directly in the copper itself with a diamond point, or a steel graver or burin. The graver has to be pushed with some force by the palm of the hand, and thus the line acquires a severe character. There is no doubt that the Juvenile Drama prints were etched, but direct engraving may sometimes have been used in conjunction with it; for ordinary purposes, however, the prints have always been referred to as engravings.

When the biting is completed the plate is dried, the ground is cleaned off, and the engraved plate is ready for printing. Copper-plate printing ink was made from any pigment with sufficient body, ground rather stiffly, with burnt linseed oil. The black pigments in common use were Frankfort black and heavy French black which were used to give 'body' to the ink, and a much lighter pigment obtained from the smoke of burning paraffin, which was mixed with either or both of the others, to give surface tint. The oil was prepared by boiling the linseed oil in a cauldron, and then setting fire to it; it was continuously stirred in this state, and the longer it was allowed to burn the thicker, and the more like varnish it became. The black pigment was now ground with the oil, and produced a heavy and rather stiff ink, which was applied thickly all over the plate with a dabber, to drive it into all the lines. While printing the proof the plate was often warmed over the heater so as to assist the manipulation of the somewhat stiff ink. The ink on the plate was now wiped off with a pad of printing muslin or canvas, leaving ink only in the engraved lines; to make the plate as clean and bright as possible it was often finished off with a rub with the palm of the hand. A sheet of printing paper was then laid on top of the plate, the roller was passed over it, and the first proof was ready.

It was not too late to make small alterations. There is in the British Museum a proof of Jameson's *The Heart of Midlothian*, with the pencilled remark, 'Hat not half so large'—it would have saved a lot of trouble if he had made the correction on the artist's drawing. Publishers, however, often changed their address, reissued their plays with new dates, or, as we have seen, bought up other publishers' plates and wanted to insert their own names and addresses instead. Small alterations could be made by burnishing the spot smooth and engraving again over it; if the area was already cut deep, it could be scraped into a smooth hollow, and then the level of the plate could be knocked up from the back upon a smooth anvil; a pair of callipers was used to indicate the correct spot at the back to be hit, and the small end of a hammer or puncher was used for the knocking up.

This was the way, in an atmosphere whose stinking concoctions and secret processes remind one irresistibly of a witches' Sabbath, that the Juvenile Drama was printed. I have purposely ignored the finer points of proof correction, as these plates obviously had to be printed quickly and cheaply; despite this, the results were amazingly good. In later years other processes were introduced; some time after the middle of the century a publisher called Archibald Park issued scenes for *The Miller and his Men* and other plays that seem to have been drawn in chalk and printed by lithography; the results were not very successful. Cheaper publishers who began to spring up about this time issued plays printed from woodcuts; these were usually extremely crude. At the end of the century lithography was established as a far cheaper and easier process of printing than the laborious etching procedure that I have described, and the plates of Redington and of Webb were transferred to the stone. In this process only one smooth stone slab is required; the drawing or print that is to be reproduced is placed upon it, and, by a special treatment, the tones of the original are transferred on to the stone; this is now coated with ink, which only adheres where there is an element of grease present, i.e. where the tones are dark; and from this the sheets are printed. When no more are required, the stone can be cleaned and a fresh impression taken of another print. Carefully handled the results can be quite satisfactory, but they inevitably lack the clear impression of a true engraving.

Hayward Marks, an experienced printer himself upon a hand-press, has left this interesting account of Mr Pollock's lithographic printing press. He visited the shop in Hoxton Street shortly after old Mr Pollock's death. 'In the shop I met the son,' he wrote, 'who had been trying a little printing but had got into difficulties. It seems that the stone was scummy in between the work itself, not round the work. This I attributed to weak ink. The son had bought from Winstone's ½ lb of Press Black Litho ink and some thin varnish, this last they had supplied him with on their own recommendation, he not knowing what to ask for. He had only bought ordinary turpentine, instead of spirits, not knowing the difference. He had neither resin or French chalk. I suggested that I might be allowed to try my hand at the stone, and he being agreeable lent me an apron. I first scraped one of the rollers. There were four of these, all in excellent condition, nap rollers, not polished as I had expected to find. I mixed some fresh ink, using very little varnish, the weather being warm. Then I washed out the stone; this had been gummed badly and had dried in blotches, but the old ink came off quite easily. On rolling up I found that the stone needed a slight etch, and that it was impossible to proceed until this was done. There was no resin, but one of the sisters went out to the oil shop to get some. She came back with ordinary lump resin, which is not what I am accustomed to use, though I was told that old Mr Pollock used to have a little muslin bag with it in, which he "kept dabbing on the stone". This I am inclined to doubt. Probably he kept powdered resin in this bag. Seeing that it was little use doing anything else, I gummed up the stone with some gum I had brought, containing a little acid, and rubbed this well in.

'In the course of conversation afterwards I learned the following facts. Redington used to do his own letterpress printing, but sent his litho printing out. Pollock did the reverse. Of late he found it very expensive; the last two plays cost him £15 for a thousand copies of each. He was very conservative and would never allow his sons to do any of the printing; the most they were allowed was to keep the stone damp while he served in the shop. Pollock used to transfer his designs from the copper plates on to the stone, and then re-transfer from this stone so that he could print four on of the smaller sheets, and two on of the larger.' Mr Pollock's litho printing press was eventually presented to the Ravensbourne College of Art, where it continues to render excellent service.

Now, at last, the plates of characters and scenes are finished. But they are not yet ready for printing; the lettering has yet to be applied. Engravers of lettering were often specialized workmen; they could not engrave drawings, and ordinary artist engravers could not equal their exquisite calligraphy. Whether these specialists were often called upon to inscribe Juvenile Drama plates one cannot say, but there was ample scope for them, and many a sheet owes much of its charm to the flowery cursive of its inscription.

The first sheet of characters was regarded as the title page of the play, and the full particulars were enumerated there. Usually the space equivalent to a couple of characters in the top row was occupied by some elaborate scroll or indications of a set scene, within which the lettering was displayed. In the early sheets the normal heading was 'Principal Characters in such and such a play', but as we have seen, with the movement towards completeness, the 'principal' was soon omitted. Sometimes the publisher placed his own name in front, and often the nature of the play was stated, and the theatre at which it was performed, giving such full round titles as 'West's Characters in the Grand Historical Ballet, called *La Perouse, or the Desolate Island*, as performed at the Theatre Royal, English Opera House'.

The next most important information was to state how many sheets were necessary to complete the play, and so we almost invariably find such an addition as 'in 4 Plates, Plate 1st'. West and Jameson published many plays of characters alone, and when they did issue scenes as well, the fact was never stated on the 'title sheet', but after Hodgson all the later publishers gave the full particulars of the play's make-up. We have, for instance, 'Hodgson's Characters in *The Maid and the Magpie*. Plate 1st. In 5 Plates, Characters and Tableaux and 6 scenes', or 'Green's Characters and Scenes in *Whittington and his Cat or Harlequin Lord Mayor of London*. 8 Plates of Characters, 13 Plates of Scenes, 3 Plates of Tricks, 4 Plates Wings, No. 6, 10, 28, 30'. The sheets of wings were of certain set types, such as forest, town, cottage, or palace, and could be used with any play.

This much information was invariably set out, but individual publishers often boosted their plays by increasing the blurb; many of West's plays, and some even of Orlando Hodgson's have inscribed after the name of the theatre, 'By permission of the proprietor', sometimes the name is given, as 'By permission of R. W. Elliston Esq.'. West's *'The Black Prince . . .* as performed with applause at the Royal Coburg Theatre' is even inscribed, with what must be a sly dig at an unpopular character, as 'Done without the Permission of **Mr W. Barrymore**'! The later publishers often referred to the book of words, as in the phrase 'With a book adapted to the above only.' A few other advertising puffs that may be mentioned are West's note on his Portraits, 'Superior to Creed's at 2*d.*'; Creed was a small publisher who used to boast that his portraits were 'published from original drawings'. Hodgson and Co., too, to impress the fact that they were the original publishers, sometimes headed their plays 'Hodgson's Theatrical Characters from Original Drawings'. R. Lloyd made the proud claim, 'The Trade Supplied with everything Connected with the Juvenile Drama.' And Dyer inscribed the following verses upon the title sheets of some of his plays:

> Ask for Dyer and Co.'s Plates or Scenes,
> Depend they are the best,
> Do they sell much? crie all the Spleens.
> Ah! More than all the rest.

(I commend this use of the word 'Spleen'—in the sense apparently of 'a young blood'—to the attention of dictionary makers. It is not thus recorded in the O.E.D. or in Partridge's Dictionary of Slang.)

One thing that was never mentioned was the author of the play; as I have already suggested, the playwrights were the least important figures in this period of theatrical history. The other sheets of characters carried only a condensed form of title; the scenes carried their own number as well as a plate number, so we get 'Scene 1, No. 1', or upon a backcloth that appears in several scenes of the play 'Scenes 2, 4, and 6, No. 2'. The later publishers found an excellent way of economizing by making the same scene do for several different plays. This worked out quite well in practice, as the same stock situations continually required the same stock setting of cottage, forest, castle, street, or palace. The toy theatre was, of course, only reproducing the current practice at any other theatre. Some of the publishers, however, carried this a little too far, Green's *Tom Thumb*, for instance, did not contain a single original scene, and when Redington published *Oliver Twist*, and wanted a room in Mr Brownlow's house, he solved the problem by using an Oriental interior from Green's *Forty Thieves*!

So much for the 'Title'. The next thing to do was to inscribe the name underneath each character. As we have seen, the early publishers often also stated the name of the actors and actresses as well. Although this practice began to die out very early, it was never entirely forgotten, and Green gave the names of the actors in the pantomimes he published as late as 1854. One might suggest that the children, for whom these plays were now solely intended, might have seen the actual pantomime, which by this time had been accepted as the children's Christmas treat, and so might be familiar with and interested in the names of the performers. Some publishers, wanting to make everything as easy as possible for their young patrons, even described underneath what each character was doing, and we find from Lloyd such rather unnecessary explanations as 'Volther (with Knife)', 'Mathews (Reading)', or 'Therese (Fainted)'.

Finally, usually at the bottom of the sheet, we must have the publisher's imprint. This, as well as the names of the characters, was lettered in italics, and was sometimes the work of an apprentice to the chief calligrapher. 'Published as the Act directs July 30th, 1811' was the style in which the early sheets were dated; this phrase was not peculiar to the Juvenile Drama, and is found on all prints of the period. I do not think there is any mention of this Act after the days of West. This dating, however, which should prove such a help to the student of the Juvenile Drama is only too often a snare and delusion; when plays were reprinted the dates were altered, and it is quite common to find two identical sheets bearing widely different dates. A great many of West's sheets are dated in 1824, but this was not the date of the original publication, which may have been eight or ten years earlier, as in 1824 West seems to have gone through his old stock and reprinted a great deal of it, altering the date at the same time. Presumably this was done to make the plays appear new issues and up to date, but it may also have been done with the idea of extending the period of copyright; as we have seen, this only lasted for twenty-eight years, and the publishers may have imagined (without any real legal authority) that a redated sheet could carry its twenty-eight-year copyright from the new date.

Almost all the early sheets are dated, but after Orlando Hodgson this was very seldom done. Green, alone, punctiliously dated his plays; the prolific Skelt, and even the comparatively recent Redington and Webb, present a more obstinate problem to the toy theatre historian than do many of the earlier publishers, because of the complete absence of dates on their sheets. But when dates do appear, helpful though they are, the possibility—even the probability—of their being second or third issues, must be constantly borne in mind.

After the date came the name of the publisher and his address, sometimes with a description of his premises. These are sometimes quite informative: we have W. West 'at his Circulating Library, 13 Exeter Street, Strand' in 1811, 'at his Theatrical Print Warehouse, No. 13 Exeter Street, Strand' in 1812, and at 'Exeter House, Exeter Street, Strand' in 1816; the progress towards respectability cannot be ignored. Other descriptions of what were, in fact, only small stationers and print-sellers were Jameson's 'Theatrical Print Warehouse', Straker's 'Juvenile Dramatic Repository and Public Library', and Bailey's 'Publisher's, Children's Book, Theatrical Print and Pamphlet Warehouse'. Sometimes, here, too, might be mentioned the names of any agents who stocked the plays. Green was particularly fond of giving a list of two or three retailers; they were introduced by the phrase 'And Sold by', followed by their names and addresses.

And finally, the price was usually marked on the sheet. We have already seen the question of price arising in our survey of the publishers, and it will be sufficient now to give a résumé of the main trends. The original price for both Juvenile Drama sheets and theatrical portraits was 1d. plain and 2d. coloured; there were exceptions: West published some sheets at 1½d. and large double plates at 2d. plain; his large-size scenes were priced at 2d. plain and

E   65

4d. coloured; the plays of Jameson were published at the same price, that is 1d. plain and 2d. coloured with a few large scenes at 2d. plain and 4d. coloured. This policy was carried on by Hodgson; Hodgson and Co.'s extra large scenes were priced 3d. plain and 6d. coloured. As far as I can tell, the first publisher to introduce a steady run of $\frac{1}{2}d$. sheets was Green in 1834; he was followed very soon by Skelt, who sold both 1d. and $\frac{1}{2}d$. plays, but from this time on the regular price became a $\frac{1}{2}d$. plain and 1d. coloured; large-size scenes and superior portraits were now 1d. plain and 2d. coloured. When Robert Louis Stevenson wrote his famous essay on the toy theatre in 1884 he entitled it 'A Penny Plain and Twopence Coloured', which is more phonetically pleasing, but a quite inaccurate description of the price of the sheets at that time, though it could have been applied to the portraits. The phrase, however, so often and unpretentiously printed upon so many cheap prints, has something of the magic of the toy theatre in it; the words, immortalized by Stevenson, have become part of the language, and are used continually by people who have never seen or heard of the Juvenile Drama. The phrase as a phrase, was, how-ever, not invented by Stevenson; a few years earlier, in *Routledge's Every Boy's Annual* of 1874, we find a Mr Samuel Highley referring to 'the fixed 'stage-struck'' attitudes of the "penny plain and tuppence coloured" style of the ordinary toy theatre "characters"'; it was evidently already a current quotation. A few years earlier a poem by Henry Leigh entitled 'Coloured and Plain', had used as its motif the line 'For twopence coloured and a penny plain'; and as early as 1848 Albert Smith in *Christopher Tadpole*, disparaging the cheap watercolours sold in the shops, could write that 'the children sighed for the brilliant hues of the "twopence coloured" prints', indicating that this description applied not only to theatrical characters but to Valentines, the frontispieces of dream books, and so on. No light at all is thrown upon the origin of this common phrase by any of the standard dictionaries of quota-tions, but there is no doubt that it is derived from these toy theatre sheets. The Juvenile Drama itself will perhaps never be anything but a passion and a delight among a few select eccentrics, but in this phrase at least it has left words on our tongues that will probably never be forgotten.

And so, at last, with brows dripping sweat and ink-stained hands, the printer can bed the finished plate in the press. The paper is cut and stacked ready for printing; the plate is inked; an assistant stands by to feed the clean sheets into the press; another is ready to remove the printed sheets; and now with every run of the roller a penny plain is achieved. But what of two-pence coloured?

Many, probably most sheets, were sold uncoloured, and coloured by the purchaser at home. But for double the price what a transformation was there! The publisher's colouring possessed a true theatricality, a bright, vivid sweep, that no amateur could hope to surpass; the colouring on these prints, over a hundred years old, is as gay and splendid today as when it was put on; and with what a sure touch it takes the paper! The quality of colouring follows the quality of printing; with West, Jameson, and Hodgson it is exquisite; with Orlando Hodgson less exquisite, but more dramatic; with Skelt less careful, but still thrilling. Green's colours stood no chance on his cheap paper, but the old flamboyance was there, and those of his plays coloured only a few years ago in the authentic manner by Miss Pollock still shine as 'gorgeous as summer flowers'. It is only in the coloured sheets that the Juvenile Drama attains its full charm; how was this brilliant colouring achieved?

In the first place the materials were of the best. West claims that his plays were 'printed on fine drawing paper purposely for colouring', and simply to feel this old paper is a pleasure in itself. In later years the 'wrong' side of the paper was sometimes printed, as it held the colours better. And then the colours, like the printing inks, were not bought at shops, but specially mixed to old and secret formulae, and applied while still fresh. A great mystery was made of the colouring, and many were the rumours of the secret ingredients that were added to obtain such bright hues; gum, sugar, and a few drops of beer, it was said, were mixed to make the yellow gleam as if it was burnished, and the crimson make blood, in comparison, look like water. I cannot refrain from boasting that I have been honoured to receive from Miss Pollock and from Mr How Mathews, two of the last surviving publishers of the Juvenile Drama, their own special recipes for mixing their colours. But in these days, when every print-seller in town has his private establishment for turning one pound plain into two pounds coloured, wild horses would not drag the secret from me! I have, however, ensured that the tradition is not lost and that the formulae and technique have been passed on to worthy hands.

I can, however, reveal here that only three primary colours were used: carmine, gamboge, and a light blue. From these three every possible shade could be obtained. The typical brilliant crimson, for instance, is produced by applying deep pink over strong yellow. My friend, Mr Stanley Bult, once went to the trouble of analysing some of Miss Pollock's coloured sheets; one scene only showed four distinct colours, but most had from ten to fifteen; in one scene from *Cinderella* he counted 4 browns, 4 blues, 2 yellows, 2 pinks, 2 greens, and 1 each of red, violet, and grey; in all, 17 distinct colours. All these were obtained from three primaries! The amount of brushwork, too, is incredible; in the pantomime of *Baron Munchausen* sheet 4 contains 122 separate pieces of colouring, and scene 13 has 167 strokes with the brush. All this was provided for an extra halfpenny or penny!

But it would be a mistake to give the impression that the colouring was detailed or finicky. It was, in fact, quite the reverse; these sheets had to be coloured quickly and cheaply. The procedure was to have a model sheet coloured with some care; in the British Museum there are several uncoloured proof sheets marked with West's directions to the colourist; these are the colours he demanded for one plate of characters: red, copper, dark brown, yellow, black, flesh, buff, light blue, steel, brown, pink, and white. Then there is a colourist's proof marked with the terse and very 'toy theatre' comment, 'colours a great deal brighter'. When this model sheet was properly coloured, it was given to a family with a gross of plain sheets, and was copied at home; most of the colouring seems to have been a home, and probably a very sweated industry. Each member of the family or group would have one colour only to apply, and the sheet would pass from hand to hand round the table gathering fresh colours all the way. Payment was by results, so there was every incentive to work quickly, and in fact, these colourists seem to have become amazingly deft with their fingers.

The late Mr How Mathews, about whom I shall have plenty to tell presently, described the process to me as follows: 'Speed would come with practice; a pair of legs would be done with one stroke of the brush, starting up one leg and down the other, narrowing and widening the brush, in about two seconds; about the same time for a jacket, right and left arm. The whole figure would take about eight seconds. A sheet of ten characters, say, eighty seconds, or, say a gross of 144 sheets would take four to six hours; at two shillings a gross this would work out at fourpence an hour.' I think this rate and general description applies to the later toy theatre period at the end of the century. Skilful colourists, working for the best publishers, such as McLean or Ackerman, could earn good money by working long hours. J. B. Howe recalls that his father with three other colourists had earned as much as fifty pounds between them in a good week, colouring botanical prints or tinting landscapes. This was in the late 'twenties. The rates paid by West and Hodgson cannot, I think, have been so very much less.

Speed compelled a broad treatment which gives these coloured sheets their great charm; there was no nonsense about painting every button or every finger; a coat was one flat colour, trousers another, and the hat the third; a dab of flesh tint on the face and hands, and the figure was finished. The results were splendid.

When competition became fierce and cheapness essential the colouring was done by stencils. This involves cutting a hole in sheets of cardboard so that the aperture in each board corresponds to the position of one colour on the painted sheet. Thus, for a sheet requiring the application of seven different colours, there would be seven differently cut boards. Applying colour with an ordinary brush through a stencil frame is not very satisfactory, and what were known as sable pencils were used. Given care, stencil colouring can be quite satisfactory, and it is quicker and requires less skill than direct brushwork; but there is always the danger of the stencil slipping, and when used carelessly, the results can be very horrid.

At one time, Webb is said to have employed twelve families to colour his sheets; this was long past the heyday of the trade. At its height, from the 'twenties to the 'fifties, there must have been hundreds of families in high attics and dark basements, where the women and the children spent long days round the table with brush and paint; their tired fingers and straining eyes, rewarded by a few shillings at the end of the week, were sacrificed for the lovely colouring that we can still enjoy today.

And by the time the sheets were ready, the book of the play had to be printed. I do not propose to discuss these books in detail here, as they can conveniently be considered when we go into the problems of practical performances; but briefly, what was necessary was to cut down the original play-book to a satisfactory length, and insert relevant instructions for toy theatre performance. The books of words were not normally printed by the publishers themselves, as they probably did not possess a suitable type-printing press; the books of West, for instance, were printed by E. Thomas of Denmark Street, and Elliot of Holywell Street, but fortunately it is hardly necessary for us to delve into the bibliographic underworld of the playbook printers.

The books were at first priced at 6d. each, but the very last book published by West in 1831 was reduced in format and price to 4d.; in the 'twenties Allen was already publishing cheap books at 3d. each; all Hodgson's books were 6d., but after that Skelt and Green published their books cheaply printed at 4d. Most of these had frontispieces, usually showing a tableau of how the characters should be placed at the fall of the curtain, but with the constant cry for cheaper production, these came to be omitted. Green's *Jack Sheppard* in 1839 shows a momentary return to the grand manner, with 36 pages and an engraved title page opposite the frontispiece, priced at 6d.; but the days for this sort of thing were over. At the end Pollock's and Webb's book were reduced to 2d., and rival playbooks were sold for 1d.

The book of words is a subject in itself, and, as we shall see, a careful study of their characteristics throws a great deal of light on the history of the Juvenile Drama.

This, then, is how the plays were published. And all this work would have to be done as quickly as possible if we were publishing a new play that had just been performed for the first time; the speed, indeed, at which these sheets were prepared is quite remarkable. West's earliest play of which we know, *The Peasant Boy*, was performed on January 31st and published on February 28th, a period of four weeks. By the next year this had been cut down to a fortnight; *The Spanish Patriots*, for instance, being performed on September 22nd and published on October 5th. The quickest publication that I can trace is that of *Ferdinand of Spain*, performed at Astley's on April 19th, 1813, and published by West on April 21st, a period of only two days! Even if this is the publication date of only the first sheet it represents an amazing achievement.

6 The Artists

Who, then, were the artists, the designers, and engravers, who drew these sheets and etched these plates? We have already seen how fragmentary is our knowledge of the publishers of the Juvenile Drama, derived almost entirely from the bare indications of name and address printed upon the sheets. Of the artists we know almost nothing; a name here and there, a few stray hints, some untraceable rumours, alone relieve the obscurity. Hack artists earning a pound or so at some cheap stationer's, their work was disregarded and their names never even remembered long enough to be forgotten.

There is, however, a little that can be gleaned. Some of the sheets issued by the early publishers are signed; many of West's prints, especially the large 2*d*. scenes, bear the inscription 'W. W.' or 'W. West fecit'; less often 'West del.' or 'West del et sculpt'; this signature, however, appears below quite a variety of styles, and it has been suggested that it was only inserted out of vanity or as a trick of the trade; the authority for this suggestion is provided by William Archer, in 1887, who says, 'Mr Blanchard and Mr Godfrey Turner assert that West did not draw at all.' I have been unable to trace the original statement to either of these gentlemen, and as they were both theatrical journalists of the 'eighties it is not evident with what authority they could speak on the subject. However, some years later, in 1898, Mr Ralph Thomas, a collector of West's sheets to whom we shall continually refer throughout this book, and who had made an exhaustive life study of these prints, confirmed this opinion in a letter to *Notes and Queries*; 'West was no artist, though he may have made rough sketches in the theatres,' he says. This statement has been accepted by A. E. Wilson, but I cannot see that there is enough evidence to support such a sweeping denial of authenticity. West certainly took a great interest in the production of his plays; there are artist's drawings and proofs in the British Museum scored with his comments, and it seems almost certain that he was, at least, an engraver and printer himself. If he was an accurate engraver of different artist's drawings, it is only natural that he should have worked in several styles. The evidence is, perhaps, not conclusive, but I can see no grounds for denying West all the credit due to him as, at least, a capable draughtsman, an excellent engraver, and a very good printer.

There is no suggestion, however, that West drew or engraved all his plates. Mr Ralph Thomas identified a large number as the work of George Cruikshank or of his brother, Robert. Mr Thomas was old enough to have met George Cruikshank, and asked him about his dealings with West; 'the only bit of information I managed to get from him,' he writes many years later, 'was that West's price to any artist for a quarto plate was one pound, no more. This price did not conform to Cruikshank's ideas, he told me, which accounts for his having done so few for West. I asked him the names of the "small fry", and one or two other pseudonyms of the persons whose drawings he etched. He said he could not tell, and that he often etched sketches for publishers, and never knew the names of the artists who were frequently amateurs.' From this, the only authentic statement in existence on the subject of Juvenile Dramatic artists, it appears that George Cruikshank certainly did a few engravings for West; the price of one pound would appear to be for the engraver and not for the artist, and I am not sure if he was expected to provide the copper plate and materials out of it; but to go on from this, as has been done, even by Mr Thomas, to assign play after play to the Cruikshanks merely on the grounds of a fancied resemblance in style, is, I suggest, quite unjustified. I do not propose quoting the long list of alleged Cruikshank drawings for West compiled by Mr Thomas and printed in *Notes and Queries* of October, 1920, as I feel that it lacks real authority, but the sheets of *The Merry Wives of Windsor, Comus, The Battle of Waterloo, The Wild Boy of Bohemia,* and *The Pilot,* as well as many single portraits, have all been reasonably attributed to George Cruikshank.

A few other signatures appear here and there upon West's sheets. William and Henry Heath did some very good work, Henry in particular specializing in splendid horse combats. Dighton did some excellent pantomime figures in 1812, and also drew for Burtenshaw; this could have been Robert Dighton, who did not die until 1814, but is far more likely to have been one of his sons, Denis or Richard, to whose careers as theatrical portraitists I have already drawn attention. West's elaborate catalogue sheet was engraved by Turnbull; scenes in *Rob Roy* and other plays are signed by T. Layton, who also seems to have worked for Hodgson and Co.; some of West's plates were by C. Tomkins, who may have been a scene painter; R. Scruton, the scenic artist at the Coburg, published some scenes through West, which are certainly reproductions of his designs at the theatre; the names of 'the late celebrated' (but now forgotten) John Varley and Alfred Cocking, together with William Heath, are mentioned by Edward Draper as having coloured for West; the names of J. Wright, T. Bradley, and D. Brooke appear on a few sheets; and there are a few excellent plates signed with the monogram 'W.B.'.

Discussing the meaning of this monogram, a gentleman named Godfrey Turner, in an article in *The Theatre* in 1886, is bold enough to state, 'I am able to tell with positive certainty. It was William Blake. Blake was one of West's most industrious limners. The monogram combining the two letters W.B. appears again and again on these penny sheets.' This statement, like a great many others with no more authority, has been uncritically accepted by A. E. Wilson, and has now found its way into almost every article about the toy theatre, and it will unfortunately be necessary for us to digress a little in order to examine it more carefully.

The statement itself is a gross exaggeration. So far from appearing 'again and again' the 'W.B.' monogram is only found on the sheets of one play— *The Broken Sword,* on West's show card, and on a portrait of Miss Dennett as Columbine. 'W. B.' was apparently an engraver, not a designer; an original drawing for *The Broken Sword* exists, and bears no signature, but the print is inscribed 'W.B. fecit'; similarly the original of West's show card is unsigned but the print is inscribed 'W. West del. W.B. fecit'. Whoever 'W.B.' was, he was a good artist; all these sheets are very accomplished and professional pieces of work; but who was he?

As we have seen, George Cruikshank could not recollect the names of any other artists who had worked for West. Edward Draper, who wrote an article in 1868 displaying some knowledge of the subject, made no reference to 'W.B.'; John Ashton who contributed the first real attempt at a history of the Juvenile Dramas in 1894, has nothing to tell about 'W.B.'. And yet, this Mr Godfrey Turner, in 1886, has no hesitation in assuming that 'W.B.' stands for William Blake! The next year, in *The Art Journal*, William Archer, a critic of some discernment, disputes this ascription, pointing out, on the authority of Sidney Colvin, the keeper of the Print Room at the British Museum, that the 'W.B.' monogram, though similar, is not the same as that used by Blake. But Mr Ralph Thomas, whose opinion must carry authority, does seem to have come to accept the Blake theory, though he certainly never orginated it; writing in 1898 he goes so far as to say that the characters in *Guy Mannering* 'are in Blake's style' and he also 'thinks' West's show card is by Blake. Coming from a man who never failed to stress the high 'artistic' value of West's sheets this must be considered a doubtful claim. But stories like this are easier to start than to stop, and Godfrey Turner's 'positive certainty' has gone round the world.

A. E. Wilson describes Godfrey Turner as an 'authority' on the matter, but I cannot see what claim he has to that title. He was writing seventy years after the sheets were drawn, and if he had any private source of information he does not reveal it; he only seems to have written one article on the subject, and although he undoubtedly had a real love and appreciation of these prints, his whole approach was that of an imaginative journalist.

One last test remains—that of style. Godfrey Turner again says, 'But the mannerism of Blake is almost sufficient—for remember it was a signature in spite of itself and was not likely to be obtruded. West's purpose was to subdue all these designs to one style, an ideal of his own.' There is a lot of truth in this last sentence, but no competent student will agree that even the handful of sheets signed 'W.B.' are self-evidently the work of William Blake. Some years ago I showed the original sketches and the finished prints in the British Museum collection to Mr Geoffrey Keynes, who is the bibliographer of and a recognized authority on Blake. He told me that he did not accept the attribution of any of this work to Blake, and that the signature was not in Blake's handwriting.

The situation is further complicated by the fact that there do exist plates signed 'E. Blake' or simply 'Blake'. A Portrait of 'Mr H. Kemble as Massaniello, in *The Fisherman of Naples*', published by West in 1825 is signed 'Blake fecit', and there is a similar one of Kean as Richard III; but these are wooden lifeless cuts, without a trace of genius or even professional competence in their execution, and are certainly not the work of William Blake, or even 'W.B.'. Similarly, several of the scenes for *The Dumb Savoyard and his Monkey* and *The Pilot* published by Straker, are signed 'E. Blake' or 'Blake'; but—though they may be connected with West's 'Blake' portraits—they obviously have no connection with 'W.B.'. One can only assume that Godfrey Turner put two and two together, equated 'Blake' with 'W.B.', and instead of putting forward a reasonable and interesting surmise, boldly announced 'with positive certainty' that 'it was William Blake'. This ascription remains a possibility about which there is doubtless more to be said, but for the time being it can only be regarded with critical scepticism.

No student of the Juvenile Drama will take any pleasure in demolishing one of its most cherished legends; but I feel that this popular cheap form of what is essentially a folk art does not need the attraction of the names of famous artists to advertise its wares. It was born in the gutter, and though for a time it flaunted itself in quite high company, the anonymity of the gutter is its true resting place.

Of the artists who worked for other publishers than West there is little that can be said. Mr Ralph Thomas has written that 'the Cruikshanks drew more for Jameson, the juvenile theatrical publisher, than for West. In fact, I believe all Jameson's are by the Cruikshanks.' To anyone who has seen some of the crude sheets issued by Jameson in 1811 this statement is quite incredible, but he did undoubtedly publish some very well-drawn plays in later years, and the Cruikshanks certainly worked for him then; some of his portraits are signed 'Cruikshank' or 'I. R. Cruikshank'. Some sheets issued by Jameson are signed by J. Findlay.

The brothers Heath did some of their best work for Hodgson and Co.; they were very accomplished artists, and William Heath especially was quite well known as a book illustrator of the Cruikshank school. A few of Hodgson's sheets are signed with the name of W. Hornegold. Writing many years later, in 1868, John Diprose in *Some Account of the Parish of Saint Clement Danes* recalls as a remarkable character, until recently resident in the parish, a certain 'George Honygold, of eccentric habits. . . . He was an artist of no inconsiderable talent, and possessed a large share of originality. The drawings of his celebrated theatrical characters were delineated with strict attention to the costumes they wore in the dramatic representations they were intended to represent, to which were added sketches of the scenery incidental to the pieces performed. From this arose the toy or model stage, which not only became a favourite with the juveniles, but also a great boon to the theatrical professors. . . . This style of printing or drawing was adopted by many printsellers, and is still a thriving trade. Honygold was a very agreeable companion, having collected a rare and racy fund of anecdotes; this led him much into company, and caused him to indulge too much in intemperate habits, which ended, we regret to say, in an untimely death. He constantly used the noted "No. 9", a gin-palace in Clare Market. He afterwards frequented the "Fountain", No. 4 Clare Street. In this house he imbibed his last drop; he had been indulging freely, and when the house was cleared, being deeply intoxicated, he fell down. He was taken to the Charing Cross Hospital, where he expired, at the age of sixty-nine, in the year 1866.' It is the too familiar story lying behind so many gay and innocent toy theatre sheets!

No sheets signed with the name Honygold are known to exist, and it seems reasonable to equate the subject of these memories with W. Hornegold, and perhaps with the more common initials 'W.H.', which may not necessarily always stand for William Heath. John Diprose was a curious journalist-publisher-antiquary, and seems to have been writing from personal knowledge; he was himself a resident in the parish of Saint Clement Danes. Later historians of this London district, such as Charles Heckethorn and Beresford Chancellor, have misquoted Diprose and described 'Honeygold' as 'the originator of the toy or model stage'—an ascription for which there is no vestige of authority.

The extra large scenes published by Hodgson and Co. are mostly signed 'G.C.'; at one time, these, too, were attributed to George Cruikshank, but Ralph Thomas, who here seems to speak with authority, has declared them to be the work of a certain George Childs, and sheets do exist signed with this name; Childs, it appears, was an artist and scene painter; he illustrated Captain P. M. Taylor's *Sketches in the Decor* in 1837, and exhibited at the Royal Academy between 1825 and 1873, so these sheets must be the work of his youth; they are undoubtedly very good examples of contemporary scenic design. After Hodgson had shut down, these large scenes were bought by

Lacy, the predecessor of French, for the use of scenic artists. The names of W. Nicholls and A. Courcell appear on some of the portraits and combats published by Creed and Cole; P. Roberts signed a few fine portraits for Orlando Hodgson; A. Burcham drew portraits in the 'thirties; and some of the equestrian portraits of Ducrow, published by Lloyd, are signed by W. Cocking as artist and by Lloyd himself as the engraver. Apart from West, other publishers who signed their own names as 'del.' or 'fecit' were G. Creed, Pyall, and J. L. Marks. Other names mentioned by Godfrey Turner as artists of the Juvenile Drama are Flaxman, Crowquill, and William Finden; I do not know of any evidence to support these names, and in themselves they are most unlikely; Flaxman, for instance, was a professor of sculpture at the Royal Academy, and Finden was an illustrator of elaborately pretentious picture books; the idea that they would have stooped to drawing cheap theatrical prints is quite ridiculous.

We do not find any more signatures on prints after the time of Hodgson; toy theatre sheets were not considered worth signing, and the artists were unknown hacks whose names meant nothing. Arthur Park is said to have been an artist and engraver, and probably not only drew his own, comparatively few, plays but worked for other publishers as well, notably Hodgson, Cole, and Skelt. W. G. Webb was apprenticed to his brother Archibald, and some of Park's portraits appear to be in his hand; the original drawings in my possession suggest that Webb also drew some of Skelt's plays during this time. Later Webb, who was a very capable artist, drew and engraved all his own plays. None of the Skelts could draw or engrave themselves, according to a letter I have seen from Mr G. Skelt, and employed two engravers—one for characters and one for scenes—hard at work for five or six years. As I have already mentioned from the same authority, the drawings were done in great detail by separate artists, and special lettering engravers were employed. Old Mr Webb once said in an interview that the artist who drew Skelt's pictures died in the workhouse.

The plays published by Redington were perhaps drawn by himself, for he surely could never have found a professional artist to produce such crude work. And so we come to the last of the Juvenile Drama artists, a certain Mr Tofts, 'a man of substance—a wonderful designer—a draughtsman he called himself'—perhaps a toy theatre customer with a love for these toys—who enlarged and improved the small scenes of *The Sleeping Beauty* for Pollock, Redington's successor, in 1883. These delightful magic forests, ogre's kitchens, royal palaces, and fairy lakes are as pleasant as anything ever drawn for the toy theatre; even in its last decline its artists' pencils had not lost the magic touch.

7 Selling the Play

When the sheets were drawn, engraved, and coloured, how were they sold? Individual sheets could be purchased separately, or sometimes the entire play with the book of words was 'neatly done up in a Case', which might be embellished with an attractive cover. All these publishers kept shops; in the literary world generally the distinction between publisher and bookseller was not yet finely drawn; and it was in these circulating libraries and theatrical print warehouses that the Juvenile Drama was set before the public. I once took the trouble to mark on an old map of London, the addresses of all the Juvenile Drama publishers, and it was interesting to see how they congregated round certain areas; the great centre was the congeries of narrow streets north of the Strand, in the shadow of the great theatres of Covent Garden and Drury Lane; Wych Street and Holywell Street, the heart of this district, acquired a very disreputable character later in the century for their display of pornographic literature, and eventually the whole area was razed to the ground to make way for the Kingsway improvement. There was a small colony round Smithfield, and another further east in the Minories district, by the Tower of London, to serve the East End. West of Trafalgar Square there were only a few scattered publishers; all this area was far too residential and respectable. There was another colony, south of the river, nestling near the transpontine theatres, and yet another group in north London, Islington, Finsbury, and Hoxton, to satisfy the patrons of Sadler's Wells and the Britannia.

Several of the publishers have left us drawings of their shops as Harlequinade scenes in pantomimes; this was entirely in the spirit of the theatres, who used to allow firms to advertise their names upon the facias of the harlequinade street scene backcloths. We have already seen what West's shop in Exeter Street looked like; at the end of the toy theatre period, in the 'fifties, we have a view of Webb's shop in Old Street. It has the usual many-paned window, with a side door; inside the shop, on the counter, can be glimpsed a stage with a full scene in position; in the window there are closely displayed, from top to bottom, rows of combats, single portraits, joke figures, and writing paper. Some of these shops had specially painted signs hanging outside; Lloyd's, for instance, depicted a Clown and Harlequin, and Redington hung a complete stage above the pavement to proclaim the business that was transacted inside.

We have seen that toy theatre publishers did not restrict themselves to these prints alone, and in later years we find them dealing in a wide variety of goods; Green offered fifty different sorts of juvenile and pantomime books, and, in addition to his toy theatre stock, he lists 'Scraps, Varietys, Lotterys, Childrens' Toys and Playing Cards, Conjuring, Conversation, Fortune Telling and Oracular Cards with directions. Sentimental and Comic Valentines. Valentine Writers, Draught Boards and Raffle Papers. Improved Card and Paper Window Bills of every description, 500 sorts.' The prices of these articles ranged from a farthing to sixpence.

To what extent the early publishers sold their plays at retail agents I am not sure, but the striking show card published by West, with the inscription 'West's New Theatrical Characters Sold Here—Magic' can only have been designed for display in the windows of his retailers. The plays of Skelt and Green, however, were certainly sold at a large number of retail stationers; there is a drawing by Leech showing the inside of one of these shops in *The Struggles and Adventures of Christopher Tadpole* by Albert Smith, published in 1848. The shop was known as 'Smedlar's Library'; on the shelves behind the counter is ranged a small stock of books, in the doorway hangs a notice of the latest titles, headed 'Lent to Read'; in front of the counter is placed an advertisement for *Mabel the Mildewed*—the sort of romantic title that would be popular with the servant girls who patronized the library. Another notice in the doorway says 'Now Ready, *The Murder at Midnight*'; this was doubtless a boys' 'penny dreadful', appearing in weekly numbers. But the shop stocks other things besides books; there is a bundle of smart canes, there are two figures in the windows advertising cigars, and on the counter is a complete set-up toy theatre, with proscenium, wings, and back drop in the familiar six-inch by eight-inch size, with a cut-out character gesticulating on the stage. In the windows of the shop may be seen a selection of 'Theatrical Portraits of heroes in very determined attitudes'.

This is the only contemporary view of the interior of one of these stationers, and it may be taken as typical of thousands of shops in London and in the provinces at which the halfpenny toy theatre sheets were sold; only occasionally did their names appear on the sheets of the plays.

We have descriptions of one or two of these toy theatre agents. J. F. Wilson has described a shop in Drury Lane at which he 'bought many a set of Skelt's

The interior of a circulating library which also sold toy theatres. From *The Struggles and Adventures of Christopher Tadpole*.

Theatrical Characters' in the 'thirties; it was kept by a blind man named Cox, 'whose sense of touch was so acute that he could pick out the newspapers and periodicals required by his customers, and take money and give change with perfect accuracy'. This unpretentious establishment was quite a meeting place of down-at-heels actors: 'here would gather utility gentlemen, the ladies of the ballet, columbines, harlequins, pantaloons and clowns, while occasionally a tragedian would stalk in, or the representative of second low comedy would condescend to make a hurried call and crack his latest joke. Newspapers being dear commodities in these days, it was a privilege to have the use of this place as a reading-room, and scan the criticism of last night's performances without being expected to buy anything.'

The trade was always mainly confined to London, for the interest of the plays was closely bound up with the London theatres, but West's catalogue of as early as 1811 advertised 'Country Orders Punctually attended too' [sic], and in the later toy theatre period we find one or two provincial publishers. There were also undoubtedly stationers acting as agents in almost every town; at Brighton, for instance, in Church Street, or at Cambridge in King Street, there were shops where the plays and all the accessories could still be bought within living memory; and it was in Edinburgh, in Leith Walk that Robert Louis Stevenson first saw, in a stationer's windows, those plates of 'robbers carousing' that inspired his early love of the toy theatre. This shop is still standing today, at number one, Union Street; it is an old-fashioned newsagent's, with steps up from the pavement, but the Juvenile Drama has not been sold there for many years.

These then were the shops where the toy theatre was sold, and it was here that a whole generation of boys came with pennies in their hands to learn the mysteries of its art. It must be emphasized that they were not toy shops; from its first proud stilted title to the end the Juvenile Drama was very jealous of its semi-adult status; *The British Theatre in Miniature* was how Straker described his publications; Cole titled his catalogue *The British Stage in Miniature*; 'W. Webb, Printer and Publisher' was elegantly displayed above his shop. Towards the end of the toy theatre period, however, the sheets do seem to have found their way into toy shops; in 1866 a writer in *Every Little Boy's Book* informs us that 'having decided on the play you intend to represent you may purchase the characters, which are sold in sheets at almost all the smaller toy-shops, and at many booksellers'; but during its heyday the trade was undoubtedly carried on from the stationers; the boys would not have their plays rubbing shoulders with dolls.

There is no record that these publishers ever advertised their wares by any other means than displaying them in their shop windows. The books of words were often provided with an outside wrapper of thin coloured paper—green, blue, or yellow—upon which the firm's list of plays and toy theatre accessories might be detailed; but in the early 'thirties Robert Lloyd, apparently an enterprising fellow, struck an original note by printing an advertising blurb in doggerel verse on his playbooks; this is crude, but not unamusing. The opening verses are as follows:

THE INVITATION

Tune—*The Calais Packet*

Come all ye friends of amusements Theatrical
Listen a minute and hear me rehearse,
Where ye may purchase the whole Corps Dramatical,
Tragedy, Comedy, Opera, Farce;
Managers would you be, come then attend to me,
Here you may quickly see, shown in my verse,
How you may Stars engage, first Actors of the Age,
Ornaments of the Stage—with a light purse.

Lose no more time then, but quickly into Surrey go,
Bridges are plenty—the best's Waterloo;
Passing the Coburg, as you in a hurry go,
GIBSON STREET, 40, is full in your view;
Lloyd's is the shop, well-known to all the lads in Town,
Sign of the funny Clown, Harlequin too—
Both seem to point the spot, where ONLY can be got,
Drawn from the life, I wot—CHARACTERS NEW.

Similarly, William Cole, who took over the Hodgson and Co. stock, inserted a price list of plays and stages at the back of a little book of children's poems published by him in 1829 under the title of *The Parent's Poetical Present*. This same volume contains a pleasant poem in praise of the Juvenile Drama, adorned with, I think, the earliest illustration of an actual toy theatre performance in progress; the poem is entitled *The British Stage in Miniature*, in thirteen verses, from which I cull the following:

All people talk of London sights,
For London's all the rage;
But that which most a *youth* delights
Is called 'THE BRITISH STAGE'.

There's 'LIFE IN LONDON', Tom and Jerry,
There's also 'LIFE IN PARIS';
There's 'FAIR STAR' and her darling 'CHERRY'—
Nay, ev'ry thing that rare is.

For there are *Combats*, great and small,
And *Portraits* out of number;
Processions, Cars, Stage-Fronts, and all!
To fill one's mind with wonder.

The *Drama*, too, call'd 'Juvenile',
Portrays each sep'rate Part,
And, while we thus our time beguile,
We get the Play by heart.

80

Selling the Play

Then, let us haste to *Newgate Street*,
And find out *Number Ten*,
For there 'THE BRITISH STAGE', complete,
Delights both boys and men.

It would be interesting to know how many of these sheets actually were sold. Sales of millions have often been vaguely referred to, but this is certainly an exaggeration. I have calculated that a sale of one thousand copies would have yielded a small profit to the publisher; and I think it probable that in the early period the maximum sale of any play was in the region of five thousand sets; other plays probably only sold a few hundred copies and failed to make money. It must be borne in mind that the population of London in 1820 was only just over one million; this represented about 200,000 families, of whom half were illiterate and living without any pennies at all to spare for toys; if two out of every hundred literate families purchased Juvenile Drama sheets we are left with the figure of 2,000 as a maximum sale.

The halfpenny plays of Skelt and Green must have been sold in many thousands to cover their cost, especially as they largely relied on a wholesale trade. By this time the business covered the whole country, and the sale of popular sheets probably ran into hundreds of thousands during this period.

Despite its great popularity, no one ever seems to have made more than a bare livelihood out of the toy theatre. The Wests were said to be well off in their old age, but they lived in squalor and wretchedness; Skelt died in the workhouse; there were no fortunes to be made in the toy theatre business.

The revolving disc from I. Green's 'Punch's Show' a form of paper toy that may have preceded the toy theatre

8 Georgian Home Amusements

After the sheets were sold, what happened then? There is no difficulty in describing the children's performances of the later toy theatre plays, of which we have ample documentation, but it is not at all easy to decide exactly what was done with the early character sheets of the Juvenile Drama. We have approached the subject correctly, I think, from the standpoint of the theatre; let us now look at these sheets from the other angle. What was the background of the home?

Domestic life in the early nineteenth century followed a pattern not fundamentally different from our own, but the emphasis was varied and the day was divided by meals into segments that are still familiar in Scotland and the North of England, but have been forgotten in the South.

Among well-bred families, breakfast was often not eaten till ten, but a great deal of the work of the day was completed before it; there then followed, thus soundly fortified, a lengthy 'morning' devoted to work in the house, shopping, visiting, or outdoor exercises and pursuits; this morning was interrupted, but not concluded, by a midday luncheon that might consist of sandwiches or cold meat, but which was eaten informally in the breakfast-room, and never made the excuse for a social occasion. After luncheon the morning's work and pursuits continued until dinner. This was *the* meal of the day, and was eaten at about five o'clock—sometimes a little earlier in the country, and sometimes a little later in fashionable town houses. Here the famous trenchering of our ancestors took its leisurely course, the table was covered with plates and cutlery, soup was sent round, the master of the house cut venison or goose, puddings crowned the repast, and wine was drunk in informal toasts. After this, the cloth was removed and the table relaid with dessert and fresh wine; the formality of the dinner table might be lessened, chairs pushed out, or pulled round the fire, and conversation grew more general.

The ladies now retired to the drawing-room, and the gentlemen remained with their brandy or port; coffee was served separately. After a decent interval, the gentlemen left the dining-room, singly or as they chose, and joined the ladies; the time might now be half past six or seven, work for the day was finished, and a long evening lay ahead.

If one left at once, there was time to reach the theatre before the play started; sometimes there were balls or routs; but inevitably, in most middle-class families, most evenings were spent at home.

After an hour or more, at about eight o'clock perhaps, tea was served, accompanied by cakes; this was a social function in itself, and visitors who did not want the formality of a dinner engagement were sometimes invited to tea. And then, at last, the day came to a close with an informal light supper between ten and eleven; a cloth might be laid and the company adjourn to a supper-room, or more often, a tray with elegant sandwiches and glasses of Madeira would be handed round. The family could now make its way to bed.

How were these long evenings occupied? In conversation and gossip, in music and singing, sometimes in reading aloud (but for quiet private reading one retired to the library), in making knick-knacks and fancy work, but above all, in cards and paper games. Whist was considered a serious game for four; five or more could play for high stakes at loo, and piquet or backgammon were popular gambles between two gentlemen. But there were many other frivolous round-the-table games, some played with cards and some with special counters or ivory fish, at which any number of ladies and gentlemen, young or old, could amuse themselves: casino, commerce, andro, speculation, vingt-un, consequences, lottery tickets, or quadrille. In this way the hours between tea and supper were cheerfully occupied.

The children's lives followed the same pattern as their parents, within the boundaries of the schoolroom, and under the direction of a governess, who supervised the education of young ladies up to the age of fifteen or sixteen—if they were not sent to boarding-school. Study seems to have largely consisted of exercises in mnemonics; girls of thirteen or fourteen, we learn from Jane Austen, could name the principal rivers in Russia, repeat the dates of the Kings of England and of the Roman emperors, recite the chief characters in heathen mythology, and reel off a list of all the metals, semi-metals, planets, and distinguished philosophers; they were also instructed, as a matter of course, in music and drawing. This curriculum was not, however, as one is sometimes led to imagine, driven home with nothing but tears and the rod; the ingenious minds that had developed so many entertaining games for adults also produced a whole crop of amusing and instructive games for children, to reinforce their regular tuition.

For geography, there was 'A Complete Voyage round the World, a New Geographical Pastime', 'The Panorama of Europe', or 'The Panorama of

London, a Day's Journey round the Metropolis'; these were coloured folding sheets, mounted on canvas, across which counters were moved by spinning a tetotum (dice were not approved of in the nursery), with hazards and accelerations whose awful warnings and happy outcomes drove home the lesson of their natural features. Jigsaw puzzles of the map of Europe could also be had, in which each country was to be fitted into its appropriate place. Finally there appeared 'A Geographical Panorama exhibiting Characteristic Representations of the Scenery and Inhabitants of Various Regions', which was in effect a model stage, upon which could be mounted nine different and most attractive views, with cut-out native inhabitants, mounted on cardboard, to be displayed before them. As this was published by Harvey and Darton in 1822, it must, however, be regarded as an offshoot rather than a forerunner of the Juvenile Drama. Geographical, too, and even more elaborate, were the peepshows, but these, too, in the form of 'Areaoramas' and 'Perspective Views', were not adapted for the home until about 1825.

For history, there was 'The New Game of Human Life', 'A Game of the History of England; an Historical Pastime', 'Who Wears the Crown', or 'The Royal Game of British Sovereigns, from Egbert to George III'. With such attractive coloured sheets, neatly folded in their slip-cases, every branch of knowledge was pleasantly diverted; we find 'An Arithmetical Pastime; intended to infuse the Rudiments of Arithmetic under the Idea of Amusement', 'Science in Sport, or The Pleasures of Astronomy', 'A Grammatical Game in Rhyme, by a Lady', and 'A Musical Game for Children invented by L. M. Drummond, Esq.'; contemporary history was taught by 'The Life and Military Adventures of the Duke of Wellington from 1787 to 1815'; and ethics were even instilled with 'The Mirror of Truth, A New Game calculated to Inspire a Love of Virtue and Abhorrence of Vice', or 'The Road to the Temple of Honour and Fame, an Instructive and Entertaining Game'.

But by no means all these paper games were educational or instructive; there was 'The Game of Goose', 'The Royal Pastime of Cupid; or the New and Most Pleasant Game of the Snake'; 'The New Game of Emulation', the Games of the Jew, the Monkey, and the Swan, and 'The Magic Ring, a New Game, replete with Humour'.

And so with tetotum and counters, with young tempers lost and tears of disappointment, with puny rages and little triumphs, with reconciliations, with fun and laughter, these games of the late eighteenth and early nineteenth centuries diversified the leisure nursery hours.

There were other paper toys, too, pretty or constructive, rather than competitive. The most interesting of these, for our purposes, were the 'Turn Ups' or Harlequinades; these were first published a little before 1770 and remained in circulation until the end of the century; the best, and probably the first, were issued by Robert Sayer, but other publishers, such as H. Roberts and Laurie and Whittle, who published children's books in the late eighteenth century, also issued a number of these delightful toy picture books. American booksellers too, such as Nobel's Juvenile Library in Boston or Samuel Wood in New York, displayed them in their windows, and publishers like J. Rakestraw in Philadelphia or P. B. Goodsell in Hartford continued to print them for more than twenty years after they had disappeared from the English stationers.

The original 'turn ups', which can best be described as 'flap picture books', seem to have been based on the contemporary stage harlequinades. Their interest, then, as forerunners of the Juvenile Drama is obvious. These picture books displayed some of the antics and adventures of Harlequin in a novel and amusing manner by means of folded paper flaps, which could be raised or lowered to effect the transformations and change the scenes; each book consisted of four engravings, usually hand-coloured, and each engraving was hidden under two flaps, which, when dexterously lifted up, progressively and totally transformed the scene. The normal size of these books was what is called narrow octavo, that is to say, as high as a modern novel, but about half as wide, and they were issued bound in paper wrappers.

The titles selected were mainly those of the pantomimes in which such Harlequins as Woodward were most delighting the town; we find *The King and the Clown* in 1767, *The Elopement, A New Harlequin Entertainment* in 1771, and so on. In all, fifteen titles were issued by Sayer at sixpence plain and a shilling coloured; only a few imitations seem to have appeared, and it seems reasonable to conclude that the experiment was a comparative failure. In 1797 Laurie and Whittle, Sayer's successors, were 'remaindering' these booklets at four shillings and eight shillings a dozen. (Today they are worth something like fifty pounds each!)

Early in the nineteenth century the 'turn up' developed into something very close to our subject. In 1803 the firm of T. Hughes announced for publication a series to be known as 'The Juvenile Theatre'; this was to consist of 'Dramatic Delineations . . . of all the most Favourite Spectacles, Pantomimes, Ballets', etc., presented at the principal theatres. J. Harris, Champante and Whitrow, and other well-known booksellers were appointed agents, and at least seventeen titles were issued between 1803 and 1807, ranging from *Harlequin's Habeas* to *The Wood Daemon*. Nearly half of the titles were melodramas. For this reason I would enter a plea that the term 'harlequinade' which has generally been used in the antiquarian book trade to describe these booklets is not really appropriate, and that the term 'turn up' is more suitable. In style and format this series closely follows the Sayer's turn ups, and has little resemblance to West's first sheets of theatrical characters, but it is without doubt a link between the turn ups and the Juvenile Drama, and is of very great intrinsic interest.

Hughes's enterprise seems to have encouraged other publishers in the same direction, and we find the famous publisher of children's books, Tabart, issuing booklets that once again draw their illustrations from contemporary theatrical performances. In 1804 he announced editions of *Cinderella*, *Blue Beard*, and *Valentine and Orson* 'with coloured representations of the scenes contained in the last spectacle at Drury Lane', and in 1809 a turn-up edition of '*The Exile*, as performed at the Royal Theatres'. *The Exile*, which was first produced in 1808, is neither a pantomime nor a children's story, but—like much of Hughes's Juvenile Theatre—a typical melodrama of the period.

The connection with the Juvenile Drama must not be pushed too far; no publisher of turn ups ever issued any Juvenile Drama plays; these books were simply designed as pretty and amusing toys to look at, and the business of lifting up a flap was within the ability of any young child; there was no sort of practical cutting out required. But the similarities cannot be ignored; here was a children's toy that was directly derived from the contemporary theatre. As a record of eighteenth-century pantomime they have a unique interest; they were extending their range into nineteenth-century melodrama; and they died out in England in the very decade that saw the birth of the Juvenile Drama.

I do not think that these 'harlequinades' can be described as the origin of the toy theatre; but there is a certain affinity in style, and they can, very accurately, be described as forerunners of the Juvenile Drama. It was to a public already familiar with turn-up books of pantomime harlequinades and melodramas that the first sheets of theatrical characters and scenes were offered; their influence cannot be compared with the toy theatre, and they constitute only a minor chapter in the history of English children's books, but I hope that one day someone will write them the monograph that they deserve.

Young children would be satisfied with picture toy books, but as they grew older they liked something to make and do themselves; the paper dolls, introduced in about 1790, were designed to answer this need. These consisted of a sheet printed with the figure of a lady in her underclothes and with her other and various articles of clothing shown separately; these were all cut out and the lady could be dressed, piece by piece, until she appeared elegantly arrayed in all the latest fashions. These sheets were exported to France, where they were known as 'English' dolls.

Similar to these were the cut-out figure books published by S. and J. Fuller between 1810 and 1815; the idea here was that the same paper head could be placed upon a number of different paper bodies, to represent the same person in a variety of costumes. About seven to nine coloured cut-out bodies, one or two movable heads, and usually three or four head-dresses were provided in a slip-case with a small story book. The book told some story that the characters could illustrate; it might be a simple tale such as *The History and Adventures of Little Henry, exemplified in a Series of Figures, Phoebe, the Cottage Maid, The History of Little Fanny*, or *Ellen: or the Naughty Girl Reclaimed;*

or it might be some anecdote more directly designed to display the hero in his many costumes, such as *Frank Feignwell's Attempts to Amuse his Friends on Twelfth Night, exhibited in a Series of Characters*, or *Young Albert, the Roscius, exhibited in a Series of Characters from Shakespeare and other Sources.* Here, with these cut-out theatrical figures published in 1811, we are again very close to the Juvenile Drama. These cut-out heads and bodies cannot be regarded as the origin of the toy theatre; there was no suggestion of performing them on a stage, indeed one could not do more than arrange and rearrange them as they lay on the table; and they are in no way derived from the adult theatre. Moreover, they appear to have been contemporary with, rather than to have preceded, the first sheets of theatrical characters, and S. and J. Fuller never published any Juvenile Drama plays. But their affinity with the toy theatre is obvious, and these too must be accepted as interesting forerunners of the toy theatre as a nursery pastime.

So far we have found some suggestions of the Juvenile Drama in the paper toys of the late eighteenth and early nineteenth centuries, but they have all hitherto lacked movement—the very essence of the toy theatre. We do, however, find this in the 'movable pictures' that were just beginning to appear at this time. Later in the century, story books with figures that could be gently jerked to and fro were not uncommon, and there are several such books still published today; the most popular seems to have been *Punch and Judy*, which intrinsically lent itself to such treatment. I do not think this type of publication was common before about 1840, but I have in my possession a single sheet depicting a Punch and Judy show, which appears to date from very early in the century. The opening of this could be cut out and a revolving disc pinned behind, upon which the various incidents of the drama were displayed. And when we look for the publisher's name, what do we find? The name of I. Green, 1 Clements Inn Passage, Clare Market. Could this be I. K. Green, 'the original inventor and publisher of Juvenile Theatrical Prints'? It is impossible to make any precise judgment upon the date of this sheet, or its place in our story, but there is here, anyway, the beginning of movement with paper figures.

Pursuing our search for anything that may have suggested the Juvenile Drama, we must mention the painting books, which were being published by the second half of the eighteenth century. *Punch, or a Collection of Droll Figures proper for Youth to draw after*, for instance, was published by Robert Sayer, the harlequinade publisher, in about 1780; it contains sixteen plain engravings, two to a page. Children were quite accustomed to using their camel-hair brushes and watercolours by the time the first penny plain sheets were presented for their embellishment.

These then were the paper toys with which young children in the years before 1810 found pleasure and amusement. At a time when most books for children were considered bound to inculcate some moral principle, these gay and pretty little sheets express the very spirit of fun and gaiety; the nurseries were happy where their ingenious manipulation provided employment for many little hands. Here and there, as we have seen, there are suggestions of the toy theatre, and these paper toys undoubtedly prepared the way for what was to follow; but I do not think any of these publications can really be described as the origin of the Juvenile Drama; the first sheets of principal characters, as published by West, for example, strike an entirely different note; they are neither childish—even in the best sense of the term—in inspiration nor in execution, and as I have shown, their true origin lies elsewhere. These paper toys, however, undoubtedly trained the children of England in the careful use of scissors and paste, of brush and crayon; children who had successfully overcome the complexities of turn ups and movable heads were in a fair way to commence the management of a model theatre. The Juvenile Drama was, in fact, an amalgamation of the first more or less adult sheets of theatrical characters with these cut-out paper toys, and it is only with both these influences in mind that one can really understand its rather anomalous position in the home.

If one tried to simplify the whole thing, and construct a genealogical tree of the toy theatre, I suggest it should be arranged something like this:

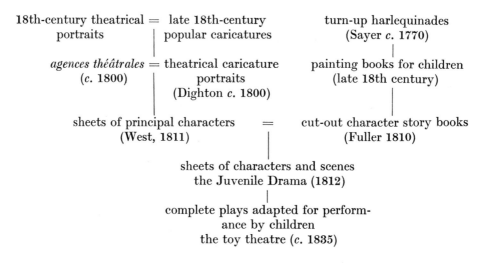

18th-century theatrical = late 18th-century   turn-up harlequinades
    portraits | popular caricatures   (Sayer *c.* 1770)

agences théâtrales = theatrical caricature   painting books for children
    (*c.* 1800) | portraits   (late 18th century)
               (Dighton *c.* 1800)

sheets of principal characters   =   cut-out character story books
     (West, 1811)   (Fuller 1810)

sheets of characters and scenes
the Juvenile Drama (1812)

complete plays adapted for performance by children
the toy theatre (*c.* 1835)

9 The Toy Theatre in the Home

These paper toys that we have been considering were essentially designed for young children, at least under the age of ten. I am not sure at what age children joined the family table for dinner, but the ruling that children should be seen (occasionally) but not heard, seems to have been less observed in Georgian than in Victorian days; some time about the age of ten, children must have begun to feel themselves growing up, and new interests claimed their attention.

For girls there was a positive host of accomplishments of which every young lady made herself mistress; for the next century drawing-rooms were to be submerged beneath a vast accumulation of feminine ingenuity. Objects were coated with gold paper, screens were painted or worked with wool, purses were knitted, tables were painted, samplers were stitched, carpets and rugs were woven, china ornaments were imitated, landscapes were contrived from coloured silks, footstools were covered, windows were obscured with transparencies, artificial flowers were created, filigree baskets were produced from entwined rolls of paper, and scrap books were filled with cyphers and trophies, rhymes and riddles, watercolours and prints. And beside all this, music, singing, and dancing had to be carefully cultivated. Children grew quickly to maturity in those days; it was a matter of pride if a girl married at sixteen; after marriage there was the housekeeping, children, the flower garden, servants, the poor neighbours, and children again.

So much for the girls. But what of the boys? They too came to an age, earlier even than the girls, when the toys of the nursery were rejected; a little later, when they too were sixteen, they would be young gentlemen, hunting, shooting, and fishing in the country, young bloods, Corinthians, budding mashers, in the town. But till then, how were they occupied?

The Toy Theatre in the Home

Surprisingly, the theatre played a big part in these boys' lives and up-bringing; in nonconformist homes, no doubt, everything to do with the stage was forbidden, but among the ordinary middle-class well-to-do families, to whom all these descriptions mainly apply, the stage was a constant interest. That careful observer and accurate chronicler of contemporary life, Miss Jane Austen, has left on record the 'love of the theatre' and the 'itch for acting' that was 'so general and so strong' among young people. Elocution and good speech were encouraged, and schoolboys would be summoned before their fathers to declaim favourite passages from the great dramatists: 'Friends, Romans, Countrymen', 'To be, or not to be', or 'My name is Norval' (from Home's *Douglas*) were recited in many boyish trebles. Miss Austen, again, describes even a typical country squire, who did not approve of mixed private theatricals, as having 'a decided taste for anything of the acting, spouting, reciting kind'. At school, Edward Draper tells us, writing of the early 'thirties, 'one of the daily reading lessons was usually taken from the drama', and there are numerous references to the end-of-term plays performed by the pupils at many a scholastic academy.

The craze for amateur acting was in full swing; private representations were given in country houses, and there were several small London theatres that could be hired by ambitious amateurs, and were indeed in constant demand; young men in their early twenties, no doubt, were the chief enthusiasts, but their younger brothers too were infected with the contagion. There is, moreover, some evidence that boys were not infrequent spectators at the theatres themselves. The question of how often and how young boys went to the theatre in the early nineteenth century throws an interesting and largely unexplored sidelight upon social history; the truth would astonish those whose ideas of the period are based upon a few distorted late Victorian impressions.

At the end of the eighteenth century, in Bath, Southey saw Fielding's comedy *The Fathers* and Walter Scott saw *As You Like It*, both at the age of four; Charles Lamb saw *Artaxerxes* when he was six years old; Charles Dickens was taken to see *Richard III* and *Macbeth* at the Theatre Royal, Rochester at about the age of eight in 1820, and at the same age he saw Grimaldi in the Covent Garden pantomimes. These are examples, of course, of exceptional and early visits to the theatre, but it would seem that children in their early teens were not infrequently regular theatre-goers; Thackeray, for instance, describing in *Vanity Fair* the lives of two boys in London in the year 1826, tells how 'they both had a taste for painting theatrical characters; for hard-bake and raspberry tarts; for sliding and skating in the Regent's Park and the Serpentine, when the weather permitted'; and, unexpectedly, 'for going to the play, whither they were often conducted . . . by Rowson, Master George's appointed body-servant; with whom they sate in great comfort in the pit. In the company of this gentleman they visited all the principal theatres of the metropolis' and 'knew the names of all the actors from Drury Lane to Sadler's

Wells'. The age of Georgy Osborne, one of the boys in question, was eleven. Even girls were by no means barred from the theatre; in 1813 Jane Austen took a family party to London, and visited the theatre twice in the company of her two nieces, aged twelve and thirteen; among the plays they saw were *Midas* and the pantomime version of *Don Juan*, which were both published for the Juvenile Drama. On the other hand Fanny Kemble has recalled how she clamoured to be taken to see Mrs Siddons in a special revival of *Douglas* in 1715, when she was only six years old, but was at first refused as she was considered too young. At the age of eight, however, judging from 'The Baby's Debut' in *The Rejected Addresses* of 1812, a girl might be taken by her parents to Drury Lane, and there is another reference from Thackeray in *Pendennis*, when young Arthur Pendennis, who is only seventeen, takes his family to see Miss Fotheringay act, and little Laura, who is nine, is included in the party.

It would appear from these references that, in Regency England, visits to the theatre were unusual, but not unknown, for a child of six, and usual for children of twelve. Mr Vincent Crummles, some twenty years later, in *Nicholas Nickleby* has described a great theatre-going family of six children, who brought six grown-ups to hold them on their laps and fill the family box at the provincial theatre. There is no doubt that English children were reared on the drama from an early age; and it must be remembered that there were no such things as special children's plays; even pantomimes only accidentally catered for children's tastes.

Among artisan and 'mechanic' families, visits of young boys to the theatre were probably much more frequent than among the middle classes, and there is rather more documentation on this point; I might mention, among several references, the memories of J. B. Howe, who describes his frequent visits to the Bower Saloon, the Albert Saloon, the Queen's, and Sadler's Wells during the early 'forties, when he could not have been much older than ten or twelve. 'From this time,' he writes, 'I had a decided mania for the stage . . . I neglected everything for the theatre.' In 1827 we find John Forster, at the age of fifteen, writing 'A Few Thoughts in Vindication of the Stage' for the benefit of a lady who had admonished him on the evils of theatre-going. By that age many boys were enthusiastic patrons and, doubtless, not unworthy critics of the contemporary drama.

This then was the society, of boys and young men mad on the stage, and of boys grown out of their childish pastimes, upon which the toy theatre was launched.

Punchs and puppets had been played with at home by both boys and girls during the eighteenth century; in Italy and Germany home marionette theatres of great elaborateness and cost (there is a fine Venetian example in the Bethnal Green Museum) had been constructed, but it is doubtful whether these things ever appeared in English homes. The earliest actual model theatre of which I have found record in England was one belonging to young William Macready at Birmingham in about 1802; David Cox, who had been trained as a painter to the toy trade, was employed from 1800 to 1804 at the Birmingham Theatre, under the management of Macready's father, first grinding colours, and then as the scene painter. He was always fond of children, and during this period, according to Charles Kent, 'he painted scenes for little Macready's Toy Theatre, which were long preserved in the family'. One of these, we learn, was a diorama on rollers, representing a flock of sheep being driven to market. Macready was ten years old in 1803, when he left for boarding-school at Rugby. I think that this theatre must have been specially constructed, like the scenery, probably by the stage carpenter, and cannot be accepted as evidence of any general popularity of toy theatres at that time. It was nearly ten years later that the first signs of an organized toy theatre trade became apparent, and even then the exact significance of the first sheets is not entirely clear.

We must now examine in more detail, the most difficult question of all that is presented by a history of the toy theatre. What were the early sheets really intended for? We have already seen the difficulty of describing them as children's toys, but it may be convenient to summarize the relevant facts again.

The first sheets published by West, Jameson, and other early publishers were in no sense of the words toy theatre plays, or even Juvenile Dramas. They were sheets of the principal characters in various popular plays; the name of the theatre was always, and the names of the actors, often given. They must be regarded as souvenirs of the performance, and were bought by the theatre enthusiasts—who were in fact the stage-struck boys and youths of the middle class, who could scrape together enough pocket money for a seat in the pit or gallery.

Whether these character sheets were intended to be cut out is a little difficult to determine, but it was a very obvious move; and once cut out they needed a background. And so, by 1812, we find sheets of scenes accompanying the characters; but it was a long time before a full quota of scenery was provided for every play. I think there is no doubt that boys must have started contriving some sort of performances at home with these scenes and characters as soon as the bare elements were provided, but it is quite certain that the early plays were not primarily adapted for actual performance, and considerable ingenuity must have been required to make them actable at all.

West, whose sheets are so attractive pictorially, never seems to have really studied the art of practical performance, and often important characters were provided in only one attitude; this makes things very difficult, and John Oxenford, writing of the 'twenties, complains that he has 'seen Sir Lilliput Cardboard glide through three acts of a serious drama, with a drawn sword, always ready to be plunged into the heart of an enemy, whether that enemy was on the stage, or behind the scenes'. Toy theatre performances are, indeed, difficult enough when everything is provided, and the representation of these early plays was certainly beyond the capabilities of mere children.

The choice of plays, too, indicates that a theatre-going and not a nursery public was being catered for. No less than a dozen plays from Shakespeare were published; and, although the censor's ban zealously barred the least suggestion of immorality from the stage, such plays as Garrick's *Cymon*, or *The Libertine*, which was an adaptation of Don Juan, both published by West, can hardly have been considered suitable for children.

The early toy theatre was, in fact, never intended for children, in the sense that the paper toys were. It was quite obviously intended for the enthusiasts of the theatre, who were mainly young men and boys; and it was the boys who insisted upon making the thing work, and compelled its evolution from souvenir sheets of characters to complete plays. As John Oxenford says, describing the period of 1825, 'this little stage was regarded as something above a mere toy; and its management was deemed neither a childish nor an effeminate pursuit. The young ladies of the family might assist with their scissors or their camel's-hair pencil, and the children might gape, as the growing wonder matured to perfection before their eyes; but in a well-regulated household, the manager and proprietor was always a boy, beginning to think himself a man.' It was a drama not for children, but for the young people — for juveniles in the same sense as in the theatrical term 'juvenile lead'.

Several contemporary references could be quoted to define more closely the exact significance of this term. From Jane Austen, for instance, in *Sense and Sensibility*, of 1811, a jovial country squire who was fond of summer picnics and winter balls is described as being 'a blessing to all the juvenile part of the neighbourhood'; or Charlotte Brontë in *Jane Eyre* can refer to 'the juveniles, both ladies and gentlemen'. Between the child and the young lady or gentleman lay the juvenile—and hence, the Juvenile Drama.

This term 'Juvenile Drama', which I have adopted as the best name for what was a mixture of so many different things, does not ordinarily appear on the sheets at all, but in the books of words. It was thus used by West and Hodgson and Co., and its first recorded appearance is, I think, in Hodgson's books in 1822. It was not the original name; West described his publications as theatrical characters; but by the 'thirties we find R. Lloyd and Straker using it to express everything connected with toy theatre plays. It was never a name much on the lips of the public, but it was, I think, the normal description of these articles in the trade. It was used by Skelt and Green, and continued to appear upon the title pages of Webb's and Pollock's books until the end. In its stiff and pompous verbiage it correctly unites the juvenile and the dramatic elements that had given it birth, and it seems to me to convey all the stilted charm of the sheets which it so aptly describes.

For any practical performance, not only the characters and scenes, but the words were necessary. No books of words earlier than 1822 have been preserved, and it is extremely unlikely, I think, that any were issued for the early plays. If the purchaser of any of the early sheets of theatrical characters or scenes had required a book of the play, he could always buy one in the acting edition; indeed, some of Dyer's plays, issued in the late 'twenties, years after the Juvenile Drama had established itself, are marked as adapted for the various unabridged acting editions; *The Bear Hunters* was 'adapted to Duncombe's book', and *Paul Jones* 'adapted to Cumberland's book'. A copy of West's *The Secret Mine*, of 1812, exists in the Stone collection, in which the sheets have been bound up with a contemporary manuscript copy of the play; this very interesting item further supports my view that special books were not issued for the first ten years or so of the business, and that the complete unabridged acting edition was considered the right and suitable accompaniment to the sheets of characters and scenes.

Hodgson, who was the first publisher to appreciate the value of making his plays really actable, was, I think, probably the first publisher to issue special books to accompany them; they are, at any rate, the earliest to be preserved. No books for Jameson's plays are known to exist at all, and the earliest books of West's that have survived date from 1827. But these early books, although printed for the Juvenile Drama publishers, are hardly adapted for practicable toy theatre performance at all; when their texts are collated with those of the acting editions, they often prove to be merely reprints, sometimes slightly abridged or rewritten, of the original versions; the directions for actual toy theatre performance are either extremely sketchy, such as '(Plate 2)' after a character's name to indicate from which sheet the figure should be selected, or quite non-existent; some of West's playbooks were, in fact, bound up and sold by Lacy as the ordinary acting edition. As late as 1832 Orlando Hodgson's book to *Chevy Chase* is quite frankly a reprint of the full acting version; 'printed from the acting copy', it is proudly inscribed, 'to which are added, a description of the costumes, exits, relative positions of the performers on the stage, and the whole of the stage business. As now performed at Astley's Royal Amphitheatre.' But there are no directions at all for toy theatre performance, and indeed such a procedure would be impossible; how could a pasteboard Douglas 'look angrily at Elwina—then as if to drown all thought, snatch a huge goblet and pledge the Knights who all join in the toast'? Or what could a drawing-room stage manager make of this direction, 'Lord Douglas and Elwina express their different emotions'? A close comparison of the text and the sheets of characters and scenes shows that they did not in many ways correspond; there were situations and scenes in the play that could not be represented from the plates, and vice versa. It must have needed a very ingenious performer to put these plays over on a model stage.

Elegantly lettered within a scroll at the heading of West's catalogue of plays is displayed the somewhat obscure motto: 'Encouragement promotes Ingenious Performances.' I wish I could trace the origin of this motto—it was also adopted by the Lupino family. Ingenious the performances certainly must be, but from whence was the encouragement to come? Is this a delicate plea to brothers and sisters to restrain their mocking, and parents their tedium, while the intricacies of production are carefully mastered?

This sort of thing was all very well for the original purchasers, boys and youths who were more interested in the real theatre than in the model, and who bought the plays mainly to remind themselves of what they had already seen. But a new generation of boys was growing up who found these plays already in their homes, and who began to perform them, at a younger age and for the sake of the performance alone; for them these acting editions were incomprehensible, and the plays were too expensive. It was this new class of public that compelled the price of the sheets to be halved, and altogether simpler books to be prepared.

Even the great West felt obliged to change his style; his early books, well printed and boldly displayed as always, are lettered on their title pages as follows: 'West's Original Juvenile Drama. (Entered at Stationer's Hall and the Stamp Office)', here follows the title of the play, 'Written and adapted to West's Theatre, Scenery and Characters, with Songs, Duets, etc., adapted to popular Airs.' But, as we have seen, the 'writing and adapting' amounted to very little. There must, however, have been complaints that his books were too difficult, for in 1831 the book to *Olympic Revels,* one of the last plays he published, was issued printed in a smaller format and on cheaper paper, and with the price reduced from sixpence to fourpence. This time the title page reads, 'West's Juvenile Theatre. An Original Juvenile Drama, called Olympic Revels; written expressly for the introduction of West's Scenes and Characters with Songs, Parodies, etc., etc. Suited to the capabilities of his little patrons, the managers and real minor performers.'

Skelt and Green, publishing a few years later with halfpenny sheets, produced books that any intelligent small boy could understand. Green advertised his books of words as 'the only Juvenile Edition Published correctly marked with the Stage Directions', and the Skelts claimed that their books were 'expressly written and adapted only to Skelt's scenes and characters'; this phrase was repeated by all the later publishers. The texts were ruthlessly cut, and sometimes rewritten, and they really did contain practical directions for toy theatre performance; there is information as to which character should be put on and from which plate, and even such directions as 'Young Tom is seen in a boat saving a man, pl. 8; and Mr Turnbull and Guests rush on to know the cause of alarm, pl. 4', from one of Skelt's books, are quite practicable with a little rehearsal.

The play books of the period, with their emphasis on action, often present almost a solid page of stage directions. These to-dos had to be presented in the toy theatre book by some such instructions as these, taken for example from Green's *Jack Sheppard*:

'Scene 33. Four Cells in Newgate. Jack discovered chained.
'*Jack*. I will try to get myself free again. I can but die! (Jack to be drawn off behind the chimney, and Jack, Fig. 2, to come in his place.) I have broke part of my irons; one more effort. (To be drawn off as before, and Jack, Fig. 3, to take his place.) I have succeeded; now to get one of the bars from the chimney. (To be drawn off as before; the bricks from the chimney to fall, to be done by the trick in the Set Piece, plate 2. Jack, Fig. 4, to appear with iron bar.) This may be of service to me; now to break through the flooring of the cell above. (Exit behind chimney again. Calaban, plate 15, to be seen asleep in No. 4 cell, enter Marvel, Set Piece No. 2.)'

This sort of thing is certainly rather bewildering at first, but it really can be managed after a good deal of practice.

C. Scrummidge drinking   C. Scrummidge Reading the Newspaper   C. Scrummidge asleep

Changing attitudes at table from a small inset scene in *Jack Sheppard*

The quality of the book adaptations varies from publisher to publisher in the same way as the sheets. Some of them were quite well done, and even improve upon their ornate and long-winded originals, but normally the cutting was ruthless, sometimes leaving obscure ragged edges and grammatical errors. Green has been particularly blamed for the crudeness of his cutting, but the effect of these truncated speeches is often unintentionally highly amusing, and far more suitable to the miniature characters on the stage than any more spacious dialogue. Webb's plays are very carefully cut and are far fuller than any of his other contemporaries, but—to my taste at least—they are a little *too* long for actual toy theatre performance. Plays and speeches were sometimes entirely paraphrased, but these plays contain hardly any 'writing down' to their young performers; the Skelt and Hodgson Shakespeare plays are rewritten in rather bald prose, but Green's edition of Home's *Douglas* is in the original blank verse; the pantomimes, also, are invariably in rhymed couplets. *The Silver Palace*, a water pageant originally forming part of George Almar's *The Cedar Chest*, was written in splendidly histrionic rhymed couplets in imitation of which Skelt's adapter could produce only a puerile versification; Green's anonymous adapter, however, not only possessed a virile

96

pen of his own to produce very acceptable alternative verses but eked out a, no doubt, ill-rewarded talent with a judicious borrowing from the classics: a dozen or so lines are lifted almost unchanged from Pope's translation of the *Iliad*!

Theo Arthur has described the playbooks as 'masterpieces of adaptive art', and commended the way 'all the big, big D's' were carefully suppressed; and the Hodgson books were advertised as containing 'no sentiment or expression improper for the tender minds of youth'; but as a matter of fact these plays were quite sufficiently bowdlerized in the original by the censor, and what is really remarkable is how completely adult they remain in their toy theatre versions. If Theo Arthur had ever read the text of Redington's *Don Quixote*, for instance, he would perhaps have been surprised and shocked at an unmistakable *double entendre* on the subject of 'tarts'!

It might be of interest to compare the way the same passage has been adapted by different publishers. For instance, the opening speech by Kelmar in *The Miller and his Men* runs as follows in the full acting version:

'What more sacks, more grist to the mill! Early and late the miller thrives. He that was my tenant is now my landlord; this hovel that once sheltered him is now the only dwelling of bankrupt, broken hearted Kelmar. Well, I strove my best against misfortune, and thanks be to Heaven have fallen respected even by my enemies. So, Claudine you have returned. Where stayed you so long?'

Webb reproduces this almost in full:

'What more sacks, more grist to the Mill. Early and late the Miller thrives. He that was my tenant is now my landlord. This cottage that once sheltered him is now the home of nigh broken-hearted Kelmar. So Claudine you are returned. Where stayed you so long?'

Hodgson and Co., in an attempt to simplify, only produce a bald paraphrase, not very much shorter:

'Here's more grist to the mill!—This miller's fortune increases, for he was my tenant once, and now I am a beggar compared with him.—But never mind; although I am poor, I am still respected for my honesty.—Heyday! here comes Claudine.'

Green, as usual, is the most concise:

'Ha! 'tis sunset, and the mill at work; Grindoff, the Miller, appears to thrive; he was my tenant once, now he is my landlord. But here comes Claudine.'

And Skelt, in this case at least, the most illiterate:

'What, I see the mill at is usual work, turning to the advantage of the Miller Grindoff, so has times turned round with me; for he was my tenant once, and now he is my landlord. But here comes my Claudine.'

This, then, is the story of the Juvenile Drama in the home, as reconstructed from the sheets and the books. Unfortunately there are no contemporary references for the earliest years; no one thought it worth while to chronicle in his diary, or in a letter, or in a newspaper article, that theatrical characters were on sale in Exeter Street, or to give us an inkling as to who was buying them; or if they did, their record has disappeared. The earliest literary mention of the Juvenile Drama would appear to be in 1847, in Thackeray's *Vanity Fair*, but this passage is actually describing life in the year 1826; the quotation about the boys visiting the theatres, which we have already given, goes on to tell how they 'performed indeed many of the plays to the Todd family and their youthful friends, with West's famous characters, on their pasteboard theatre'. So here we have boys of eleven, performing at home the plays they had already seen in the theatre.

The same year provides us with another contemporary memory; in Forster's *Life of Charles Dickens*, Dr Henry Danson, a fellow pupil at Wellington House Academy, tells how 'we mounted small theatres and got up very gorgeous scenery to illustrate *The Miller and his Men* and *Cherry and Fair Star*. I remember the present Mr Beverley, the scene-painter, assisted me in this. Dickens was always the leader in these plays, which were occasionally presented with much solemnity before an audience of boys and in the presence of the ushers.' Dickens himself in an essay called 'A Christmas Tree', written in 1850, recalls the pleasure he had 'in the getting up of *The Miller and his Men* and *Elizabeth or the Exile of Siberia*'. Dickens attended Wellington House Academy from 1824 to 1826, between the ages of twelve and fourteen.

John Oxenford, the dramatic critic of *The Times*, writing in 1870, has recalled the toy theatres of forty-five years earlier and gives us an excellent account of how boys managed their theatres in 1825: 'A small artificial stage,' he says, '. . . was the most valued treasure that a boy in his early teens could possess,' and he compares the toy theatres of 1870, as sold by Redington and Webb, unfavourably with those of 1825. 'With all their improvements in certain details' (such as being more practicable for actual performances) 'the modern Toy Theatres . . . are on a much smaller scale than those that satisfied British youth in the Georgian era, and are comparable only to the small stages, with penny scenes, which were considered toys for children only, and widely distinguished from those more imposing edifices, the uncoloured scenes of which commanded a price of threepence or even fourpence, and necessitated a heavy outlay for millboard.' These threepenny scenes were, of course, the extra large size published by Hodgson and Co. and drawn by George Childs. There is here an interesting comparison between the large scenes which were used by grown-up boys for their performances and the small penny scenes (this is before Skelt and Green cut the prices) which had already become mere children's playthings.

There is one more reference to this period; Edward Draper, writing in 1868 of the early 'thirties, says 'nearly every boy had a toy theatre' and goes

A home performance. From a playbook published by Myers.

on to tell of his ambition 'to carry out a play' and 'the final fruition in a state performance on the parlour table before an admiring party'.

A few years later we find references to altogether younger children playing with toy theatres; the halfpenny plays and the abridged books were introducing a new public. J. B. Howe, describing his life in the year 1840, at the age of eight, tells how he spent much time with the two sons and two daughters of Mr Lightfoot, the property master of the Adelphi Theatre, at their small cottage in Westminster Broadway; 'I can remember,' he said, 'more than one Christmas night spent in their society and more than one stage manufactured with my own hands with "Skelt's" characters and scenes, and what was to me the greatest charm of all, real gunpowder to blow up the mill, and real foil paper (brought from the property-room of the Adelphi) to stick on the characters. Oh! Those indeed were the "good old days of the drama".' The reference to gunpowder blowing up the mill is, of course, to *The Miller and his Men*, that classic of the juvenile stage.

In 1845 Albert Smith described how young Frederick Scattergood, aged ten, on going to Merchant Taylor's School for the first term, packed his box 'with a cake, an accordeon, conjuring tricks. . . The Lothairs and Grindoffs [from *The Miller and his Men*] of departed theatres were also included, pasted upon cards of the Infant Orphan Asylum, and weak in the ankles.'

Right up to the end of the century young children went on performing plays on their toy theatres; banished from the parlour they found a refuge in the cellar, and here, for an admission of a farthing, boys and girls would witness the old dramas jerking along their old familiar way. Mr Pollock once told me how these farthing shows were regularly staged by the children of the Hoxton streets. Here, in these dank cellars, behind the guttering footlights with the slum kids rapt and silent round, nineteenth-century melodrama and extravagance ran its final course. It was positively the last appearance upon any stage.

Older boys did not entirely give up toy theatre performances, but I think they came to despise the cheap halfpenny sheets as fit only for children. Richard Doyle, the well-known illustrator of *Punch* and Dickens, made a delightful pictorial diary in the year 1840, when he was fifteen years old; the entry for Tuesday, April 21st is as follows, 'I have been most of the day making little figures for a Pantomime which Frank is going to act tonight. After toiling at them all day I ran out for a short time and when I came home I found a little thing named Glandville in the house who was come to witness the performance of *Bombastes Furioso* and a new comic pantomime in two acts. All the characters to be supported by Master Frank Doyle. The first piece went off rather tamely, but the pantomime called forth such peals of merriment from the wit displayed therein, which was all brewed on the spot by the spirited manager, that I don't know what might not have happened if a supper had not been announced.' There is an interesting sketch illustrating this performance. *Bombastes Furioso*, which was a famous burlesque, was never published by any real Juvenile Drama publisher; the stage illustrated appears to be a traditional model, but I think it is obvious from this passage that the figures were drawn by the boys themselves.

A few years later, in about 1845, we find young Charles Dodgson performing plays upon a model theatre at Croft Rectory; the future 'Lewis Carroll' was thirteen years old at this time. This theatre, which has been preserved, bears no resemblance at all to the traditional English type; it is a good deal larger than anything put on sale hitherto, the characters were moved by wires from above, and it appears, in fact, to have been a contemporary German model. The plays performed were written by Charles himself.

This movement for children to draw and compose their own plays was, of course, an excellent development, and one which modern educationalists (who tend to be a bit sniffy about the old-fashioned toy theatre) have done much to encourage. One could go on for a long time detailing the famous people who have made their own model theatres—Aubrey Beardsley, C. B. Cochran, G. K. Chesterton, Orson Welles, and so on—and the splendid results obtained in schools where model theatres and puppets have been taken up as craft subjects. But these artistic and educational developments really lie outside the scope of this book, and require a rather different approach. We must concern ourselves rigidly with the genuine article, the plays drawn by professionals and produced for profit, the crude and 'inartistic' impressionism of their design, the highly uneducational subject matter of their dramas, the real ranting, roaring, romantic Juvenile Drama.

10 Performing the Play

We have saved our pennies, we have made our choice, we have brought our play home. How do we set about performing it?

A great deal depends upon whether we have bought it plain or coloured. Amateur colouring could never compare with the professional brilliance, but it was a matter of pride for a really capable household to do its own colouring —besides it was so much cheaper. John Oxenford remembers that in the 'twenties 'even the purchase of coloured scenes and characters was deemed an effeminate operation. Though he was nothing of a pictorial artist, the boy of fourteen who could not do all the painting that was required for a moderately spectacular drama would have been looked upon as a very poor creature indeed.' Writing of a rather later period Robert Louis Stevenson recalls, 'I cannot deny that joy attended the illumination; nor can I quite forget that child who, wilfully foregoing pleasure, stoops to "twopence coloured".' Here all the family could assist, and even sisters were invited to bring their paints and brushes to the common task. Collectors (I have done it myself) on finding muddy colours or a too nice detail upon a rare sheet may murmur scornfully 'amateur colouring', but these home-made efforts are precious indeed with the many hours of quiet happiness that they have absorbed.

Once coloured the sheets had to be stuck on cardboard and cut out, and the larder was raided for flour with which to brew a good paste with no lumps in it. There was a special art in this operation too; John Oxenford, again, tells us, 'By a careful manager, the characters were first painted, then carefully cut out from the sheet, and then pasted on cardboard, from which, when dry, they were again cut out, and then they were in condition to appear. The cutting-out was somewhat tedious work, and lazy boys would seek to diminish their toil, by pasting the whole sheet of characters on cardboard at once, so that one cutting would suffice. To this method there were two objections. In the first place the thickness of the material to be cut was materially increased; in the second, much cardboard was wasted, and this was one of our most expensive articles. If the stage was large, the scenes, when coloured, were pasted upon very thick millboard.' I must confess that I have always been, by Oxenford's standard, 'a lazy boy'; but with twentieth-century scissors and razor blades, it is perfectly satisfactory, though still tedious, to do the whole process in one operation.

'One of the great advantages pertaining to the toy theatre was the quantity of time that it occupied,' John Oxenford goes on to say. 'A boy with his bare wooden stage yet unprovided with proscenium or curtain, with his sheets of scenery and characters yet uncoloured, was supplied with ample employment for all the spare hours of his winter holidays. Hence, when at some of the West End toy-shops I see a little theatre, evidently offered for sale complete with all the performers and decorations, brilliantly illuminated, and ready for immediate action, I sometimes wonder how it can find a purchaser. In my day the preparation for the performance gave infinitely more pleasure than the performance itself, and the gift of a theatre with a piece that could be acted at once, would have been regarded with the indifference with which an angler would contemplate a basket of killed fish offered as a substitute for his expected day's sport.' That is the key to the long popularity of the toy theatre; it was a creative art.

For the boys these long hours of preparation was the initiation to the shrine; only when you have explored with your brush every sash and every belt, and traced, with fingers raw from the scissors, the outline of every spear and every nodding plume, may you enter into the toy theatre country, wander as a native among its beetling cliffs, or dwell within the splendour of its palaces.

Now, at last, the play is ready; but what of the stage upon which it is to be performed? The early publishers provided paper prosceniums often copied from existing theatres, and sometimes orchestra strips, but there is no evidence that they provided the actual stage framework. At first there is little doubt that the stages had to be made at home; later, when the ingenuity of the boys had led the way, the shops began to put out their models, but they seldom figured in the publishers' lists; I think the stage-making must normally have been carried out by the individual shops selling the plays, and not by the publishers themselves. It would appear from the passage just quoted from John Oxenford, that one could buy a bare wooden stage and fit the curtains and prosceniums afterwards; but there were elaborations, and he also refers to 'a small artificial stage . . . with wings that changed by mechanical means, and a sliding trapdoor at the back' as 'the most valued treasure that a boy in his early teens could possess'. John Ashton, describing the stages of the same period, notes how 'clouds hung from the top swaying in the most natural manner in every breeze, whilst the scenes mounted on stout millboard were brought from the top through proper grooves. There were one or two trap doors but they were difficult to work and except in pantomimes were seldom required.'

These traps were normally of the drawing 'graveyard' type, but Mr Webb used to provide a 'rising trap' with his stages that, even though it sometimes stuck, showed a very fine sense of theatrical carpentry.

The earliest stages of which I have seen any kind of printed advertisement are those offered by William Cole in 1829; these models were almost certainly put on sale by Hodgson and Co. some years earlier. They are described as '*Wooden Stages*, with Machinery for the Scenes, etc., adapted to the three sizes—first size, 6s.; second size, 10s.; third size, 18s. These are made to take to pieces, and printed directions are given with them for their use.'

The stage illustrated in *Christopher Tadpole*, at the middle of the century, is of very simple construction and lacks even an orchestra, but is probably representative of the cheaper 'shop models' of the period. A little later, in 1866, an article in Routledge's *Every Little Boy's Book* tells that 'the stage may be bought ready-made, but you may save the expense, and earn the praises of your companions by constructing it yourself', and considers that 'a few practical hints upon getting up a stage will not, therefore, be out of place'. According to Brett's advertisements in *The Boys of England*, the usual price for a skeleton wooden stage at this time was about two shillings.

The elements of a toy theatre stage are very simple. All that is required are four wooden uprights around a platform, which must be raised a few inches from the table if the trapdoors are to be used. The proscenium is mounted on cardboard and bent to fit upon the front. Across the top of the stage there must run a series of thin boards mounted close together in pairs, with a groove between through which the scenes and wings can be inserted and held. The 'mechanical means' of scene changing, which Oxenford boasted, must have been some kind of weight and pulley by which wings and backcloths could be 'flown' with a tug at a string. The curtain, which was normally of the simple 'drop' type, was made of calico, either red or green, and preferably the latter as this was the standard colour in the real theatre. Some stages, including the very excellent models made to the last by Pollock and Webb, were designed to fold up, but in its elements the toy theatre stage was never anything but a very simple framework within which to display its characters and scenes.

The lighting of the stage must at first have been done by candles, and this is the only form of illumination shown even in Richard Doyle's drawing of 1840; but little tin footlights for oil-burning wicks were being developed; 'these footlights were reservoirs for oil with six wicks requiring constant attention and trimming—a proceeding which they resented by emitting a most powerful odour of oil and dense black smoke which condensed into greasy

The orchestra at Richard Doyle's performance of *Bombastes Furioso*

smuts'. This is John Ashton's description, and every elderly gentleman who remembers today the toy theatres of his childhood can recall the pungent smell of the colza oil, the spluttering illumination, and only too often, the grand incendiary climax in which his toy theatre, emulating to the last so many of its adult exemplars, perished in a burst of flame and a tower of smoke. John Ashton goes on, 'Besides this brilliant illumination in front of the green glazed calico curtain there was a single-wicked lamp placed on the side which brought into greater prominence the beauties, architectural or arboreal of the wings.' Beneath a bright but soft light these gay scenes seem to glow with colour; they are never so magical as when they shine upon the stage in a blaze of light within a pool of darkness.

The movement of the characters upon the stage was something of a problem. 'In my days,' writes Oxenford, 'they were placed in slides, which were about four in number, and were slipped through grooves, cut into the stage. In the case of a grand "discovery", a host of card "supers" could, of course, be placed on separate stands, and massed together at the back, while the scene in the front groove concealed the operation; but the principal performers were confined to four strips of the stage, parallel to the footlights, and were obliged, after entering at one wing, to "exit" at the wing directly opposite, unless they preferred, like the Ghost in Hamlet, to walk backwards. "Crossing" was, of course, out of the question.' The same arrangement is described in an essay by John Ashton: 'the stage was provided with grooved slides for the reception of the characters but if used they provided an unnatural effect, as for instance, if William was on the same slide as Black-Eyed Susan they must remain absolutely quiescent throughout the whole duologue because if William were to advance his Susan would retire precisely on the same ratio and William would be no nearer to his love.' Although it is not explicitly stated I think it can be accepted that these 'slides' were of wood, with a slit into which the base of the character could be inserted. The figures must have appeared to stand very naturally upon the stage, but the restriction upon their movements was quite unacceptable and a very much better method was devised; 'the modern plan,' wrote Oxenford, 'is to set them in tin stands to which long wires are attached. A command of the whole surface of the stage is thus obtained, but the wires clash together disagreeably.' This was the perfected method, as used to the end. Oxenford's complaint (he is otherwise a very sound observer) is frivolous; the slides only clash when you make them —as in a duel, when the resulting noise is highly suitable.

I think it is probable that the tin footlights and tin slides were introduced at about the same time, probably in the 'thirties or 'forties, along with halfpenny sheets, condensed books of words, and practical stage directions. A real performance was now very much what was aimed at.

The final touch to a successful performance was some 'Red Fire'. Redington, for instance, advertised 'Blue, green, amber, and every coloured fires'; these were various kinds of chemical powders, which, when ignited, gave forth a mysterious flickering coloured light; they might be burnt in special 'firepans', which were also sold at the toy theatre shops. This effect was very popular as a grand climax with which to bring the curtain down.

And so, at long last, armed with the book of words, we are ready for the performance. There is no doubt at all that these plays *were* performed, despite all the difficulties; the climax, the goal, the final fruition of all these preparations was 'a state performance on the parlour table before an admiring party'. But it seems that there were many who fell by the wayside; Robert Louis Stevenson, by his own admission, never achieved an actual performance: 'But when all was painted,' he wrote, 'it is needless to deny it, all was spoiled. You might, indeed, set up a scene or two to look at; but to cut the figures out was simply sacrilege; nor could any child twice court the tedium, the worry, and the long-drawn disenchantment of an actual performance. Two days after the purchase the honey had been sucked. Parents used to complain; they thought I wearied of my play. It was not so; no more than a person can be said to have wearied of his dinner when he leaves the bones and the dishes; I had got the marrow of it and said grace.' Even when the performance was achieved it was not always an unqualified success; 'the actual performance,' Oxenford admits, 'was not a very brilliant affair, the only persons really amused being the manager and his assistants, if he had any, so that yawns were frequent among the audience long before the final descent of the curtain. The dialogue read in a schoolboy voice became lamentably dull as the piece proceeded, and to fancy that it was uttered by those flat Lilliputians who glided over the stage was beyond the power of the most unbridled imagination.'

Alas, many boys must have succumbed before what Dickens described as the 'besetting accidents and failures' of the toy theatre. 'The working of a toy stage is to this day a mystery to me,' wrote William Archer; 'I never saw one in action and cannot conceive that any human soul could find pleasure in pasteboard performances.' 'In the many years of devotion to the cardboard drama,' A. E. Wilson confesses, 'I cannot recall that I ever actually completed the production of or went through a whole performance of any play.' And so one could go on with one melancholy confession after another; in 1936, at the exhibition mounted in honour of Mr Pollock's eightieth birthday, Mr J. B. Priestley admitted that he and Sir Cedric Hardwicke had been completely unable to make head or tail of the toy theatre that I myself had proudly sold him!

But is this the whole story? Unfortunately the people who have written so discursively and so charmingly about the toy theatre have usually been rather unpractical, 'literary' types; the practical boys who made the thing work never seem to have written about it afterwards. I know several boys, even in the twentieth century, who have staged successful performances, and a number of grown-up men and women, among whom I am proud to count myself, who have not thought it beneath their dignity to re-enact upon a toy theatre these old dramas that graced the living theatre a century or more ago.

It must be admitted that a smooth and finished toy theatre performance requires a great deal of rehearsal and is really an altogether adult venture. This does not imply that it is not worth while for children to attempt performances; indeed I can well remember numerous successful performances that I gave when I was a boy of about ten to fourteen. I had inherited a Pollock stage from my elder brothers, but my eldest brother Robert, who became a well-known actor, was hopelessly clumsy with his fingers and could never work the thing, and Hugh, the next brother, went through a highbrow schoolboy phase and used to do Shakespeare on it, so that I was the only one to perform the real toy theatre plays. My favourites were *Douglas* and *The Corsican Brothers*; I do not think the audiences were too bored, and I remember that Hugh, who was then at Oxford, used to bring his Varsity friends to see my shows. But five years later, when I was quite grown up and began giving shows again, I found that a terrible lot of hard work had to be put into rehearsing in order to present a polished performance.

As I have quoted so many damning criticisms of toy theatre performances, perhaps I may be permitted to reproduce a few kind remarks that have been printed in the Press about my own shows; not with the idea of boosting myself particularly, for these remarks could apply to any of my 'rival' producers, but just to show that these old literary pundits never really understood the toy theatre properly at all. I yield to no one in my love for the charm of these old sheets, or in my appreciation of their historical and social significance, but they were inspired by living performances and they were, after the first few years, designed for performance themselves; delightful though it is to handle and brood over the sheets, they only really fulfil their destiny and come alive upon the stage itself. Before the footlights were they conceived, and to the footlights let them return.

'A charming and amusing little entertainment; to the grey and bald in the audience the experience was a pure delight', wrote *The Star*; 'to the children the whole thing was a fresh and wonderful thrill, of the effectiveness of which they made no secrets', countered *The Morning Post*; 'this spirited and spectacular performance; very amusing without showing any condescension or intending any satire', from *The Times*; and so one could go on, but surely Robert Louis Stevenson, William Archer, and the rest are sufficiently answered.

It might be of interest if I were to describe briefly the way I carry out my performances; it is not, of course, the only way, but it is, I think, the best way to obtain what one must always put first—dramatic effect. I use an ordinary toy theatre wooden stage, with no special effects; several of my friends have constructed elaborate model theatres, with flying back-drops and wings, and specially enlarged scenes. Although all this is fun in itself it means that one man can no longer control the performance; the ordinary large size toy theatre, designed to take the twelve-inch by eight-inch size scenes, is as large as one man can manage by himself; he can lean over it, see what is going on, and manipulate characters from both sides at the same time. To change scenes it is quicker to pull one scene out by hand, leaving another one behind it, than to play about with a lot of strings and pulleys. I always try to make the scenes follow each other with great rapidity by placing one behind the other, and working from the front to the back of the stage, or the other way round; the width between the upper slats must be enough to allow thick cardboard to slide easily between without sticking.

I consider that the old-fashioned period atmosphere is half the charm, but for the lighting I have been compelled to make some concession to modernity; I still use the tin footlights, but in place of colza oil, I have small electric torch bulbs fitted behind each shade; this lights the proscenium and the front of the stage nicely, but is not enough to illuminate the back of the stage, and I have a long strip light on a batten across the top of the stage, concealed by the foremost curtain top piece; this lights up the scenery very brightly, and I have an arrangement by which different coloured strips of gelatine can be placed across it, to give all the lighting effects one could desire. This is much simpler than any kind of elaborate lighting switchboard.

I use the original tin slides, as made by old Mr Pollock, but paint them and the floor of the stage black, so that they are inconspicuous; the black stage also helps to set off the highly coloured scenery. It is essential to have a separate slide for every figure, as you cannot possibly spare the time to change them over during the performance. The characters should be stuck on thin stiff cardboard—visiting-cardboard would be ideal—and when you cut them out you must write on the back who they are and from what plate they come, as that is the only way of identifying them. They must all be arranged on the table on either side of the stage, ready to be pushed on, and during the rehearsals you must get to recognize them immediately *from their back view*, that is from their attitude and not from their costume or inscription, as that is the view you will have of them as you stand behind and over the stage during the performance.

Personally, I insist on doing the entire production single-handed; it makes it all rather hectic, but you know exactly where you are, and the movements of the characters will exactly fit the words that are being spoken; I think the performance gains zest and speed and cohesion. I am lucky in having a very adaptable voice, and can speak in about six different male and three different female voices; but there is no reason why you should not have quite a company of speakers behind the scenes, provided they keep out of the way of the manipulator, and their timing has been well rehearsed.

The toy theatre convention is to indicate which character is speaking by a slight movement of its slide, the degree of movement depending upon the emphasis of the speech; this may seem silly at first, but one very soon accepts it as perfectly natural. It is absolutely essential to know all the words by heart, as your eyes and hands are more than fully occupied in pushing the right characters on and off, and jigging them about as necessary when on the stage. Always keep something moving; the audience will tire quickly if you don't.

For music I insist upon a musical box—one of the old-fashioned Swiss kind that is wound up and will then play for a quarter of an hour without attention; the delicate tinkling exactly matches everything else about the production.

The ideal length of performance is about half an hour; it is a great mistake to go on for much longer than this, as it is quite a strain for the audience to concentrate on such small figures, and they will soon tire if they have to keep it up for too long. I try to get through any play with one interval only, and apart from this, no appreciable pauses between scenes.

It must be appreciated that the number of people who can see a toy theatre performance at one time is very limited; it is essentially an intimate drawing-room entertainment. You want at least ten to get enough 'audience reaction'; probably about twenty to thirty is the happiest number; if you have more than this number, and I have often played to fifty or more, you may have a jolly crowd but some of them will only get a poor view of the stage.

At one time I thought it was essential for the performer to be screened, so that the audience could not see him bobbing up and down behind the stage. When this is done it certainly adds to the magic and enchantment of the atmosphere. But in later years I have tended to give my performances un-screened, so that those in the audience who can see very little of the action on the stage can at least see something of the action of the performer. I am not sure if this is a very 'pure' approach to my little art, but I am told that seeing the performer does, in fact, often add to the effect of the performance.

More, I think, than in any other kind of theatrical art, the audience must be an integral part of a toy theatre performance. They must cooperate; they must applaud the heroic and moral passages, and they must hiss the villain. Inevitably, there is ample scope for guying whenever one presents a nineteenth-century melodrama or pantomime before a twentieth-century audience; but I am sure that it is cheap, easy, vulgar, and fatal for the per-former to self-consciously guy these plays at all. He must play them dead straight, with just the most delicate touch of exaggeration, and they will guy themselves, and an intelligent audience will pick up all the points for them-selves. The heavy-handed 'funny business', to which we have been treated so lavishly in recent Victorian revivals, is only painful to an audience of any susceptibilities. Beware of the easy laugh!

But these plays, especially the melodramas, *are* funny—and even more amusing in the toy theatre with all its little crudities than in the living theatre. I know nothing more stimulating than giving a toy theatre show to a really responsive audience; it must be the aim of the toy theatre performer to break down his audience's reserve of shyness or false politeness; he must encourage them to laugh if a character falls over (this happens at almost every performance), and to throw themselves with abandon into the spirit of the production. If they have dined and wined well this is all the easier. Once this atmosphere is achieved—and it seems to come most naturally from children and rather simple or rather sophisticated people—nothing could be more magical.

11 Portraits and Tinsel

Characters and scenes for specific plays were not the only manifestations of toy theatre art. On the scenic side there were drop scenes, copied from the theatres, sheets of top pieces and foot pieces—these last were useful for hiding the tin slides—orchestra strips, and prosceniums. The first proscenium was apparently issued by Green on January 1st, 1812, and Green, about whose early publishing activities one is bound to feel rather severe, can certainly claim credit for thus early recognizing the potential *acting* qualities of the Juvenile Drama; in the early years West, too, issued tasteful and accurate reproductions of the stage fronts at Drury Lane for 1s. 9d. (this was a masterpiece), and at Covent Garden and the Lyceum for 9d.

Character sheets representing favourite performers were sold in large numbers: harlequinade characters, highwaymen, brigands, fairies, and the Knights of Christendom were displayed sixteen, eight, six, or four to a plate. And then there were the combats; every melodrama boasted its broadsword fight, and if there was not one in the evening's programme, the manager often put one in as a special attraction between the plays. These trials by battle and grand combats were faithfully and eagerly portrayed in special sheets by the Juvenile Drama publishers; 'Trial by Battle, in which will be portrayed the ancient mode of decision by Kemp Fight, or Single Combat', for instance, presented as the opening piece at the Coburg in 1818 was very soon the subject of two sheets from the house of West. Then there were the nautical combats, with ferocious pirates wielding their cutlasses against brave British tars; and best of all, the equestrian combats, with memories of Astley's and the smell of sawdust and ammonia in, for instance, the 'Grand Combat between Kerim and Sandballet' from *Timour the Tartar*, portrayed by both West and Hodgson. Equestrian, too, were the many prints issued by Lloyd of the famous Ducrow,

Mr. J Reeve as Cupid

Mr. Blanchard as Robinson Crusoe

Characters from plates of Fours

as 'The Courier of St Petersburg', as 'The Chinese Enchanter', as 'The Indian Hunter', and even as 'The British Tar', with guns pointing broadsides from the flanks of his horse.

Some of these equestrian combats were issued in an exceptionally large size—about four times as large as the ordinary character sheet. Exceptional too, were the tableaux published by Hodgson and Co.; these were the size of three or four character plates placed lengthwise, and depicted battle scenes in such plays as *Edward the Black Prince* and *The Infernal Secret*; the figures themselves were of the same size as on the ordinary character sheets, and they were intended apparently to be drawn across the stage in the same way as a diorama. Similar to these were the plates of processions that adorned many a toy theatre play; some of the finest of these were published by West for *The Coronation*, a spectacular reconstruction of the coronation of George IV at Drury Lane in which Elliston played the King, and, it is said, 'fancied himself really so, for he wept when with outstretched hands he blessed his people'. Queen Caroline, one gathers, was not represented.

The 'sixes' and 'fours' were normally designed to portray individual actors in favourite rôles, but this type of portraiture found its full expression in the single portraits themselves. We have seen how the Juvenile Drama seems to have evolved out of the theatrical portraits of the early nineteenth century but, when we come to the Juvenile Drama publishers proper, it is a little difficult to say which is the egg and which is the hen; the characters are the portraits in miniature, and the single portraits are just exactly the characters grown large. West, Jameson, and the other early publishers were

111

issuing single portraits in 1811, and throughout our history all the chief publishers issued portraits as well as plays. There were several other publishers who only issued theatrical portraits but, where these are of the 'twopence coloured' school, they are necessarily included in any survey of the Juvenile Drama.

The characteristics of a 'twopence coloured' theatrical portrait are perhaps more easily sensed than described, but the genre is unmistakable. The character is always displayed full length, he is striking an habitual and dramatic pose, and there is a bare suggestion of distant scenery to be glimpsed beyond his legs. There is inherently about these prints an element of exaggeration and flamboyance, although the faces themselves may be quite accurate likenesses. They are, in fact *theatrical* portraits.

These portraits, as well as the combats, were normally printed on the same size of sheet as the character plates—that is six and a half by eight and a half inches. They always gave the actor's name, usually in such a phrase as 'Mr Cooke as William in *Black Eyed Susan*'; sometimes the name of the play was omitted. The theatre, the manager's permission, and other such particulars that were often given in the character sheets, were seldom, if ever, printed on the portraits. Underneath this came the normal publisher's imprint and date. Occasionally there was a warning against copying, to which these portraits were particularly liable; on Bailey's Portraits of 1830, for example, we see 'All piracies of this or any other of J. Bailey's Prints will be dealt with according to law', and Fortey's crude portraits of a later period were inscribed 'Caution (Copyright)'. There was just as much eagerness to publish these portraits as soon as possible after the first performance as with the plays; we have already quoted one example, that of Mr Kirby as Clown in *Jack and Jill, or the Clown's Disasters*, which was published by West on August 1st, 1812, only two days after the play's first performance at the Lyceum. Portraits were often numbered by the publishers, usually at the top right-hand corner; several publishers ran more than one series of a hundred or more each, and it is only from these serial numbers that we can estimate the large numbers of portraits that have now entirely disappeared. Lists of portraits were hardly ever published; in fact Lloyd with a list of sixty-five single portraits and fourteen 'fours' on the back of his books of words in 1830 was, I think, the only publisher to prepare a printed list at all.

The price of single portraits followed that of the character sheets; they too were a penny plain and twopence coloured, although some of the most popular were sold by West at threepence or fourpence coloured, while he did publish a few on cheaper paper at a halfpenny plain. West, Jameson, and Hodgson maintained the same high quality in their portraits as in their plays, and in addition, we find some very good examples from Smart, Dyer, and Bailey. Later these portraits became less and less recognizable as portraits; plates passed from publisher to publisher, and not only were the names of the

1 West's characters in *The Pilot*, a nautical drama adapted from Fenimore Cooper. *Victoria and Albert Museum, London*

23 and 24   Characters and a scene from Skelt's penny version of *The Children in the Wood. Victoria and Albert Museum, London*

publishers, but also those of the actors erased and changed to bring them up to date. A portrait published by West, for instance, of 'Mr Wightman as Richard III' appeared years later over the imprint of W. G. Webb as that of 'Mr Rickards'. There is even a case of the portrait of a male performer being translated into that of a female; Mr C. Dillon, portrayed by Skelt as Richard III, was pirated to serve as the likeness of Mrs Lewis in the same rôle! But while the likenesses degenerated, the attitudes, the gestures, and the costumes flowered into ever more histrionic blooms. A new influence was at work: these portraits were now designed for tinselling.

The art of tinselling consists of embellishing an engraving by sticking various kinds of material on to its surface; the face is left untouched, but anything else, particularly the costume or armour, may be 'built up' in a most elaborate way. As far as I can trace, the earliest examples of this kind of thing are the 'patch portraits' of the early eighteen-hundreds; these consist of quite ordinary head and shoulder engraved portraits, non-theatrical in style, with 'patches' of silk or other material suitably cut out and inserted in place of the dresses and hats; the effect is a little tame compared with the later manifestations of the art, but these undoubtedly are the forerunners of the theatrical tinsel portrait. The idea of these patch portraits is said to have been introduced by French prisoners of war in England, and the earliest examples appear to date from the end of the eighteenth century; it was inevitably adopted as an excellent occupation for the home. I cannot say when 'twopence coloured' theatrical portraits were first embellished in this way, but the full-length portraits published by the Juvenile Drama publishers were eminently suitable for this treatment, and there is no doubt that by 1820 the idea was beginning to catch on. A tinselled copy of Denis Dighton's Theatrical Portrait of 1811 has been found, but I am not satisfied that the tinselling is contemporary, and the earliest example that I have actually confirmed is in the Stone collection and represents Kean as Richard III, published by West; according to a contemporary written inscription the tinselling was done by 1823, and the velvet and silk used were part of the coronation robes of George IV. This is such a highly finished piece of work that it must have been preceded by a great many more experimental efforts, but it is nevertheless a very early example; tinselled examples of West's portraits are extremely unusual, and it was not until the eighteen-thirties that tinselling really became a popular pastime.

The distinguishing characteristic of the true tinsel portrait is the use of metal foil to represent armour, and it is this which is properly described as tinsel. Originally the amateur tinseller must have had to buy sheets of different coloured metal foil, and cut it himself to fit upon the portrait he was tinselling, but by the 'thirties the trade was organizing itself for this popular and profitable sideline to the Juvenile Drama, and ready-cut tinsel and materials could be bought to be applied to any particular portrait. From

The development of theatrical portraits from genuine likelinesses to vehicles for tinselling
By West and Orlando Hodgson (above)
By Park and Redington (below)

this it was an obvious development to design new theatrical portraits so that existing stocks of cut tinsel could still be used, and so we find that the design of these portraits tends to become stylized, with the same shaped dots, stars, helmets, daggers, and so on, appearing again and again upon one print after another. Charming though a tinselled portrait can be, the rage for tinselling undoubtedly stereotyped an already highly conventionalized style of theatrical portraiture, and in prints published after about 1830 the idea of portraiture has been sacrificed to that of decoration.

The actual procedure of making a tinsel portrait was as follows. You first of all selected the actor or the character that you fancied, and almost certainly bought it uncoloured for a penny; at the same time you examined it carefully for anything that required tinselling, such as swords, helmets, pistols, spurs, in fact anything that was made of metal. All these decorations could be bought at the shops which sold the portraits and plays; they were manufactured by a **Mr J. Webb**, a gunsmith, who had a range of steel punches or dies for stamping out all the shapes and sizes required. The metal foil itself could be had in several different colours—steel, bronze, and, most popular of all, a kind of snaky shiny green. The copper foil had to be backed with paper, so that it could be easily stuck on to the portraits, and it is this business of making the foil adhere to paper that has defeated all attempts to reconstruct modern tinsel portraits; the secret is said to have been lost, and the original formula to have died with **Mr J. Webb**. **Mr Jonathan King**, a great collector of these prints, is reported to have consulted chemists and trade journalists about this problem, and to have experimented with gum, paste, fish glue, varnishes, lead paint, and other likely substances, but without success, as the action of punching the designs out invariably dislodged the paper backing from the tinsel. It would seem that all the resources of modern science are unable to solve this mystery. (Since these words were printed in the first edition of this book I have been told that the copy of it in the Royal Society's library in Dublin has been annotated at this point with the comment: 'The secret is Friar's Balsam'!)

Mr Webb's specimen book of tinsel ornaments appeared for sale in a bookseller's catalogue in 1953, and was found to contain 1,919 different specimens of tinsel ornament, each offered in a variety of colours, so that there were, in all, over 13,000 different ornaments mounted in the volume. The prices ranged from small sequins at sixty a penny to elaborate shields or devices at one shilling each. These were probably wholesale prices. The paper of this volume is watermarked 1836 and it was probably compiled during the 'forties. A great opportunity was lost when this unique record was not acquired for the nation.

The shops used to keep specimen cards with every kind of tinsel ornament displayed in their windows. Albert Smith, in his description of the little stationer's shop in Lambeth in the 'forties to which we have already referred, describes how 'the window was enclosed by theatrical portraits of heroes in very determined attitudes. Mr Huntley as El Hyder was violently opposed to Mr Macready as William Tell; and there was a horse combat between Kerim and Sandballet of a fierceness that threatened to annihilate everything'; later he notes that an increased demand for theatrical prints led the young proprietor 'to add to his store a collection of gorgeous tinsel dots, and stars, and lions, to adorn the different heroes. And as a specimen of their effect, he had Mr Hicks, as "The Avenger", in a panoply so dazzling that no eye might have borne him in the sun.' As well as the tinsel ornaments, the shops offered pieces of silk or satin or velvet, cut to fit the figures in the portraits, and specially shaded to appear realistic; these cost anything up to sixpence each, but it was considered more enterprising to cut these out at home; *Every Little Boy's Book* of 1866 says that 'many tinsellers employ regular paint-colourers to shade their silk and satins, but we strongly advise the reader to trust to his own abilities'.

The number of bits and pieces required for one portrait might be quite considerable; a typical Smuggler, for instance, needed the following: a doublet of blue, a collar of cream, a waistcoat of old gold, a white apron, and a scarlet sash, all in satin, boots cut in suede leather, and a cap with gold lace cover, epaulettes, pistols, cutlass, etc. in tinsel; in all about thirty-eight separate pieces. A Crusader, covered all over with shiny armour, was far more elaborate and needed over 130 pieces for a single figure. In all eight or ten shillings might be expended, in weekly instalments, in embellishing a really ambitious example.

At last all is ready and taken home; apart from the few tinsel portraits made up by the shops as specimens, tinselling was entirely a home occupation, and nobody thought of buying one ready made. First of all the sheet is coloured, but only the hands and face and the background really need this, as everything else will be replaced; then, to quote *Every Little Boy's Book*, 'the artist should neatly cut away those parts of the engraving which represent drapery and place under the spaces thus formed, satin, silk or velvet of the proper colour, which may be secured to the back of the picture with a little gum'. Upon this foundation the tinsel ornaments are now gummed, the boots are covered with real leather, and small feathers are stuck on hats as plumes. Finally, a few clouds are lightly painted in the background; sometimes tinsel figures were mounted upon specially enlarged backgrounds of Bristol board that could be bought from the shops. The finished result was usually proudly displayed in a frame of walnut, rosewood, or bird's-eye maple. A great many hours must have been pleasantly employed before all was finished.

The greatest expert in the 'clouding' of Bristol boards was a certain Mr Young, the proprietor of a sweetstuff shop in Union Street; according to Jonathan King he was to be seen in the daytime 'at work in his shop window, with all his pots and saucers of colour around him', and in the evening at the local 'Free and Easy' where he was chairman of the music hall, announcing the artists with gusto and quelling ribald remarks with ignominy. It was of one of Mr Young's cloudy skies that a Royal Academician is reported to have said, 'I can paint a picture and get it exhibited; but for the life of me I cannot match that sky, though I have tried hard.' These clouded backgrounds were sold by Redington for twopence!

The most prolific publishers of these single portraits, explicitly designed for tinselling, were Fairburn, Park, Johnson, and Webb. There is a family likeness about them all, imposed by the conventions of the tinselling technique. These portraits continued to be priced at a penny plain, twopence coloured even when the character sheets were reduced to a halfpenny, but right at the end of the period Redington issued a run of halfpenny portraits that, to a certain extent, broke free from the usual convention; these portraits of Redington's were very crude, cheaply printed, and sometimes atrociously drawn, but their naïveté has all the attraction of a child's drawing and they appear very engaging to modern eyes. They were on sale at Pollock's up to a very few years ago, and are probably represented in the casual purchases of almost every amateur of the toy theatre.

It is easy to despise the later examples of these theatrical portraits. Edward Draper, writing in 1868, recalls that thirty years earlier, at West's shop, there might be had 'capitally drawn and, when coloured, as gorgeous as summer flowers, engraved character portraits of all the dramatic celebrities of the past generation and these—we allude to the larger prints—were really good characteristic portraits; not as now, mere outrageous, idealized figures sprawled into impossible attitudes to fill four corners of the sheet'. But this is too severe. As facial likenesses only the earlier portraits have any value, but as records of contemporary acting the histrionic stance with which they take the paper is only too true to life; these actors really did stand thus, magnificent profiles displayed to the audience, the body cast back, the rear leg bent at the knee, the front leg straight, the arm thrown up; the clash of colour, the clink of armour, and the innumerable appurtenances which they wielded or carried about their persons—the swords, spears, dirks and daggers, the cutlasses, the pistols, the lamps and torches—these too were displayed before the footlights. And when, in their last phase, these figures plunge in some abandoned ecstasy into wilder and ever wilder contortions, they enter the world of pure fantasy, and evolve from the cartwheel of their legs and arms decorative patterns of imaginative beauty. Gleaming with tinsel, they acquire something of the character of an ikon. Many a fine print has been spoilt by clumsy tinselling, but at their worst these tinsel portraits represent one of the most interesting of the many 'fireside occupations' of the Victorian era, and at their best they constitute a form of decorative art that is, I believe, unique in the history of this or any other country.

Theatrical portraits must have been sold most readily to stage-struck youths, but we find them displayed wherever bright popular decoration was required—in the parlours and tap-rooms of public houses, or—as sketched by Boz—in the windows of a theatrical hairdresser in the Waterloo Road, or upon the transparent lampshade of a kidney-pie stand in the New Cut. Like the toy theatre, tinselling was apparently a boy's occupation, but girls and adults, too, sometimes tried their hand at it. I think it flourished essentially among the working classes; the gleam of tinsel, the extravagance of gesture, the vulgar strident colours, the luxurious velvet and satin dresses, were the natural qualities of folk art in the slums. The tinsel picture is in the same tradition of popular art as the costume of 'pearly kings', the galloping horses on fairground roundabouts, the painted decorations of narrow boats, and the lush magnificence of 'saloon bar baroque'. Like the theatre from which it had sprung, it was a craft of escape, a fantasy of luxury and wealth.

There are surprisingly few literary or contemporary references to what must have been a very popular hobby; J. B. Howe, whose fascinating memoirs have already thrown light on many obscure points in our history, describes how, in 1844, when he was a boy of twelve, there were published 'characters as played by Phelps, done in lithography, which were the first seen in this new style of art, for a penny plain and twopence coloured. There was one which had a special charm for me, on a large scale, which when coloured made a good picture, but when tinselled a better; that was "Hamlet". I saved up my pocket-money, bought the tinsel and did it myself, worshipping it for years.' Fifteen years later tinselling was still a popular boy's pastime, and in the 'sixties tinsel was given away with numerous 'Penny Dreadfuls'; *Turpin and Bess. A Romance of the Road,* for instance, was issued in parts by E. Head of 9 Red Lion Court, and as an inducement to subscribers it was announced that '£5 worth of Tinsel given to every subscriber. A series of tinselled pictures given gratis with this work. Dick Turpin, Tom King, etc.' The tinsel was attached to slips that were placed at intervals between the pages. Even if one takes the '£5 worth' with a grain of salt it appears that a mass of tinsel must have been going cheap, and I think this indicates that the original trade must have begun to decline at about this time.

However, the article in *Every Little Boy's Book* of 1866 shows that tinselling was still an active industry; 'should the reader feel inclined to try his hand at tinselling', it says, '. . . he ought to procure one of the best-known figures, as he will then have no difficulty in procuring the embossed gold and silver work with which it is adorned.' The trade may have lingered on during the 'seventies, but by the 'eighties I think it must have died out; no new plays for the toy theatre were being issued, and the theatrical portraits could not survive alone.

In its heyday, from about 1811 to 1850, every important and many a minor actor of the British stage was delineated in a theatrical portrait. Edmund Kean in all his important rôles—Richard III, Othello, Macbeth,

Portraits and Tinsel

Shylock, Lear, Brutus; J. P. Kemble, Liston, Farley, and Grimaldi were all portrayed by West and Jameson. Hodgson and Co. turned their attention to the minor theatres, with portraits of such actors as H. Kemble, Bradley, and Huntley, who were the reigning stars at the Coburg. From now on it is chiefly the minor actors who grace these sheets; Mr Braham, Mr Osbaldiston, Mr Yates, Mr Day, Mr Hicks, and so many others, are now remembered only in these portraits of highwaymen or buccaneers—Tom Tug, Mat Mizzen, Harry Hallyard, Jack Steady, Black Ralph. The faces may not be photographically true, but their characters come alive.

The actresses fared less well in this theatrical portrait gallery. There were few great actresses, the boys were not yet ripe for the appeal of feminine allure, and their costumes were less suitable for tinselling. But there are nevertheless some fine feminine portraits: Mrs Siddons, who retired in 1817, stayed long enough upon the stage to be portrayed by Jameson; the rather elusive charms of Mrs Egerton, Mrs West, and Mrs Honey are recaptured; and Madame Vestris, with her many imitators in 'breeches parts', Miss Vincent and Miss Louisa Pyne for instance, sport their shapely limbs to make a fine and graceful showing. Complaint is often made of the excessive plainness of these nineteenth-century actresses as portrayed in the twopence coloured plays and prints; A. E. Wilson, for instance, writes that 'there was a uniform ugliness and hardness of feature over all the portraits. . . . The insipidity and uniformity of feature among these ladies grieves the heart and affronts the eye,' and Stevenson wrote of 'the extreme hard favour' of the toy theatre heroines. This is a complaint that I cannot share; I think these ladies are magnificent! They were delineated in an age that had not yet been corrupted by the vice of the Dickens conception of the 'child-wife'; the waning, wilting Victorienne was not yet the ideal woman; nor was the plucked-eyebrowed, tilted nosed, baby-face of the nineteen-twenties extolled as the acme of beauty. These actresses were proud to be every inch a woman, with poise and dignity in their carriage and character in their face. They could be soft, they could be impassioned, but fundamentally their rôle was that of a foil to the histrionics of the actors, and their standard of beauty lay in repose and regularity.

Allegorical subjects, such as Britannia, St George and the Dragon, or St Andrew and the Winged Serpent, for instance, published by Park, proved very suitable for tinselling; there were also portraits of Her Gracious Majesty, on horseback in company with the handsome Prince Consort, or of national heroes—Nelson or the Duke of Wellington. These represent a movement to free the tinsel portrait from its dependence upon the stage, but though individual examples are in themselves delightful, they were not enough to constitute a sustained source of inspiration. The tinsel portrait is inextricably bound up with the theatrical portrait; and the theatrical portrait is an intrinsic part of the Juvenile Drama.

135

12 Decline

We have seen in our survey of the Juvenile Drama publishers how the trade began to decay from about 1850; how the prolific industry of Skelt and Green petered out into drunkenness and bankruptcy; and how, by the year 1870, only two genuine publishers were still in existence, both trading largely on old stock. We must now trace the causes and the melancholy story of this decline.

In the year 1857 a firm of educational agents in Leadenhall Street, Joseph, Myers and Co., included in their lists, along with prismatic dioramas, the polyorama, and a moving panorama, a number of toy theatre plays from Skelt, Park, or Green, and described them as 'The Lilliputian Theatre'. 'The whole theatre may be had complete and ready for immediate perform-ance,' they announced; 'but those juvenile patrons of the drama who may prefer to exercise their ingenuity in arranging the various parts of the theatre themselves, can be supplied with the characters, scenes, etc., in sheets either plain or coloured.' Is not this the beginning of decadence, with its offer of plays ready cut out and fit for immediate performance? The original creative enthu-siasm must have begun to wane. In the same list there is also offered 'The Juvenile Theatre; a larger size and improved form of Theatre, for the amuse-ment of young people with Characters, Scenes, Stage, etc., complete, together with Text of the Play.' The titles in this 'improved form' were *The Daughter of the Regiment, Oberon, The Czar and the Carpenter, Ali Baba,* and *Cortes.* These plays were published in Vienna; it was the beginning of the German invasion.

Along with German bands and Christmas trees, in the full flood of mid-Victorian fashion, came the German toy theatre. The plays for which Myers acted as agent were published by Trentsensky in Vienna; the sheets were longer than in the English style, and only carried one row of rather larger characters; the drawing was accurate, unmannered, and naturalistic; the quality of the paper was good; the colouring was by hand, careful and artistic; the whole effect is vastly different from the cheap, exaggerated, popular style of the Juvenile Drama. Most of the plays issued by Trentsensky had an international appeal, such as *Hamlet, Mary Stuart,* or *Der Freischutz,* but there seems to have been a two-way exchange as there are versions carrying the name of Myers, but almost certainly executed by Trentsensky's artists, of *The Winter's Tale* and *Henry VIII,* based upon Charles Kean's productions at the Princess's Theatre in 1856. Trentsensky's sheets were printed both in German and English; I do not know at what price they were sold, but it must have been a great deal higher than the English toy theatre sheets. These plays were still being sold by Myers at the end of the 'eighties. I have a large number of Trentsensky sheets and admire them very much, but their appeal is really that of the costume plate; they lack *theatricality.* For all their high quality they are not the Juvenile Drama.

The Trentsensky sheets are unique, but other German publishers were now issuing toy theatre plays in a style that became as standardized as that of the Juvenile Drama. There was normally only one sheet of characters to each play; this contained usually eight or ten figures in two rows, in the English style, but the size of the characters and of the sheet was about three times as large. The drawing is very competent and fully professional, though the attitudes tend to be a little wooden. The scenery was on a very large scale, two or three times as large as the large size of the English toy theatre. The earlier German toy theatre sheets were coloured by hand, but not in the rich vivid English style. Later, beginning in the 'sixties, they were printed by colour lithography, and this became the standard technique. The chief publishers of these plays were Winckelmann in Berlin, Gustav Kühn, and Oehmigke and Riemschneider in Neuruppin, Joseph Scholz in Mainz, and J. F. Schreiber in Esslingen; Schreiber's plays were still on sale in Germany at least up to the First World War. The titles were mainly chosen from German folk tales, popular nursery stories, and opera; pantomime of the English kind was unknown; we have, for instance, *Bluebeard, Snow White, Hansel and Gretel, Robinson Crusoe, William Tell, The Flying Dutchman, The Magic Flute, Lohengrin,* and *The Barber of Seville.* There is no indication that the plays are based on any actual stage performance. The lettering on the sheets was often printed in German, English, and French.

These German toy theatre plays are not without their value or interest. They represent an entirely praiseworthy attempt to provide a high-class and artistic type of children's entertainment; they utilized the latest technique in colour lithography; they were not dependent upon the adult theatre, and could embrace the whole field of children's stories in their repertoire. They are not without their charm; the earlier sheets possess freedom and movement.

but by mid-century stiff Teutonic characters move against the expressionless façade of the Burgstrasse, or the rich horrors of a middle-class Hauszimmer. But when all is said, they lack the warmth, the vigour, the exaggeration, the amusing crudity of the English toy theatre; the lithography is ugly; the manner stilted and pretentious.

Today we look back across a century, and smile with indulgence or with enthusiasm at the popular art of the English toy theatre; but the mid-Victorians were not amused; to them the German style was incomparably more refined and artistic. Samuel Highley, F.G.S., for instance, writing on the

Trentsensky's characters in *The Winter's Tale*

model theatre in *Routledge's Every Boy's Annual* of 1874, notes with some contempt 'the fixed stage-struck attitudes of the "penny plain and tuppence coloured" style of the ordinary toy theatre "characters",' and describes 'the ordinary toy theatres of the shops, manufactured for the delectation of British boys' as 'but of a primitive kind and small size', comparing them unfavourably with 'the German Stages made in Vienna'. He admits, however, of the figures, that 'though they are more artistically drawn, there is less "go" in them than in their English counterparts'. Of the scenes, Highley says that the Germans 'are larger and constructed on the "perspective system"', that is to say, the back scenes are smaller than the front scenes, and the sets of side-scenes run "small by degrees", so that the stage is arranged on the converging plan'. The outside measurements of the German proscenium front (this is probably Trentsensky's 'Juvenile Theatre') are given as thirty inches across and twenty inches high; this is the same height as, but somewhat wider than, the normal large-size English stage.

From this time on the high-class toy theatre trade went to the Germans; there is an entertaining story by Percy Fitzgerald called *The Model Theatre*, dating probably from the end of the century, which describes a party given in a country house to which carriages came from twelve miles round. It commenced with a model theatre performance in the ballroom, at which *Black Eyed Susan* and *The Princess Bellamarine, or The Enchanted Doll* were presented upon an elaborate stage with a 'gorgeous façade, or opening, some four feet high', which had been 'Imported from Germany' and was supplied by a West End shop in a box, all ready to be unpacked and performed. The performers were a couple of young gentlemen and a young lady, apparently about sixteen or seventeen years old; during the rehearsals the young gents quarrel over the girl, and they have a real fight in the middle of the performance—much to the lady's secret gratification. After the show there was a dance, at which all was made up. This is a very different world to 'the quiet homely evenings', and the getting up of *The Miller and his Men* with real gunpowder and foil paper round the fire, of the eighteen-forties.

The attraction of the German toy theatres must have been their large and 'modern' scenery; performances with such a small range of characters cannot have been very realistic. John Oxenford, in the 'seventies, describes how the manipulation was effected in at least some models: 'in those German ready-made theatres I see in the toy-shops, the figures, fitted with wooden stands, have each a wire attached, which rises through the flies, and derive their mobility from above. Facility of movement is thus obtained, but the wires are perfectly visible and very ugly.' This, it will be remembered, was the type of theatre with which 'Lewis Carroll' played as a boy; indeed this model, which was in use in 1845, must be one of the very earliest German stages to have reached England. The Dodgson family had visited the Continent a year or so previously, and so we cannot be sure if they had bought it on their travels abroad or whether German theatres were already, by that date, for sale in English shops.

Germany, though the most enterprising, was not the only country from which superior toy theatres were exported to England; in Denmark the 'Dukke Teater' or children's theatre, published by such firms as Jakobsen and Prior, had been in common use since the 'sixties; the colour lithography is less heavy than in the German sheets, and the results are quite pretty, often with an Art Nouveau flavour. France had an indigenous toy theatre, from the famous publishers of *Imagerie Populaire*, such as Pellerin in Epinal, which had been introduced in the first half of the century. All these continental theatres were ranged in competition with the English Juvenile Drama;

they offered imposing stages that could be quickly erected, large scenes all ready printed in colour, a mere handful of characters to be cut out, and sensible children's stories to perform; labour and trouble were reduced to the minimum. Before this competition the Juvenile Drama was driven into the back streets, while German elegance was displayed in the West End and enshrined in all the best homes. But the toy theatre could not long sustain its independence of the living theatre; with no roots in the national tradition and no links with the national drama, these foreign intruders did not long maintain their Empire here; these ready-made stages demanded no sacrifice and elicited no devotion from their patrons; and with the twentieth century there grew up a generation of boys in whose lives the toy theatre played less and less part.

While foreign and refined models secured the patronage of the gentry, what of the cheap and popular trade which had become the toy theatre's province by the 'fifties? As might be expected, the poor preserved the traditions of the Juvenile Drama more tenaciously than the rich; but in the constant competition for cheaper and still cheaper plays the original style and technique became dangerously strained. There was no lack of popularity—if anything, there was too much popularity, bringing decadence in its trail. Its apotheosis came in the 'sixties with a development that was to have far-reaching effects upon the Juvenile Drama.

The mid-nineteenth century witnessed an extraordinary literary and social revolution with the birth and enormous popularity of the 'penny dreadful'. Unfortunately, it is not possible to consider the 'penny dreadful' in any detail here, but the outlines of the subject would appear to be as follows. Sometime in the late 'thirties the technique of publishing popular stories in weekly parts at a penny a time was exploited with great success, notably by Edward Lloyd, who is said to be the brother of Robert Lloyd, the Juvenile Drama publisher; between then and the middle 'fifties Edward Lloyd issued over 200 'bloods' in penny numbers; they were mostly written by Thomas Peckett Prest, and included Dickens piracies, such as *The Penny Pickwick* of 1840, domestic romances, such as *Amy, or Love and Madness*, or *Rose Somerville, or the Double Crime* of 1847, and Gothick horrors such as *Varney the Vampire, or the Feast of Blood* or *Angelina, or the Mystery of St Mark's Abbey* in 1849. In fact, the common run of romanticism! There are many common titles with the Juvenile Drama, and the 'bloods' must have fed the enthusiasm for the plays. Single stories continued to be issued in penny numbers, and became more and more exclusively designed for boys, but the idea of serial romances was extended to support a vast number of boys' weekly journals; Lloyd had issued *The Weekly Penny Miscellany* and *The Penny Atlas* in 1843, and the rival weekly *Reynolds' Newspaper* had appeared in 1846; with these there went much more respectable and educational publications as Charles Knight's *Penny Magazine*, *Chambers's Miscellany*, or *The Family Herald*; by the 'sixties they were already in such competition with each other that some additional bait had to be offered to prospective subscribers. And now toy theatre plays, which had previously only been linked to the Boys' Journals by a general similarity in subject matter and appeal, were given away, sheet by sheet, with the magazines themselves.

As far as I can trace the earliest instance of this was in 1865, when sheets of characters and scenes for *The Red Rover* were given away, at the rate of one sheet each week, with a journal called *Black Eyed Susan* published by the Temple Publishing Co. On the 27th November of the next year a new magazine called *The Boys of England* was launched with a great flourish of trumpets by Mr Charles Stevens; with this, it was proudly announced in the initial issue, 'given away to the Boys of England a complete new play entitled *Alone in the Pirate's Lair*, consisting of eight scenes, seven sheets of characters, six wings, footpieces and a large stage-front. N.B. The above entertaining gift is especially designed for our younger readers.' 'Alone in the Pirate's Lair' was the title of the serial story in the journal, and so this is the first instance of an English toy theatre play that had not previously been performed upon the stage. In this case, however, the toy theatre version preceded the stage performance by only a few months, as this story was soon adapted for the stage and presented with great success at the Britannia.

After the tenth number *The Boys of England* was taken over by Edwin J. Brett, and managed by him very successfully for many years. Brett continued to issue toy theatre plays, often of stories that were serialized in his paper; he no longer gave them away free but he made a small, almost nominal, charge; in all, *The Boys of England* published seven plays of sixteen sheets each, price 4*d*. plain, 8*d*. coloured, and six plays of twenty-four sheets each, price 6*d*. plain, 1*s*. coloured. The book of words cost one penny, and the plays could be bought mounted and cut out for about three and a half times the coloured price. These plays, extensively advertised in the Brett publications, were half the price of the cheapest halfpenny sheet plays of Webb or Redington; they were printed from woodcuts, but the drawings were quite good, and in themselves they are quite effective productions. The coloured sheets were not very successful, being more in the nature of tinting, owing to the poor quality of the paper. Among the old favourites issued by Brett were the inevitable *Miller and his Men, Blue Beard*, and *The Forty Thieves*; these were all quite original publications, and his *The Roadside Inn*, which is a copy of Skelt's *Mary, the Maid of the Inn*, is the only instance of pirating. Some of the 'new' plays issued by Brett were *Jack Cade, Tom Daring*, and *Harkaway among the Brigands*. Brett also advertised complete wooden stages for 1*s*. 3*d*., lamps 5*d*., and slides 4*d*. a dozen, but there appears to have been a hitch and it is not certain if these phenomenally cheap articles ever actually appeared on the market.

The Boys of England found it worth while to sell comparatively well-drawn plays at cheap prices, but there was now fierce competition between a host of cheaper journals all trying to increase their sales by giving away toy theatre sheets with every number. Brett presented some large character sheets, well drawn in the contemporary style of illustrations, with another of his magazines, *The Rovers of the Sea*, and with *The Boy's Budget*, a halfpenny rag, there were given away a whole run of cheap and vilely printed sheets for many of the toy theatre classics. Other publishers joined in the competition, with Hogarth House, Henderson, *The Boy's Standard*, and *The Wild Boys of London* all flooding the market. There was even an interesting hybrid in 1870 entitled *The Boy's Halfpenny Weekly Budget of Plays, Stories, Characters and Scenes*, price a halfpenny plain and a penny coloured. What chance had Webb and Redington, dignified purveyors of the now aristocratic single halfpenny sheets, against this sort of competition?

The peak of this 'periodical' period seems to have been in the early 'seventies, and I think the craze was passing by 1880.

Brett himself died in 1895, and *The Boys of England* ceased publication in about 1900. Edwin J. Brett can claim to be the last great toy theatre publisher; he brought a new style of production and a new technique of salesmanship to revivify an old art; his plays are fresh with an original approach; they must have given great pleasure to his generation; but it was the last convulsion of a dying tradition. The movement, with which Brett's name will always be principally associated, must have gone far to ruin the 'genuine' trade of Redington and Webb, and it carried the toy theatre further and further down the cheap and nasty slope towards extinction. The field was open for the 'Penny Packets'.

At about the same time as *The Boys of England* publications in England,

Jim Binks, the Pirate.

A character from a play given away with *The Rovers of the Sea*

an indigenous toy theatre was beginning to emerge in the United States. English toy theatre plays had been introduced into America at an earlier date, as in about 1825 some of Hodgson and Co.'s sheets list Turner and Fisher, of New York and Philadelphia, as agents for the plays, but I doubt if they ever gained any great popularity across the Atlantic. In about 1870, however, the firm of Scott and Co., 146 Fulton Street, New York City, has been identified as publishing what it described as 'Seltz's American Boys' Theatre'. The sheets were woodcuts and hand-coloured, and bear a certain resemblance to *The Boys of England* publications. Seven plays are known to have been issued: the inevitable *Miller and his Men* was taken over from the English repertory, but with this exception the American toy theatre evolved its own repertory with such titles as *The Pirates of the Florida Keys, The Red Skeleton, or the Dead Avenger* and a pantomime *The Fiend of the Rocky Mountain*. Each play was complete in 16 sheets, with a 12-page book of words, and cost 25 cents plain, 50 cents coloured. An advertisement boasts that 'the plays of Seltz's American Boys' Theatre are the only miniature theatricals ever published giving full directions for working, etc. Every piece of the admirable series is put together and tested by professionals before being issued to the public, insuring the correct working of every piece.' The stages measured 22 inches by 12 inches by 15 inches (approximately the same size as the smaller English models) and cost 1 dollar; a coloured proscenium cost 10 cents; slides were 35–45 cents a dozen; oil footlights cost 50 cents; and gas footlights (this was quite a new innovation with untold possibilities of explosion and disaster) cost 1.90 dollars, complete with six feet of rubber tubing to connect with burners.

Seltz's American Boys' Theatre does not seem to have had any rivals and its sheets have practically vanished today. At the turn of the century a few other American publishers were putting out toy theatre plays similar to the German sheets, but the English style of Juvenile Drama never really established itself across the Atlantic.

Meanwhile, in its country of origin, the toy theatre was entering its lowest phase in the 'penny packets'. In 1888, *Clark's Juvenile Drama*, published in Manchester, appeared upon the scene with complete plays for one penny, described as 'equal to those sold at 6*d*.', which was *The Boys of England* price. Between now and the end of the century there was a host of cheap publishers turning out these penny plays. The most prolific and the best of them was Andrews and Co. with its *Champion Parlour Dramas*; these were condensed versions mostly reprinted from Skelt's plates, which must have been bought up cheap; each play was allowed about twelve plates of characters and scenes, which were all printed on one large sheet of poor quality paper; this was folded, put in an envelope, and sold for a penny. The books of words, some of which were not too bad, were sold separately for a penny each. As the number of plates was restricted by the size of the sheet of paper many plays had to be cut down and so the Andrews plays, though performable, are often incomplete; particularly long plays were, however, sometimes issued in two parts. Andrews published fourteen plays in all, of which only one, *Amy Robsart*, seems to have been original; the others were all reprinted from previous publishers' plates. Vilely printed though they are, they are still the genuine Juvenile Drama.

It is perhaps doubtful how far that proud title can be claimed by Andrews's rivals and successors. There was *The Penny Theatre Royal*, coloured twopence, of Yates; *The King's Theatre* of Goode Bros; *The Globe Drama*, colour-printed in Germany and stamped out in thin cardboard; and then the halfpenny packets, striking still lower depths, of Gage, Bishops, and Marks. Even in the cheapest of these productions, however, the old classic titles of the Juvenile Drama still appear: *The Miller, Red Rover, Douglas, Black Eyed Susan*; though mixed with them, we find a few new titles—*Buffalo Bill's Wild West, Sweeny Todd, The Bottle.*

Andrews was still publishing in the first decade of the twentieth century; penny and halfpenny packets lingered on upon the dusty shelves of obscure toy shops until the Great War. To a generation of boys these plays must have given pleasure; dirty, smudged with grey ink, on cheap thin paper, with indecipherable texts, they yet held dim memories of their proud descent; *George Barnwell, Mazeppa, The Corsican Brothers*, what could these mean to the working-class boys of the twentieth century? What could they know of the tenuous link that bound these strange and inexplicable characters, barely recognizable from their worn blocks and hasty printings, to Skelt and Hodgson and West, to the theatre of a century before, and to the history of England? The penny and halfpenny packets were not an antiquarian survival; they were a business proposition; but here, in its last manifestation, the English toy theatre preserved its traditions; cheap and horrid, they are nevertheless in the great line of the Juvenile Drama.

The fundamental cause for the decline of the toy theatre, which we have just traced, must, I think, be found upon the stage itself. The Juvenile Drama was the creation of a particular type of theatre, it was suited to the display of romantic stories and extravagant scenery; after the middle of the century new dramatic ideas were growing up, and the toy theatre was little suited to display the tea-table comedies of Robertson or Pinero, the wit of Oscar Wilde, or the dialogue of Bernard Shaw. It is true that spectacular drama still held the field with Irving, Beerbohm Tree, and Martin Harvey, but the theatre seemed to have lost the simpleness and naïveté that had so characterized it at the beginning of the century—and the toy theatre is essentially a very naïve theatre. As it was, the Juvenile Drama never abandoned the repertoire or the stage technique that it had acquired between 1810 and 1850; it lingered on, an anachronism and a storehouse of memories, but with no new dramas to give it fresh blood, its disappearance was inevitable.

144

Decline

A second consideration that led to its decline was, I think, the morality of the late Victorian family. The Juvenile Drama had been born in the roystering days of the Regency, when the boys who had been its patrons were themselves often among the audience at the theatres; and when the education of children was left to work its own way out. Sixty years later, with a great and good queen as a moral exemplar to her subjects, and with the nonconformist conscience ruling the country, the upbringing of children was placed upon altogether stricter lines. The theatre itself was barely approved, and so the toy theatre was necessarily suspect; and the choice of plays—pirates and highwaymen and brigands with a lot of old-fashioned nonsense—was most definitely unsuitable. Cole had tried to give his list of plays an educational slant, claiming that they would 'afford endless amusement, combined with rational instruction, to the youthful classes of Society'; but this was no more than a conventional invocation to the household gods, and it is doubtful if anyone took it seriously. Without the goodwill of the parents the toy theatre could only exist in a hole-in-the-corner way, like the 'penny dreadfuls'.

In the visual arts, wood engraving of an almost photographic realism had replaced the old-style etchings, which by now must have looked outdated to eyes growing used to these new techniques. A far wider choice of outlets in activities and hobbies was opening up for the boys of the closing decades of the nineteenth century. By Queen Victoria's Golden Jubilee the toy theatre was old-fashioned and outmoded.

A final cause must be found in the children themselves. The great thing about the real toy theatre was the time and labour it occupied, the painting, the cutting out, and the preparations; in a leisurely and unhurried age this was an asset. But already, after the steam engine, the tempo of life was quickened, and ready-made and cut-out stages and plays began to find purchasers; with the motor-car, life was again speeded up. Some modern children seem able to give the attention and perseverance that the original toy theatre demands; my own son was an enthusiastic toy theatre performer for several years, and he is by no means unique; but in this century such interests engage only a minority.

One cannot blame the children for the world they are born in, nor for the surfeit of diversions that are laid before them. But if happiness could be weighed and measured I think the little English toy theatre, in its day, has brought more joy to the homes of England than any of the clever toys that have displaced it.

13 Survival

While the high-class toy-shops were displaying German theatres, and the lowly stationers offered cheaper and ever cheaper play packets to the British youth, what of the original Juvenile Drama?

We must now return to Hoxton, for it was here in this unfashionable and forgotten quarter of London that the Juvenile Drama was to survive. Hoxton lies immediately to the north of the City of London, and was once the centre of a prosperous trade in woodwork and furniture making; some of the fine pieces of the Chippendale and Sheraton period may in fact have been built by the craftsmen of this neighbourhood; today little survives from the eighteenth century and the area was until recent years largely covered by the small mean houses that sprang up over it during the first three or four decades of the nineteenth century. As trade and fashion moved to the west and the outskirts of London the importance of Hoxton declined, though it continued to be the home of cabinet-makers, carpenters, french-polishers, and upholsterers, who worked in the many small workshops that still carried on business in the district. It was a self-sufficient community, descended from master craftsmen, that maintained a modest existence largely independent of the changes and fashions outside its boundaries. To the west lay Holborn, the skilled watchmakers of Clerkenwell, and the Italian colony on Saffron Hill; to the east, Shoreditch and the fierce vivid costermonger life of the East End; to the north, the long hill to The Angel, and the modest residential suburb of Islington. Thus ringed about, Hoxton lay like a forgotten island in the stream of London's expansion; there were no old buildings or architectural curiosities to tempt the curious among its narrow streets, and it remained unknown to many Londoners and seldom visited except by those who lived within its low rows of poor cottages.

It goes without saying that here, too, the nineteenth-century theatre found a congenial home. In Islington there was the famous Sadler's Wells; in Shoreditch the Royal Standard Theatre; and in Hoxton the Britannia Theatre, managed from 1841 to 1849 by Lane, and from then until the end of the century by his widow, Mrs Sarah Lane. Under this indomitable lady's direction the theatre presented a fine run of melodramas, most of which were written by the resident dramatist, Colin Hazelwood. Here too flourished those public house entertainments that were to develop into the music hall; the Albert Saloon, opened in 1844, boasted the novelty of two stages at right angles to each other, one opening on to an open-air auditorium; and it was the Grecian Saloon, opened in 1838, which was to obtain immortality, when it had changed its name to The Eagle, in the lines:

'Up and down the City Road,
In and out the Eagle;
That's the way the money goes—
Pop goes the weasel!'

The 'weasel' was an iron used by the tailors of the district, and 'popping' it was, of course, putting it in pawn.

If the Juvenile Drama was to survive at all it would be here, among this conservative and poor community of craftsmen, nurtured by their enthusiasm for the theatre. They are as genuine cockneys as you will find; less flamboyant than the East End, with no docks or seamen and few Jews to introduce an exotic atmosphere into the district, Hoxton has maintained a sturdy English character that stretches back through Dickens to Fielding, Jonson, and Chaucer, and has preserved other things beside the Juvenile Drama. It is here, then, that we must go for the final chapter of our story.

We have already seen how the plays of J. K. Green, who died in 1860, were taken over by John Redington. Redington was born in 1819; at what date he set up in business is not quite certain; the first reliable evidence comes from the 1851 census which shows Redington established at No. 208 Hoxton Old Town, a stone's throw from the Britannia Theatre. He was a printer, book-binder, stationer, and tobacconist, and published a fascinating list of the different articles in which he dealt—every kind of printed booklet and pamphlet, paper games and toys, 'Snuff and Tobacco Boxes, Apartment Cards, Violin Strings, Jewellery, Fishing Lines and Hooks, Waistcoat Buttons, Throw Downs, every description of Paper that is made, Bodkins and Thimbles, Poetry at Wholesale Prices'. Along with all this trivia, heaped behind the many-paned window of the low dim shop, went the toy theatres. At first Redington simply sold the plays of Skelt, Park, Webb and Green, and his name appears on many of Green's sheets as a retail agent; but at some time round about 1850 he began to issue plays and a long run of single portraits for himself. Redington's plays are the crudest examples of what might

147

The 'improved' version of a Redington sheet

be called the original toy theatre; the drawing is obviously the work of a self-taught artist and is really quite extraordinary at times. They have been often abused: 'for uncompromising ugliness of face and squareness of form Redington's figures "took the cake",' complained Theo Arthur in 1891. Later verdicts have been kinder; there is a delightful crudity about these plates that pleases the modern sophisticated eye; 'the superb Cruikshankian grotesquerie' is how D. L. Murray has described his characters for the pantomime of *Baron Munchausen*. The Redington sheets were, unfortunately, not dated, and it is very difficult to establish any sort of chronology for this period of our history; many of his single portraits are of actors and actresses at the 'Old Brit'. Redington himself must, I think, have been an enthusiast for the theatre; one can, perhaps, catch a glimpse of his character from the flamboyant detail of his printed announcements; they seem designed to be read with an histrionic gusto. Evidently self-taught, theatrical, something of a showman, Redington is a not unworthy figure to have preserved and handed on the dying tradition of the Juvenile Drama.

After the death of Green in 1860 Redington acquired his complete collection of copper plates, and set about republishing them. During the next fifteen years he actually issued nineteen plays, and had at least three more in preparation. All of these were printed, very nicely and cleanly, from the lithographic stone. He also commissioned and printed large scenes, priced at a penny, for half a dozen of Green's plays. Redington died in 1876; his son carried on an independent business as a printer. The shop in Hoxton was handed down to his eldest daughter, who had married a young furrier, Benjamin Pollock by name.

Pollock was born in 1856; he must have married Miss Redington when he was quite young, and he was thus twenty-one years old when he abandoned the furrier's trade and took over the little stationer's and toy theatre shop in what was now called Hoxton Street. Six years later he issued some splendid large-size scenes to go with Green's *Sleeping Beauty*, but this was his only original publication, and for the rest he contented himself with reprinting the plays that he had inherited from his father-in-law. He continued to do this for sixty years.

While all this was going on, not far away, in Old Street, St Luke's, the Juvenile Drama was also being preserved. We have already mentioned the name of Webb. W. G. Webb was born in 1820; his father was a dealer in wool, and his uncle was the gunsmith who later manufactured tinsel ornaments; at the age of fifteen he was apprenticed to Archibald Park, an etcher and lithographer who published a number of toy theatre plays and portraits himself, and also executed work for other publishers. The original indenture has been preserved in the family. At this time, 1835, the toy theatre was at the apex of its popularity, and it must have seemed an attractive trade for a promising artistic boy to enter. Webb is said to have paid a premium of sixty pounds; he learnt to draw, and to colour, the art of etching and lithography, and the whole business of making toy theatre plays. During the time that he worked for Park he drew and engraved sheets that were published by Park and Skelt, and possibly other publishers. These drawings were preserved in his family for a hundred years, until a friend of mine and myself were permitted to become their unworthy possessors.

After seven years' apprenticeship he seems to have spent some time laying the foundations of his business, travelling and building up a connection in the provinces; in 1847 he published his first play, an old favourite, *The Forest of Bondy*, from No. 49 Old Street. During the next thirty-odd years he issued twenty-two plays and a number of portraits. With one exception these plays were all drawn, engraved, and printed by Webb himself; they are excellent examples of toy theatre art. Webb also himself abridged the acting versions of the books of words and these too are exceptionally well done, and free from the grammatical errors and inconsistencies that mar the books of his rivals. At some time during his career Webb acquired a number of Skelt's plates, intending apparently to reissue them, but the only play that he did in fact reprint was a pleasant version of *Aladdin*.

Extensive rebuilding in St Luke's compelled Webb to move his premises several times, but he invariably found a new site in Old Street. He married twice; his first wife was his cousin, the daughter of J. Webb, the manufacturer of tinsel ornaments; through her he acquired his uncle's unique set of steel dies for punching out the tinsel dots and stars, but there is no positive evidence as to whether he carried on this branch of the business himself.

Webb's last play, *The Hunter of the Alps*, is said to have been published in 1880. There is no falling off here, the quality of this, the last genuine Juvenile Drama, compares well with anything from the palmy days. In its

SCENE 4. POLLOCK'S SCENES IN THE SLEEPING BEAUTY. N° 4.

One of Mr Toft's designs for Pollock's large scenes

final performance before an almost empty house Webb's Juvenile Drama maintained its dignity unimpaired.

W. Webb died in 1890. He was the last of the old school of publishers, and a link with the grand old days. Apart from Park, he was the only publisher personally to draw, engrave, and print all his own plays. If he had lived twenty years earlier he would probably have had a brilliant career; as it was, the trade was decaying, through causes over which he had no control, almost as soon as he established himself in business. He is entitled to all the more honour for preserving the original high quality and style when everywhere else quality was being sacrificed to cheapness. To a certain extent Webb's sheets may lack the immediate charm of some other publishers'; they are too late for the Regency grace of the early years, and they are too accomplished for the crude amusing appeal of the period of decadence; their manner is faintly mid-Victorian. The professional skill with which they are executed renders them today, perhaps, less interesting than the coarser folk-art of Green and Redington. This, however, is purely a personal and subjective reaction; most 'experts' of the toy theatre consider Webb's plays as some of the best ever published, and infinitely superior to those sold by Pollock. Without embarking on any Webb/Pollock controversy, however, Webb's plays are certainly splendid original Juvenile Dramas, and his name deserves to rank very high in our history. He was a man with the fierce and even obstinate love of a craftsman for the real toy theatre.

After the death of W. Webb, the business was managed by his second wife, but it does not seem to have prospered and after two or three years the executors asked his son by his first wife, H. J. Webb, to take it over. There appears to have been some antipathy between H. J. Webb and his stepmother; anyhow, he afterwards complained that the business was ruined during this period, many of the original plates disposed of or spoilt, and that from that time 'it never had a chance'.

H. J. Webb was born in 1852. He was brought up to the toy theatre trade and assisted his father to prepare the large penny scenes that were published for ten of their plays. After he took over the shop in Old Street he never actually published any new sheets, but for forty years he continued to reprint the old plays that he had inherited. He is thus a contemporary of, and may be compared to Pollock.

The Juvenile Drama as a living creative thing had now at last died. The last play was published by W. Webb in 1880, the last sheet by Pollock in 1883. Already antiquarians and artists had turned their attention to the early Juvenile Drama, and articles extolling the charm and interest of the sheets of West or Hodgson were beginning to appear in art and theatrical magazines, but the contemporary publications still available in Hoxton were invariably ignored, or dismissed as worthless. It was in the very year after the last sheet was published that the survival of the toy theatre was first discovered and publicized by a writer and an artist.

Robert Louis Stevenson had possessed a toy theatre when he was a boy, and had bought Skelt's plays in Edinburgh; their influence on his mind was never forgotten, and when he come to London he discovered the shops of Webb and Pollock, as well as Clarke, an agent in Garrick Street who sold their sheets, and set about renewing his old passion. Mr H. J. Webb has recalled his several visits to the shop and remembers once that 'as he came in he noticed some of the coloured sheets hanging in the doorway, and at once struck a theatrical attitude. . . He used to talk toy theatres by the hour with my father.' Mr Pollock too, can recall the visits of the thin tall Scotsman who bumped his head every time against the toy theatres hanging from hooks in the ceiling; he was fond of recalling how pale and ill-looking he always was, and how he was most interested in plays about pirates and highwaymen; 'his hands were so thin you could almost see through them,' Mr Pollock once told me. In 1882 Stevenson and his wife left Britain in search of health in the South of France, but he must have taken his toy theatre sheets with him and browsed among them during his illnesses and convalescence at Hyères; all this eventually bore fruit with an article entitled 'A Penny Plain and Twopence Coloured' which appeared in *The Magazine of Art* for April 1884.

Not all of Stevenson's essays have worn well and there is an element of preciousness in his more pretentious writing, but this essay is, I think, one of the best things he ever wrote (perhaps the subject makes me blind), and there are phrases in it which ring through the mind like a bell. We must now, however, consider it more critically. It begins: 'These words will be familiar to all students of Skelt's Juvenile Drama. That national monument, after having changed its name to Park's, to Webb's, to Redington's, and last of all to Pollock's, has now become, for the most part, a memory.' The historian will note that Stevenson knew of no earlier publishers than Skelt. Stevenson goes on to dwell fondly on his childhood love, and then comes this passage: 'The name of Skelt itself has always seemed a part and parcel of the charm of his productions. It may be different with the rose, but the attractions of this paper drama sensibly declined when Webb had crept into the rubric; a poor cuckoo, flaunting in Skelt's nest. And now we have reached Pollock, sounding deeper gulfs.' Stevenson than proceeds to analyse the qualities of what he calls 'Skeltery', and concludes as follows: 'A word of moral: it appears that B. Pollock, late J. Redington, No. 73 Hoxton Street, not only publishes twenty-three of these old stage favourites, but owns the necessary plates and displays a modest readiness to issue other thirty-three. If you love art, folly, or the bright eyes of children, speed to Pollock's, or to Clarke's of Garrick Street. . . '

Speed to Pollock's or Clarke's by all means, but what of Webb? The article was illustrated with fifteen examples of 'Skeltery', all of which, except one, were in fact, taken from Webb's sheets. Why is it, then, that Stevenson suggested that Webb was no longer in existence and that Pollock was the last surviving publisher?

This problem has been discussed a great deal, and was thoroughly thrashed out in the columns of *Notes and Queries* in 1931; it is fully treated in A. E. Wilson's book, and I do not wish to deal with it at length here; it is necessary, however, to discuss the matter briefly. Mr H. J. Webb said that he remembered the circumstances perfectly (he was a man of thirty, working in his father's shop, at the time); this is his story, as told to Mr Langley Levi. During his visits to Webb's shop, Stevenson said that he would like to write an article on the Juvenile Drama, and asked old Mr W. Webb to give him some illustrations; Mr Webb made up a nice assortment, but when he had wrapped the parcel up he is reported to have said, 'Here, Mr Stevenson, where do I come in in this article?' and it seems that he was asking to be paid for his information and trouble. Stevenson was indignant, pointing out that the only interest of the article was that he was writing it; old Webb was also furious and refused to let him take the illustrations; there was 'a fearful row in the shop,' H. J. Webb said; 'when Stevenson left, he turned round to my father and shook his finger at him saying, "This is going to cost you something Mr Webb; this is going to cost you a good deal." '

That is the story; later accretions, as given by A. E. Wilson, credit Stevenson with the intention of writing a real historical monograph on the Juvenile Drama, with Webb supplying all the information, but I find it difficult to believe that the facile essayist would ever have seriously considered such a laborious undertaking. I suspect that Mr H. J. Webb, very naturally, was inclined to exaggerate his father's rôle as collaborator in the proposed history, and the story has become a little embroidered since it was first revealed by Mr Langley Levi. But nevertheless, in its essentials, I felt that we have no option but to accept Mr Webb's evidence.

To Stevenson, old Webb, with his demand for cash, must have seemed an obstinate old fool, who didn't appreciate the value of publicity. And so he left his address out of the article. It was a mean action, but Stevenson could hardly have foreseen the consequences, or that in fifty years time readers who loved 'art, folly or the bright eyes of children' would still be speeding to Pollock's, oblivious of the existence of Webb only a mile away.

A. E. Wilson and other writers have gone so far as to suggest that Stevenson went out of his way to belittle Webb by calling him 'a poor cuckoo, flaunting in Skelt's nest'; but I think it will be obvious from the passage I have quoted that this is really only a playful reference to the phonetics of their names, and he dismisses Pollock as 'sounding deeper gulfs'. It is absurd to suggest that Stevenson was pursuing a melodramatic spiteful vendetta against Webb; all he was guilty of was the light-hearted inaccuracy of the journalist, and a desire to give a helping hand to mild young Pollock, who seemed to deserve it more than the cantankerous old man in Old Street. I do not suppose he ever gave the matter a second thought. But the effects of his discrimination were far-reaching.

The immediate result of the Stevenson article was a rush to Pollock's, but even more serious was the fact that from now on the idea became firmly fixed in the minds of journalists, actors, and others who enjoyed these toys, that Pollock was the only surviving toy theatre maker. Slowly at first, and then with more and more enthusiasm the Fleet Street boys remembered toy theatres at Christmas time, rubbed up their Stevenson, speeded to Hoxton, and gave Pollock yet another splendid write up. *Pearson's Weekly* of 1902, the *Evening News* of 1908, the *Pall Mall Gazette* of 1910, the *Daily Chronicle* of 1912 and 1914, and so on; every well-meaning article repeated the same pretty myth of Benjamin Pollock, the last of the toy theatre-makers, and urged its readers to buy before it was too late. But Pollock went on and on, assisted now by his daughters after the death of his wife, and was gently lionized by the great and famous; Ellen Terry, Gordon Craig, G. K. Chesterton, Gladys Cooper, Charlie Chaplin, made the pilgrimage to Hoxton Street; Sacheverell Sitwell brought Diaghilev; the Russian Ballet presented *The*

Triumph of Neptune with music by Lord Berners and 'decor from Benjamin Pollock'. At last, in honour of his eightieth birthday in 1936, the British Puppet and Model Theatre Guild arranged a commemorative exhibition of the Juvenile Drama, from the collection of Mr Stone, at its headquarters in the George Inn, Southwark; at the opening I was privileged to present scenes from his plays upon a Pollock stage, my brother, Robert, read the Stevenson essay to the assembled gathering, and Mr J. B. Priestley made a speech. Mr Pollock himself could unfortunately not be with us, as he was lying ill in his bed in the little room above his shop where he had lived and worked for sixty years. The next year, in August 1937, he died.

Mr Pollock was himself a mild and gentle man, simple and slow, quite oblivious of the fame that was descending upon him. Mr Stone has kindly allowed me to quote this sympathetic tribute: 'the hackneyed phrase "one of nature's gentlemen" well applies to Mr Pollock. There was an air of old-world courtliness about him that charmed everybody who had the good fortune to know him. One could not fail to note the same care and attention which he gave to the small urchin who came into the shop to buy a penny bottle of ink—or some such trifle—as he did to the City man who was spending a pound or more on the plays, and one suspects that he was far from being overawed by some of the famous people who went to see him.' Pollock was a conserver of tradition, not an original publisher, but within his limits he is entitled to all the honour he has received; the plays, although lithographed, continued to be well and clearly printed to the last, and the colouring by his daughter is fresh and brilliant in the best tradition of the Juvenile Drama. The prices, though increased, were never 'fancy', and to the last a complete play could be bought coloured for about five shillings. The heterogeneous stock that he inherited from Redington was kept up, but one could always recognize the shop, even after the name on the facia was faded and indecipherable, from the toy theatre, with a set scene and characters complete, that proudly rose above the toys and oddments in the many-paned shop window in this remote side street of a North London slum.

Meanwhile, what of the forgotten rival, H. J. Webb? He finally settled at No. 124 Old Street; this was a modern stationer's and tobacconist's, with plate-glass window displays, but on the facia there was inscribed 'Toy Theatre Manufacturer', and in a corner of the window there was hung a row of stage fronts and scenes. Encouraged by none of the fashionable adulation that was Pollock's, Webb quietly went on keeping his plays in print and coloured, and constructing his wooden stages. Difficulties with printing compelled him too to transfer his plates to the stone and print by lithography; unfortunately, the results were not always very successful, and the paper used was sometimes unsuitable, so that some of these later prints hardly do justice to the original plates. The colouring too began to show an occasional tendency towards muddiness; but when Webb took pains over a special sheet the results were superb; he inherited a good deal of his father's talent and could draw and colour himself with considerable skill. He possessed a large stock of single portraits, and these are coloured as well as any that were ever put on the market. During these years the name of Webb was known to the inner circle of toy theatre enthusiasts; boys still sometimes bought these plays, but above all he had a small clientele of cronies with whom he loved to talk about the good old days of the Juvenile Drama; more than Pollock, Webb was born and bred to the trade, and he had in his possession a fine collection of prints from the early publishers, which he gradually allowed his favourite customers to purchase. In personality H. J. Webb must have resembled his father; he was a small little man, with a bushy moustache, proud and independent. Doing business with him was an art in itself; if he liked the look of you he pottered off upstairs and returned with a handful of sheets; if you dared to ask for more or argued about the price he would never sell you anything again; he was given to making dogmatic assertions about the history of the toy theatre, and would never brook contradiction. Mr D. L. Murray has written of him: 'Here was another delicious character. In spite of his tartness and his reluctance to part with his precious treasures (and I don't blame him) he melted when he found an honest enthusiast. Then he was ready to do anything.' For deserving customers he would enlarge small scenes with great skill, and at the time of his death he was engaged in preparing large scenes for a reissue of Skelt's *The Red Rover*.

The British Model Theatre Guild, which did its best to bring Webb back into the public eye, arranged an exhibition of the Juvenile Drama, drawn almost entirely from the collection of H. J. Webb, at the Faculty of Arts Gallery in 1926. For this exhibition Mr Webb drew a specially enlarged version of *Robin Hood*, that was publicly performed. Sir Nigel Playfair opened the show, and it attracted a good deal of attention; but somehow nothing could persuade the journalists of Webb's existence. A. E. Wilson's history of the Juvenile Drama, which was published in 1932, for the first time gave Webb his true position in the toy theatre saga, and should have brought him many new customers and a share of prosperity, but—with his usual bad luck in publicity—this was the moment chosen by the London County Council for yet another demolition programme in Old Street, and once again Webb was forced to close his shop. He moved this time to a private address near by, where he continued to receive his customers in the front parlour; but it was only the initiated who found their way.

H. J. Webb died a few months after this last move, in December 1933, aged eighty-one. His son, also H. J. Webb, known familiarly as 'young Harry' to the toy theatre fancy, carried on the business for a time. Young Harry was a very fine tinseller, and could colour in the traditional style. For several years he sold off the remaining stock to those who patiently waited in the front parlour; but the day came when there was nothing left.

H. J. Webb's grandson, a jolly red-headed boy who opened the door the first time I called, was killed in a bomber over Berlin.

It remains only to trace the history of the last years of the house of Pollock. After the death of her father, Miss Louisa Pollock carried on the business, assisted by her sister, who came to live in Hoxton Street. She was an expert colourist, and understood the trade, but the printing from the heavy stones was beyond her, and gradually one play after another went out of print. Life was made even more difficult by the German air raids, during which—while the two elderly sisters crouched in the cellar—bombs rained down upon Hoxton and fire raged through the City. A hundred yards up the street the old Britannia Theatre, long since used as a cinema, was gutted by flames, and ruin and devastation spread on every side. It was becoming evident that Miss Pollock could no longer carry on the business, and she looked round for an opportunity to retire from a lifetime's devoted service to the Juvenile Drama.

The possibility that the famous little toy theatre shop in Hoxton would soon have to close down had for some time distressed its many friends and patrons, and schemes had been discussed of forming a trust to take it over as a national memorial; but as is the way with such schemes in England, nothing had come of it. Now, in the midst of a great war, it seemed inevitable that the shutters must be put up for the last time, and the stock disposed of or sent for salvage. At this moment, at the eleventh hour, like one of its own plots, the toy theatre was saved!

The fairy godfather who thus appeared upon the scene was a certain Mr Alan Keen, a dealer in rare books and manuscripts. Having established himself in business at the beginning of the War he was fortunate enough to discover, within a few months, what was believed to be Shakespeare's annotated copy of *Hall's Chronicles*. Fresh from this triumph, and turning to new fields, he remembered the joy that a toy theatre had given him in his youth, and stretched out his benevolent hand to rescue the toy theatre shop from oblivion. The Misses Pollock made over the property and stock complete, and were thus able to retire upon the reasonable proceeds to the less arduous occupation of establishing a small dressmaker's business in Bournemouth. It is pleasant to think that to these, the very last of the toy theatre-makers, their trade at last brought something more than poverty and destitution at the end of their lives. Louisa eventually died in 1957.

The shop at 73 Hoxton Street closed down at the beginning of 1944, and the stock, which included 1,300 copper plates from Green and Park, as well as many thousands of printed sheets, was removed to safety. A few months later a flying bomb fell in the street only twenty-five yards away; the little brick building still stood, but the windows were blown in, and the structure badly shaken. It remained a ruin for many years and eventually disappeared in the great rebuilding programme which is changing the face of Hoxton. The facia board has been preserved by the British Puppet and Model Theatre Guild.

Survival

No chapter on the survival of the Juvenile Drama would be complete without reference to the publications of A. How Mathews. Commencing shortly after Stevenson's essay, they represent an attempt to meet the competition of *The Boys of England* plays with cheaper, but still genuine editions of the original Juvenile Drama. Starting in 1886, Mr How Mathews began to issue a series of plays more or less closely copied from the sheets of Skelt, Green, and Park; they were printed by lithography, the colouring was by hand, and some of these plays compare quite well with the original Skelt and Green productions; the titles were usually changed to give an appearance of novelty. The prices were higher than for *The Boys of England* plays, and compared with those still charged by Webb and Pollock at the 'halfpenny a sheet' rate; they ranged from 6*d.* plain for a short play like *Sailor George* to 2*s.* 3*d.* coloured for the pantomime *Little King Pippin.* Mr Mathews never kept a shop and confined himself entirely to the wholesale trade; by profession he was a music teacher and was highly esteemed by a large clientele in Acton, where he lived and from whence he conducted his toy theatre business. It was a very gallant and praiseworthy effort; Mr Mathews was a real lover of the toy theatre, and announced in 1898 that he was 'the last of the publishers of the good old English Juvenile Drama', that he had performed every available play when a boy, that there were no other names connected with the trade but Skelt, Webb, Redington, and his own, and that he had in his possession most of the plays of his predecessors and was able to reproduce them.

One notices that Mathews omits Pollock from his list. There was great competition by this time for the title of 'the last toy theatre publisher'! Webb too would not admit the existence of either Pollock or Mathews; interviewed shortly before his death, W. Webb, in his only newspaper interview, lamented, 'I am the last of them, there isn't one left now.' These gentlemen did not belong to a generation that put their salvation in combines; to the very last they pursued their independent ways, jealous and admitting no knowledge of each other's existence. Although they lived all their lives within a mile of each other, I do not think that Webb and Pollock ever met face to face!

Mathews, meanwhile, was not finding trade too promising, and he was forced to change his style of publication and put out a cheaper edition. This followed the manner of the Andrews plays, consisting of one large folded sheet of rather coarse paper, upon which were printed as many plates as possible; a much abbreviated text of the play was also printed on the same sheet. These were sold for a penny plain and fourpence coloured. He also introduced a number of the Webb and Pollock plays into his list; whether these were printed by agreement, or merely pirated, I cannot say, and Mr Mathews himself was evasive on the point; but if they were copied without acknowledgment or fee, it was, indeed, in the oldest traditions of the Juvenile Drama.

Mathews' last play seems to have been published in 1903. Although his later publications are in the style of the penny packets, they are far superior to anything else in that line and belong to the main stream of the Juvenile Drama tradition; Mr Mathews himself would have been very offended at any suggestion that he was ruining the genuine trade. The fact is that he was too much of an artist to cheapen his sheets as low as his rivals, and he was unable to stand up to the competition. He continued to display a lively interest in the Juvenile Drama until his death.

A few years before he died Mr Mathews wrote to me and offered to reveal 'the secret history of the Juvenile Drama' for a small fee; after the anticipated bargaining a price was struck (I think it was five pounds), and the letters began to arrive. I certainly had no cause to complain of my side of the bargain, and with judicious coaxing I was soon in possession of nearly a hundred closely written pages of manuscript. Mr Mathews maintained that he alone knew the inner secrets of the trade; 'I think I can claim to be the only practical authority on the subject,' he wrote, '. . . for I don't think any one has gone into the J.D. as I have. . . There is so much to write and difficult to explain and this and everything seems a great effort . . . I hope to get it all off my chest while I am here.' Unfortunately Mr Mathews was over eighty at this time, and his 'secret history' chiefly consisted of statements about various publishers and the plays they issued that were totally unsupported by any evidence except his own dogmatic assertions; where I was able to check his text against actual sheets that are still in existence I found that it was more often than not hopelessly inaccurate. With some regret, therefore, I have felt compelled to disregard a great deal of what he wrote. I am very glad to have these letters, and have drawn upon them for a certain amount of local colour, but they represent, I am afraid, the confused and rambling

A grand combat from G. Skelt's reissue of Webb's *Richard I*

memories of an old gentleman; involved and incoherent, they belong rather to the mythology than to the history of the toy theatre; as such they have an honoured place. I have, however, included a certain amount of his 'revelations' in this book—mainly in the Appendix, but always quoting the authority, which cannot, I am afraid, be implicitly relied upon.

Mr Mathews died in 1940—like both Pollock and Webb over eighty years of age; I am rather relieved that he did not live to see the critical investigation to which I have felt obliged to subject his 'revelations'. 'It will be very important to have a striking title page,' he wrote to me, and sketched out his idea of the sub-title as follows:

'. . . giving important information.

Facts imparted by [A. How Mathews] obtained from various sources, British Museum, Stationer's Hall, old directories, personal knowledge, etc.

Revealing for the first time
the *Mystery of the two Webbs*
and the sequence of *unknown publishers* from *Green* to *Skelt*.

Showing that Skelt's first 20 plays were by another publisher before them.

Also how Orlando Hodgson's plays came Skelt's way.'

In his very last letter, dictated to his daughter after thirteen months in hospital, he concludes, 'Well, I leave it with you.' I can only hope that I have been true to the spirit, if not to the letter of his injunction.

At the time that I knew him, Mr How Mathews was a bright-eyed, alert, old gentleman, with a neat white beard. Although his professional life had been passed as a music teacher, his passionate interest was in the Juvenile Drama; he came from a different class to Pollock and Webb—professional rather than shopkeeping, and his publications cannot quite be compared with theirs, but he too has his place in the roll of honour.

The source of many of Mr Mathews' theories was a Mr Conetta, who lived in Jersey, with whom he exchanged a considerable correspondence on the finer points of Juvenile Drama history for many years. George Conetta, *alias* George Skelt, *alias* George Wood, was in fact a toy theatre publisher in his own right, and his story—which has only recently come to light—is a very curious one.

George Wood was born in London in 1881, the son of a clergyman schoolmaster. It would appear that he quarrelled with his father and left home when quite young to take up residence in the Lavender Hill district with a family of Italian immigrants named Conetta, with whom he had struck up a friendship. He brought with him a facility with the pencil and a keen interest in toy theatre prints, which must surely have been implanted in his boyhood. He showed evidence, later in his life, of having actually known artists who had worked for Skelt. He would draw a sheet of theatrical figures, sell it to a print-seller, and take the whole family to the theatre or music hall on the proceeds.

There is also a story, with what foundation I do not know, that his skill as a copyist involved him in the pirating of popular sheet music at this time and that action was to be taken against him for breach of copyright. He may have needed to disappear quickly. Anyhow, for one reason or another he enlisted in the army.

But service life, not perhaps surprisingly, proved distasteful to him, and he deserted in some foreign port (it is said, Bahrein). From that time on he took the name of Conetta, and never again resided in England. Technically, at least, he was a 'wanted man'.

Between 1909 and 1919 there is evidence that he served in the Merchant Navy. He came to know many foreign countries and to speak several languages; he became an excellent cook and worked as a chef. Some time during this period he married a girl from Jersey, where he established a home.

After the Great War he set up as a scrap metal merchant in Jersey, and continued in this trade with some success for the rest of his life. His first wife died of the black 'flu in 1918, and he married twice more, having a child by each wife. His second wife also died young, and he brought up his daughters for a time single-handed. One of his daughters has given me much of the information for this sketch of his life; she assures me that his children remember him as a kind father who made a good home for them.

The annals of the Juvenile Drama are rich in eccentrics, however, and Mr Conetta was no exception. After the death of his first wife he let his hair grow long, wore large brass ear-rings, and dressed as a woman. The inhabitants of Jersey seem to have left him well alone, but visitors—often earnest toy theatre enthusiasts from England—calling, unwarned, at his home expressed some consternation at his appearance. His house was difficult to find, and the usual pattern of a visit was for a local urchin to be prevailed upon to guide the unsuspecting stranger to the door—which the urchin would indicate and then take to his heels in flight before it could be opened. Eventually the door would be flung open to disclose a long-haired unshaven figure, shouting a loud masculine welcome, and wearing a skirt. The popular—but unjustified—opinion that he was off his head left him completely unconcerned.

Somewhere in this eccentricity his old passion for the toy theatre found a niche. His daughters remember how he would settle down in the evening to a session of drawing sheets with a fine mapping pen and a magnifying glass. He would be completely absorbed in this occupation for hours on end, and would allow no interruption. He would borrow old and rare sheets and copy them so faithfully that it is not easy to tell his copy from the original print. He kept up a correspondence with collectors from all over the world. Sometimes he would inscribe a name at the bottom of the sheets he drew, and for this purpose, recalling no doubt the great publisher of his own young days, he adopted the name of G. Skelt. He claimed, moreover, that his mother was one of the Skelts.

Comparatively late in life, not perhaps until after the Second World War, he went a step further as a toy theatre publisher and had a series of sheets printed by a printer in Southampton. They were reproduced by a lithographic process, apparently in runs of five hundred copies of each sheet. It is not always easy to distinguish his hand-drawn sheets from the printed ones.

Very few of his sheets are dated, and it is impossible to establish any chronology for his publications. Sheets exist dated 1899, 1904, 1905, 1912, 1913, and 1923. The earliest carry the address 24 Clairview Street, Jersey, but it would appear that he did not move to this address until the Second World War. The explanation of this apparent anomaly is that the dates refer to the year in which the drawing was made, not to the year of publication. He appears to have continued issuing sheets until his death in 1956.

The mystery is that these prints were never, apparently, put on sale in any systematic way. Towards the end of his life he began advertising in a small way and issued a catalogue of his publications, but it came as a considerable surprise when a stock of thousands of sheets was discovered after his death. From some printings not a single sheet appeared to have been sold. When asked what was the object of this extraordinary publishing project he would merely say, 'When I'm dead you can put a match to them and burn the lot.' Fortunately this advice was not taken and the G. Skelt reprints were saved for the benefit of collectors and theatre historians; indeed, in recent years they have formed the only modestly priced examples of Juvenile Drama obtainable anywhere.

It is impossible to estimate the total of the G. Skelt publications, but after Mr Conetta's death his effects included stocks of some ninety single portraits; playbooks and sheets of characters and scenes for some twenty-five plays; and some dozens of other miscellaneous sheets. These prints are almost all meticulous copies of originals issued by such publishers as West, Hodgson, Lloyd, Dyer, Bailey, Skelt, Fairburn, and Webb. In some cases the original publisher's name was reproduced exactly, and here future collectors must be on their guard to recognize a Conetta reprint from the original; the Conetta sheets are, in fact, easily distinguished by the glossy character of the paper, the smooth surface of the litho print, and a coarsening of the stippling. In other cases the imprint of G. Skelt is added to that of the original publisher, and sometimes it appears alone. In a few examples Mr Conetta originated entirely new sheets—but in the old style.

G. Skelt is something of a mystery in our history. Like Pollock he was a preserver of tradition, not an originator, but his work is entitled to a higher recognition than has, as yet, been given it. This, the last of all the Skelts, is well entitled to the proud name he adopted.

14 Collecting the Juvenile Drama

One either understands the 'mystique' of collecting, or one does not. To the uncomprehending the whole business appears mysterious or even ridiculous; and collectors themselves hardly ever attempt a rational explanation of their pursuit for the benefit of the uninitiated. I cannot do more here than indicate a few lines of approach for those who are not instinctively sympathetic to the conception.

Life is short; and when it has passed what have we to show? Man needs creation to satisfy his immortal soul. We are not all creative artists with our hands, but there is that other creation, the collecting of created things, open to us. One hundred separate pictures or books, scattered among the houses and shops of the earth, are only one hundred separate and divided facets of a complete jewel; but gathered together (if they are intelligently chosen) they can combine to illuminate each other and together form a complete consensus of, for instance, a school of painting, or the development of a social fashion. This is a collection. It is something greater than the sum of the individual articles of which it is composed. If this result is not achieved, the collection is a failure. Collecting is nothing whatever to do with spending money, and the best collections are often made up of a large number of unconsidered trifles, in themselves perhaps valueless or of little interest, which in the aggregate support each other and create something new, perhaps small, but rounded and complete.

This is the modern approach to collecting—perhaps merely the twentieth-century rationalization of an instinct common to the magpie and to every schoolboy. It is not the spirit that animated the great patrons of the past; the aristocratic collectors of the seventeenth and eighteenth centuries filled their palaces with everything that was beautiful; the results were eclectic and brilliant, but only by accident complete. In the same spirit gentlemen filled their libraries with fine and choice editions of all the great authors. It was during the nineteenth century that fashion evolved a different approach, and interest was centred, in the realm of books for instance, not upon the finest but upon the earliest editions of 'esteemed authors'; from this grew the altogether unbalanced worship of first editions as such, from which the book trade has not yet recovered. The modern tendency in book collecting is away from vast amorphous congregations of books on all the fashionable subjects, and towards small but highly concentrated and complete collections to illustrate one particular author, or, at most, one literary school. Great attention (perhaps too much) is paid to 'original state'—that is for a book to be bound and in every way in exactly the same condition as when it left the original publisher. The same general considerations apply to whatever is being collected, though the book trade is the one with which I am most intimately familiar.

In the making of a collection it is obviously more pleasant to surround oneself with things that are beautiful and pretty, or at least instructive or amusing, but as has been stressed, the immediate intrinsic value of the articles collected is only a secondary consideration. But the disregarded toys of yesterday are the much prized rarities of today; Elizabethan chap-books are rarer than Shakespeare first folios, street broadsides of the eighteenth century are scarcer than elegant albums of gentlemen's country seats, and nineteenth-century 'penny dreadfuls' are now more sought and valued than nineteenth-century keepsakes. The cigarette cards and the match-box labels of today will be the rarities of tomorrow. But ephemera is invariably disregarded in its own generation, and it is not until it suddenly becomes almost unprocurable that it seems worthy of collecting. To this rule the Juvenile Drama was no exception.

Certainly no one thought the first cheap sheets of theatrical characters and scenes worth preserving; their normal and designed fate was to be cut up by boys, and in fact the great majority of sheets issued by the early publishers have disappeared entirely. Considering the circumstances of their publication it is perhaps surprising that any at all should have escaped the scissors, the wastepaper basket, the dustbin, and the salvage collector. Of the several million sheets printed by West, Jameson, and their contemporaries perhaps a thousand or so remain as eloquent testimony to those early years; that even these survive is solely due to the vision and enthusiasm of a handful of collectors, who, wise before their time, snatched them from the brink of destruction and guarded them for our instruction and delight today.

It was very fortunate that West continued to keep his shop open until his death in 1854. During the last twenty years the stock must have grown very thin and incomplete, but there were at least some genuine Wests available up to a surprisingly late date, and this is undoubtedly the reason why a rather unexpectedly large number of West's sheets have been preserved today.

According to Edward Draper, Albert Smith, the popular novelist and lecturer, went into West's shop a short time before his death, and bought a copy of every sheet still remaining; Albert Smith was a frequent visitor at Valentine's, the antique dealer next door, and must have known the shop well. What happened to this collection is not known; Albert Smith died in 1860, and as his effects were granted an elaborate sale it is unlikely that it was allowed to disappear. Possibly it found its way into the possession of Captain Hodgetts.

Captain Frederick Hodgetts, with the wide range of interests of which he made himself a master, is a striking example of English versatility. He was born in 1828, and was educated for a scientific career; as a boy he assisted in the arrangement of the Armoury in the Tower of London. At an early age he threw up the career which his parents had planned for him, and went to sea; he entered the service of the East India Company, and during a distinguished career afloat served as a Commander in the Indian Navy. Having learnt Russian in his spare time, he then took up the post of lecturer in practical science at the Imperial College, Moscow. He retired in 1881, returned to London, and patented the 'Hodgetts' safety slip', a revolutionary design in marine engineering. From now until the end of his life he devoted himself to writing and lecturing on archaeological subjects, specializing in the Anglo-Saxon period, and also wrote a number of popular boys' stories for the *Boys' Own Paper*, with such titles as 'Harold the Boy Earl' and 'Edwin the Boy Outlaw'. During this lifetime of constant and consuming energy he amassed, 'regardless of expense', a very large collection of the Juvenile Drama. He died in 1906, and his collection passed into the hands of Mr Ralph Thomas.

Ralph Thomas is the most important figure among the collectors of the Juvenile Drama. He was born in 1840, the son of Serjeant Thomas, who has been described as 'the curious person who used to practice at the Old Bailey, and sold violins and pictures at Stratford Place', and is supposed to be the original of Dickens's Serjeant Buzfuz. As a boy Ralph remembered visiting West's shop with his mother, who bought a set of every sheet still available; his family was very friendly with Sir J. E. Millais, and he has described how he and young John Millais, who later became the famous painter, would occupy themselves with colouring the sheets of the Juvenile Drama; the interest that was thus implanted lasted throughout his life. Later there was a quarrel between the two families, and in 1901 Ralph Thomas published a pamphlet defending his father, but this had nothing to do with the Juvenile Drama, and fortunately need not concern us here. Like his father, Ralph Thomas became a lawyer, and for a time occupied chambers in Clifford's Inn, but his early love of the Juvenile Drama became a passion, and he made it his life's work to amass the largest possible collection of Juvenile Drama sheets. For his mouthpiece he adopted *Notes and Queries*, then as now a fascinating little magazine of archaeological and historical curiosities, and it is to Ralph Thomas's contributions to this paper that a great many of the facts in this book are indebted.

Ralph Thomas, himself, described his collection as follows: 'For years I have collected West's prints published for the Toy Theatre. . . I probably have 5,000 distinct prints from copper plates printed between 1811 and 1850, and as many duplicates. Of the Skelts, I have about 1,000 different prints. The collection is almost complete.' I do not know where Captain Hodgetts or Thomas obtained all this vast collection from. It appears that there was a sale of West's effects at 57 Wych Street after his death in 1854, in which was included a box that had not been unlocked for twenty years; this must have been bought by Thomas's father, and was found to contain a veritable cache of proof sheets and original drawings. Some of the Skelt sheets were, of course, still on sale at their original price by the time Thomas grew to be a man; and of the early publishers a few dusty parcels of 'unsaleable' stock may still have lingered beneath the counters of old-fashioned stationers.

Ralph Thomas was a great disciple of West, for whose prints he had a most profound admiration. Jameson he would admit, and Hodgson he would tolerate, but Skelt was a vandal who ruined the art with cheapness, and as for Green and the rest—they were simply rubbish! He felt none of the crude amusing charm that appeals to us today in these later sheets (perhaps he was too near them in time), but though we may think that we have enlarged the scope of the subject we in no way detract from the value of Thomas's more strictly 'artistic' approach.

In 1886 Mr Thomas offered his collection to the British Museum; I understand that he asked one hundred pounds for it, but that he eventually accepted rather less. It can be inspected there today, with very little delay or difficulty, in the Print Room. The sheets are stuck down in ten large folio volumes. Only the early publishers, up to and including Orlando Hodgson, with West very much predominating, are represented; unfortunately Thomas, or perhaps the Museum, did not consider it worth while to include the 'halfpenny publishers' at all; but within its period the collection is probably the finest in existence, containing some sheets—such as the early Greens—which are absolutely unique, and a few original drawings and proof sheets as well. One hundred pounds would be cheap for this collection today, but at that time the Museum authorities might well have demurred at paying so much for mere children's toy sheets, and we are today immensely indebted to their foresight in thus securing this superb collection for the nation.

This, however, was not the end of Ralph Thomas's career as a collector; in later years he bitterly regretted parting with this collection, and he frequently visited the Museum to check it with his later purchases. I think it must have been after the Museum sale that he acquired the Hodgetts collection. Mr Thomas died in 1926, aged eighty-six. A large number of duplicate sheets had been sold to Spencer, the famous print dealer of Oxford Street, and these passed into the possession of Mr Stone. The bulk of the 'second' Thomas Collection passed after his death to Mr W. W. Nops, Clerk of the

Central Criminal Court, Old Bailey, and a friend of Judge Thomas, Mr Thomas's son. This second collection (the existence of which has been hitherto generally unknown), added to Mr Nops's existing acquisitions, was in some ways even finer than that in the British Museum, containing many very early sheets, including a number of West's large twopenny sheets that are not in the Museum and some of the excessively scarce early Greens. Mr Nops died in 1949, and I have not been able to discover what has happened to his collection. Thus the great Thomas Collection, like another Gaul, was divided into three parts, each by itself infinitely finer in its selection of early publishers than any other collection that has been, or now ever can be, gathered together.

It is no exaggeration to say that it is solely due to Ralph Thomas's efforts that a coherent history of the Juvenile Drama can be written today.

For the next great toy theatre collector we must go back to the eighteen-forties when, J. B. Howe has recalled, 'in Chapel Street, Somers Town, there was for many years a shop kept by a Mr King, entirely devoted to the sale of Skelt's characters and scenes, tobacco, periodicals, etc.' The son of the proprietor of this establishment, who later succeeded to the management, was possessed of the unusual but estimable habit of preserving for himself one copy of every piece of printed paper that passed through his stock. In this way he acquired the largest collection of Christmas cards ever brought together, requiring (it is said) fifteen goods wagons to transport it; in this way he gathered over 9,000 toy theatre sheets into his albums. In 1912, a respected elderly gentleman, with a massive face and a long beard, Mr Jonathan King generously presented his entire collection of toy theatre sheets and tinsel portraits to the London Museum; to mark the occasion he had printed a special commemorative booklet, describing his collection and reproducing the graceful letter of acceptance and thanks from the Museum authorities. According to this account, the collection comprised over 100 framed tinsel pictures, and forty large folio volumes containing about 100 tinsel pictures, and 9,000 sheets of prints, ranging between 1811 and 1860. One volume was devoted to drop scenes. The fourth volume opened with a record of the copyright controversy already quoted. Another volume contained nothing but the large scenes 'having the imprint "G.C." which is confidently believed to have been the work of George Cruickshank' (these are evidently the Hodgson large scenes, actually done by George Childs).

Unfortunately the forty large folio volumes were allowed for a time to slip out of sight, and could not be produced when I first began my research for this history. The closure of the Museum during the War and its subsequent move to Kensington Palace produced further difficulties. Search in the stores of the Museum has, however, brought this important collection to light again and a special exhibition to commemorate Jonathan King's gift was arranged by Mr Martin Holmes, the keeper responsible for the collection, in 1959. The collection would appear to be principally of the later publishers—the period of

Skelt, Green, and Park—and thus admirably complements that at the British Museum, but it also contains a number of unique early sheets.

Against the reference to King, which I have quoted, in my copy of J. B. Howe's autobiography is the pencil note 'J. King—I knew him.' This book was originally the property of Mr E. P. Prior, and it is to Mr Prior that we must now turn for the next and, in some ways, the most remarkable of our collectors. I only met Mr Prior once, but Miss Margaret Lane, who knew him much better, has kindly allowed me to quote the following description. 'Prior had all his working life been a journeyman plumber. He was about seventy when I met him (1938), and had long ago retired on account of ill-health, to a tiny house in a working-class street in Queen's Park. He was small, white-haired, distinguished, with a severe and delicate face; he can never have looked like a plumber, and at this time might have been taken for an old retired character actor of the Irving school. He was a little forbidding in manner, jealous of his own possessions and opinions, sustained by the touching certainty of the self-educated man. He had decided, he said, as a youth, that there were better things in life than women and beer; and accordingly he had looked around for a serious hobby.

'Here a childish memory had touched his fancy. He remembered, as a child of four in a tartan frock, being lifted on to the bar in his uncle's pub and being shown some tinselled theatrical portraits and a toy theatre. This memory struck a note which rang with meaning, and he fixed on the Juvenile Drama for his life's study.

'From that time, according to his wife, he never spent a penny on tobacco or drink. The dinner hour of his working day was spent in markets and secondhand booksellers' rummaging through boxes of prints and scraps in search of his quarry. In the course of fifty years he had amassed a magnificent collection, as well as a glittering quantity of tinsel portraits, a fair theatrical library and an astonishing collection of Victorian music-hall literature. All his treasures were packed into the tiny upstairs front parlour where he received visitors, and the richness of its profusion and the sequin-like brilliance of the framed theatrical tinsels covering every inch of the walls, put one in mind of a casket of stage jewels.

'He knew more than almost anyone else about the Juvenile Drama, but he was costive of information. He had come by it too hardly to be able to part with it freely to any fool who asked a question. He was suspicious of other collectors, regarding them as a circle of vultures who were waiting for him to die, as indeed with great politeness and decency, they were.'

Margaret Lane, who was eventually allowed to carry off the collection herself, has here presented Prior very sympathetically and candidly; he was something of a 'character', like all these men who published or collected the Juvenile Drama, not without his foibles; but not for one moment would one wish him any different to what he was! Moreover when at last A. E.

Wilson wrote the first history of the Juvenile Drama Mr Prior was most generous in help and advice, and the book shows his influence unmistakably.

Mr Prior died in 1939. Margaret Lane, now the Countess of Huntingdon, feasted upon her treasure for six years, and then offered it in 1944 for sale at Sotheby's. Wartime prices were high, and the lot was eventually knocked down for £260, which, it is no secret, was a good deal more than either Prior or anyone else had believed it to be worth. The collection eventually passed into the hands of a Mr Herbert Hinkins, who is its present proud possessor.

Contemporary with Prior is Mr C. H. Green, who was for some years Honorary Secretary of the Dickens Fellowship. He added to a great love of these things an expert knowledge of printing and engraving, and an enthusiasm for practical performances, for which he had constructed a fine and elaborate model stage. To Mr Green's rooms in Clifford's Inn came many, like myself, young seekers after knowledge, to beard this rather formidable lion in his den, and receive a most kind and generous welcome. Mr Green's own collection, though not quite so large, was comparable with Prior's, being very representative of the later publishers but rather thin in the pre-Skelt era. He also had a very large number of Danish toy theatre sheets, which he introduced to English model theatre performers. In 1944 Mr Green sold this fine collection to the same Mr Herbert Hinkins. Mr Green lived to a ripe old age. The last time I saw him, striding with surprising vigour through the streets of Ealing, with a broad-brimmed hat set boldly on his head and an overcoat that looked like a cape across his shoulders, he seemed the incarnation of one of the characters—say 'the Old Count, second dress, with Cloak'—that he had so long and with such understanding made his life's pursuit.

Here, too, must pass across our stage a figure as romantic and eccentric as the most extravagant character of any melodrama. Fiercely and uncouthly bearded, shabbily attired in a long ancient overcoat and a greasy hat, clutching a brown paper parcel in his hands, the figure of Mr Hiram Stead was well known to the London booksellers and print dealers during the 'twenties and early 'thirties of this century. His life was a mystery which no one, I think, ever entirely solved; he appeared to live at a choice of some half dozen attic rooms scattered over London, all of which were stacked to the ceilings with an amazing assortment of old theatrical playbills, prints, and souvenirs. Among all this the Juvenile Drama found a place. The bulk of this collection is now in the New York Public Library. Half collector and half dealer, with a passion for these relics of the theatre, and little or no sense of modern commerce, Mr Stead lived uneasily and unhappily in an unsympathetic and often scoffing world until persecution mania toppled into insanity; but as one who was privileged to know Hiram Stead as well and as intimately as seemed possible, I should like now to pay tribute to his devouring and single-minded passion as a theatrical collector.

Another eccentric figure among toy theatre collectors was Charles Dewhurst

Collecting the Juvenile Drama

Williams, a solicitor, who contributed articles on the subject to the hospitable column of *Notes and Queries* during the 'forties. His occasional forays to London from Newcastle-upon-Tyne will be long remembered by the dealers who survived his tempestuous inquisitions into their stocks of prints. But by 1949, like many collectors, he discovered that the market had outstripped his purse: 'I hear from no one and do not attempt to buy because prices are so high,' he complained in a letter to a friend. It must have been some compensation to his ghost, haunting the saleroom of Sotheby's, to note that prices had risen so much higher since then that his set of twenty-two Webb plays (which cannot have cost him more than £20 before the last War) fetched £450 in 1967.

The name of Mr Herbert Hinkins has appeared twice, and we must here welcome the latest of the Juvenile Drama collectors. Mr Hinkins is much esteemed in the town life of Oxford, where he is a partner in a large firm of building contractors. His love of the toy theatre, first instilled with a French model in his childhood, slumbered long through a busy life, until in 1944 he conceived the excellent notion of forming a comprehensive collection of the subject. As we have seen the old school of collectors was dying out, and their treasures seemed likely to be dispersed; at this point Mr Hinkins appeared, like another of the magic genii who seem to have set watch upon the survival of the Juvenile Drama, and in a couple of rapid passes gathered all into a safe haven. Mr Hinkins has set aside a room in his house at Oxford, where the collection is kept, and where all who are interested are welcome to examine it. The English sheets are complemented by a representative collection of toy theatres from other countries.

The name of Mr M. W. Stone has been frequently mentioned already in these pages. It unfortunately seems to be the case that the modern generation of collectors lacks the racy character and eccentricities of their predecessors; for Mr Stone, like Mr Hinkins, I can adduce no particularly romantic background; he was, in fact, I understand, 'something in the City'. For some twenty-five years he collected the Juvenile Drama, and in the days when he started there was still stuff to be found. The foundation of the collection was a large number of duplicate sheets from Ralph Thomas; to this was added a fine collection formed by Mr Stanley Nott, the London publisher, which was exhibited in America in the nineteen-twenties, many sheets from old Mr H. J. Webb and A. How Mathews, and another very good collection from the late Mr Ransome, which included a large number of playbills and other theatricalia of the period. In all, the Stone collection undoubtedly represents the most comprehensive ever gathered together. It cannot quite compare with the British Museum's or that of Mr Nops for very early sheets, as it lacks the early Greens, the proof sheets, and the original drawings, but all the early publishers are nevertheless well represented, and it is far superior in its array of theatrical portraits; for the later publishers it is not quite as complete as the Prior collection, lacking many of the original Green sheets that were re-issued by Redington; but as a whole, as I have said, it is a most remarkable gathering together. In 1955 Mr Stone generously presented his collection to the Victoria and Albert Museum, where it now forms one of the finest features of the Enthoven Theatre Collection.

These, then, are the collectors of the Juvenile Drama. I have not, of course, attempted to mention everybody who has ever made a collection of these sheets; these are the giants, but there are today probably a hundred people who have succeeded in acquiring a few hundred of these old sheets. We (for into this category I can scrape myself) represent an essential and important element in the fancy; it is important that at least one fully comprehensive collection should belong to the nation, but apart from that the wider and the more competitive the search the healthier.

The Juvenile Drama collectors have done their work well; there is now no excuse at all for any one to complain that he cannot examine these sheets, with their unique record of the nineteenth-century theatre. The Ralph Thomas Collection at the British Museum is magnificent for the early publishers; the Jonathan King Collection at the London Museum is strong in the later publishers; the M. W. Stone Collection at the Victoria and Albert Museum is unrivalled for a representative survey of the whole field. In the United States there are other collections, some scarcely inferior. When the Regency and early Victorian theatre receives the detailed examination that is its due from theatrical students I hope that full use will be made of the facilities thus provided by the patience and generosity of the collectors of the Juvenile Drama.

The days when toy theatre sheets could be found by grubbing through the miscellaneous boxes of second-hand booksellers are, I am afraid, gone for ever; it is not a very satisfactory subject for the modern collector, because there is practically nothing left to buy. I once formed the ambitious project of visiting the site of every toy theatre publisher's premises, in the hope of finding some old bundle of forgotten stock mouldering in the cellar! Whatever chance there was then disappeared in the wartime drive for paper salvage. The Juvenile Drama has hardly ever passed through the select West End bookshops; it was first too cheap and then too scarce. In fact it was not until the Prior sale that the subject was admitted as 'respectable' at all; at an auction sale at Sotheby's before the War, at which I was present, the room laughed when the auctioneer offered a Hodgson model stage for sale. Today they would gasp! In 1968 a Pollock stage with a set of his plays, plain and coloured, fetched £420 at auction.

There are a few collecting 'points' which, I think, might be urged for the benefit of future buyers and sellers. The first is that any sheet dated earlier than 1811 is a priceless rarity. The second is that the really scarce sheets are those of the minor and insignificant publishers. Thirdly, a complete play with its book of words is in every way a more desirable possession than the same number of haphazardly assorted sheets. And fourthly, that an un-coloured sheet as issued by the publisher is of far greater interest than the same sheet coloured yesterday by the printseller's lady colourist; some of this modern colouring is quite good in its way, and if you have two copies of the same sheet I may accept the principle, but it is nothing less than desecration to allow a unique or rare plain sheet to be touched with a modern paint brush. It is not difficult to recognize modern colouring, and if collectors of the Juvenile Drama will refuse to pay fancy prices for coloured sheets the print-seller's incentive is removed.

Tinsel pictures are a good deal more common than toy theatre sheets, as they were more likely to be preserved, and you will find them in plenty of antique and bric-à-brac shops. There are three main types: examples a hun-dred or so years old made by expert hands, examples of the same date made by clumsy children; and more recent examples, usually made 'for the market' by professionals. Many of these last were the work of H. J. Webb and Young Harry, and there were a few others who had obtained stocks of old stamped tinsel and made up their own specimens; they can usually be recognized by the bright and shiny character of the tinselling, but so long as they are genuine theatrical portraits ornamented in the traditional way they are perfectly genuine tinsel portraits and in no way fakes or frauds. An old and well-matured example, if well done, is, however, naturally a much more desirable acquisition.

There is a fascination purely in collecting; but the full value of a collection is only realized when it is used as a foundation for research. The earliest essays towards a history of the Juvenile Drama are represented by the literary articles by Edward Draper, John Oxenford, Godfrey Turner, and William Archer, from 1868 to 1887, to which I have already so copiously referred. These articles, however, though they have their value, are mainly journalistic in tone, and it is in Ralph Thomas's letters to *Notes and Queries*, covering a period from 1867 to 1920, that the foundations of a historical approach were really laid. Ralph Thomas, despite his severe attitude to the 'halfpenny' publishers, was a real authority on his subject, though he seems to have accepted Godfrey Turner's imaginative theories about the toy theatre artists upon evidence that should never have passed a lawyer's scrutiny. It is a great pity that Thomas himself never wrote a history of the Juvenile Drama; he certainly intended doing so, and in 1908 he wrote, 'I have for years intended to write an account of these prints, etc., comprised in the period 1800 to 1850. I am still in hope that I shall leave an account in manuscript.' By 1920 he could write that 'I have during the last few years completed the compilation of catalogues of every print I have seen of the juvenile theatrical series pub-lished by W. West which forms a MS. quarto of about 200 pages.' Beyond this he never seems to have gone. Perhaps he was too immersed in the details of

West to see the subject as a whole. A few years before his death Mr Thomas sent this MS. catalogue to be bound; somehow it got lost in the process; the binders refused to acknowledge that they had ever received it, and Thomas was understandably bitter about the whole matter. It is not impossible that this valuable catalogue is still in existence, unrecognized and forgotten in some high attic or deep cellar; if any one who reads these lines can throw any light on the mystery he will render a signal service to all future students of toy theatre history.

The first real history of the Juvenile Drama was written by John Ashton and printed in a volume of miscellaneous essays, entitled *Varia*, in 1894. Although no acknowledgment was made, this essay seems almost certainly based upon the Ralph Thomas collection; it is a very capable piece of work, free from serious inaccuracies, and prints a list of twenty-eight publishers and 108 plays published by West. John Ashton was something of an amateur of the curious, and has enlightened many an obscure subject with his versatile pen; this little essay on the Juvenile Drama is not the least of his accomplishments.

In the years that follow there is little but an occasional pronouncement from Thomas to enlarge our knowledge until 1913 when a Dr Francis Eagle submits an article on Webb to *The Mask*, the theatrical magazine published by Gordon Craig in Italy. Gordon Craig, who claimed to be a great devotee of the toy theatre, had been extolling Pollock as 'the only surviving man of the old school of ancient theatrical art', and Dr Eagle's sober appraisement of Webb provides a welcome corrective. This article is so good that one wishes the author had written more. He did, in fact, balance it in 1919 by publishing a privately printed pamphlet in praise of Pollock's shop in Hoxton.

The next serious attempt at a history of the toy theatre was in 1921 with a series of articles by Frank Jay in an obscure periodical called *Spare Moments*. These articles are quite a useful summing up of the already established facts on the subject, and were reprinted a few years later in an equally obscure magazine called *Vanity Fair*. Under its new title of *The Collector's Miscellany*, published by a printer in Yorkshire, this little magazine continued to print occasional articles on the Juvenile Drama, sandwiched between 'penny dreadfuls', match-box labels, and other curiosities, for many years.

This, then, was the situation in 1932 when A. E. Wilson, the dramatic critic of the *Star*, made the enterprising and ambitious resolve to write the first complete history of the Juvenile Drama in book form. As an introduction to the subject his book is of the greatest value; his publisher prepared a lavish display of finely reproduced illustrations, and by nobly undertaking this pioneer task Mr Wilson rendered a great service to all lovers of the toy theatre. Nevertheless, if A. E. Wilson had in fact written the last word on the subject there would be no reason for me to waste paper upon it now; he modestly disclaimed any special qualifications for the task beyond a natural love of the toy theatre, and it would be ungenerous to complain that his book is not a critical or comprehensive history; but unfortunately it bears some signs of careless compilation, and its easy readability masks a heavy crop of in-accuracies. One either believes that it is worth while being accurate about something like the toy theatre or one does not; personally I believe that it is. That is my only apology for writing another history of the Juvenile Drama.

So, gradually, the story is being built up. This is certainly not the end; it is only the beginning of scientific study. For too long the Juvenile Drama has relied upon a few well-worn myths and legends to support its history; this oral tradition, much of which has most fortunately been preserved by Wilson from the lips of Prior, is by no means without value; it is indeed a most important link with the past; these are the stories that old W. Webb picked up from his apprentice days, told and retold across the counter to curious gossips, forgotten, half remembered, jealously treasured. Prior and How Mathews were perhaps the last link in this tenuous chain of tradition, and happily all is not lost. But this should now be reinforced by a more sober kind of research. Because we love these old ephemeral toys we must now be critical, rational, and methodical.

Scene 12. WEBB'S SCENES IN DRED Nº 9.

Tom Gordon

London. Pub. by W. WEBB 146 Old S.t S.t Lukes

Webb's plays were being reprinted up to the mid 'thirties, and examples are still sometimes to be found

173

Collecting the Juvenile Drama

The first necessity for a fuller study of the Juvenile Drama must, I feel, be a union catalogue of the sheets preserved in the major public collections — the British Museum, the London Museum, and the Victoria and Albert Museum in England, and the Harvard Theatre Collection and the New York Public Library in the United States. With this foundation surely laid there are two lines of research open — what might be described as the interior and the exterior. The first must be devoted to the minutiae of the sheets and the publishers themselves. There are various lines of approach that have as yet hardly been explored; one of these is the evidence of watermarks on the paper; in my own collection I have examined these and found that they give some most surprising results; a sheet dated 1822, for instance, may appear printed on paper watermarked with the date 1812 (which might merely be old stock) or 1832, long after the publisher was believed to have closed down. There is no doubt that the plates changed hands continually from one publisher to another, and it will inevitably be an exhausting and baffling pursuit to trace each stage in the process — but the search has something of the fascination of a detective problem.

Leading out of this interior research, the Juvenile Drama must be linked more firmly with the theatre of the period, and an attempt made to determine upon exactly which theatrical production any given issue of a toy theatre play was based, who were the actors, the actresses, and the scene painter. This will be the natural complement to a more intelligent appreciation of the nineteenth-century theatre.

It will, of course, inevitably be urged that such a small and insignificant subject as toy theatres should not be submerged beneath a ponderous weight of criticism and research. The discussion of this point involves a complicated definition of civilization; personally I should be quite prepared to argue that a civilized society is one whose members can devote themselves to toy theatres! It is, anyhow, not a question of toy theatres instead of hospitals; the question is, can we have toy theatres as well as the atom bomb. I can only answer that we *must*! If the humane and urbane pattern of life is to survive upon this planet, man must be able to relax among toys and nonsense; a passionate interest in little absurdities is a necessary safety valve in the march of progress. In the last analysis, the Juvenile Drama was born from life and the theatre, and its study, however minute, can only illuminate, from its imprisoned mirrors, the theatre and life again.

For our justification we can hardly improve upon the motto displayed, with a nice wit, upon West's Stage Proscenium: '*Quibus minus facimus multum.*'

15 Revival

The Juvenile Drama had no sooner died than people began to wonder if it could be revived.

It was in about 1900, I think, that a gentleman named Campbell began to prepare for a revived toy theatre, modern but on traditional lines. Harlequinade characters were copied and enlarged from existing Juvenile Drama sheets to a height of about four inches; each figure was then printed back to back upon the sheet, so that it could be introduced either facing left or right; the intention was to have these sheets printed in colour, but I gather that financial backing was lacking and they never reached the market. A few of the uncoloured proof sheets have survived as a witness to this still-born enterprise.

But if the commercial value of the toy theatre was in doubt there was growing appreciation of its artistic charm, and this found expression in a series of toy theatre plays written and designed by Jack B. Yeats, the brother of the Irish poet. In 1901 there was published *James Flaunty, or the Terror of the Western Seas*, in 1903 *The Treasure of the Garden*, and the next year *The Scourge of the Gulph*; the plays were printed in book form with the texts, bound in paper covers, and sold either plain or hand-coloured; the publisher was Elkin Mathews. The art of Jack Yeats is of a clear and vivid character which certainly owes something to the folk tradition of the Juvenile Drama. These books are extremely pleasant things in themselves, and with their melodramatic piratic plots would make very jolly toy theatre plays, but I question whether they were really used in a practical way—though that was certainly the author's intention; their whole manner of production is rather 'arty', and I imagine they were bought and kept as illustrated books.

In a rather similar style are the plays published twenty years later, designed to the texts of F. J. Harvey Darton; these were originally commissioned from

Revival

Lovat Fraser, who would certainly have produced something very pleasant, and on his death the work was taken over by Albert Rutherston. In 1922 was published *The Good Fairy* and in 1923 *The London Review*; one large sheet of characters and scenes, printed in colour, was enclosed in a pocket in the cover; the publisher was Wells, Gardner, and Darton. The texts of these plays, written in heroic couplets, are very amusing, though they are far too long and profuse for toy theatre performance; similarly the character sheets are extremely gay and decorative, but quite hopeless for practical cutting out. These, too, must be regarded as artistic toys, rather than a real revival.

During the period between the wars the only toy theatre plays available in the toy shops were a few very simple children's stories, printed in colour upon cardboard; those published by Lines Brothers, with books by Kay Foster, were probably the best, and were very suitable for young children; apart from these a few firms put out toy theatres and plays as advertisements, and we find Caley's, Quaker Oats, and the London Underground entering the toy theatre trade. But the publications, though it would be vulgar to sneer at their simplicity, lack any real style of their own and owe nothing to the Juvenile Drama tradition.

In 1925 the British Model Theatre Guild was founded by H. Whanslaw and Gerald Morice, with the object of reviving interest in the old Juvenile Drama and creating a new technique of modern model theatre work. I have already referred to the excellent Webb and Pollock Exhibitions arranged by this Society; the special 'Juvenile Theatre' issues of its Bulletin, edited by Gerald Morice, are also a valuable contribution to the subject. Its attempts to promote a new school of model theatre art were, perhaps, less successful; at the annual exhibitions there were always a few stage models, and perhaps performances of grand opera, with flat cut out figures, to gramophone records; the Secretary of the Society, Seymour Marks, published a courageous attempt towards a contemporary model theatre technique with a play called *Green Jerk*; but all this amateur effort had no effect upon commercial publications. The Model Theatre Guild itself gave more and more of its attention to puppets and marionettes, and it is with this more spectacular art and its educational uses that contemporary interest would appear to lie.

It was now that a brave attempt to sell the Webb–Pollock plays in the West End was made by John and Edward Bumpus, the booksellers then in Oxford Street, and as I was the principal actor in the slightly fantastic episode which might be called 'the Bumpus revival' I must ask permission to introduce a short chapter of autobiography.

The story really begins with a very remarkable clergyman, called the Reverend J. B. Hunt, in the parish of Bishop's Hatfield in Hertfordshire; Mr Hunt was a great enthusiast for the theatre in all its forms, and in our family, I am glad to say, he found ardent disciples; urged by Mr Hunt, my father made the perilous journey to Hoxton, and returned, with hair-raising stories of his adventures, carrying a Pollock toy theatre. I have already de-scribed how the theatre fared, and was handed down from brother to brother. Eventually, when I was about fourteen I suppose, the toy theatre was laid up as being too childish a pastime, but it was never thrown away and, in fact, I have it still.

About four years later I left school, and decided to become a bookseller. Accompanied by my father I visited all the most select establishments, but trade was in the throes of a great slump and our reception was not promising. However, included high up in our list was Bumpus's which at that time, in superb premises on the north side of Oxford Street, was arranging a series of excellent literary exhibitions in what had been the old Marylebone Court House. After the usual polite regrets from Mr J. G. Wilson, Bumpus's man-ager, my father took the opportunity of complimenting him on the present exhibition devoted to Lewis Carroll, and suggested that an exhibition of toy theatres would be very interesting; Mr Wilson rose with enthusiasm to the bait, and my father then proudly announced me as a young man who knew all about toy theatres and could even perform plays on them. I was engaged on the spot!

The credit for this conception, then, must go to my father's imagination and to Mr Wilson's sporting readiness (canny Scot though he was) to take a chance. I was given a small room to myself in which a toy theatre stage was erected, and all the Pollock and Webb plays were displayed; my old favourite, *The Corsican Brothers*, which had been introduced to the English stage by Charles Kean from Dumas' novel and had then figured in Irving's repertoire, was put into rehearsal; and on the great day, shortly before Christmas 1932, the Press was invited to the first performance.

No one was more surprised than myself at the furore that was created; the journalists played up splendidly, and during a five-week season of two performances daily we had up to fifty people at every showing. Some of them stayed to buy stages or plays afterwards, and I hope that many more remem-bered Bumpus's when they next bought a book. The next year I presented *The Miller and his Men* in Webb's version, and the year afterwards Pollock's pantomime *The Sleeping Beauty*. This was the last toy theatre season; for Bumpus had to leave these lovely premises and find accommodation in a smaller shop on the other side of the street, where luxuries like free toy theatre shows could no longer be afforded.

These performances were not given under entirely ideal conditions—which call for a jolly party rather than a transient audience of complete strangers. Dramatically speaking a few of the shows were complete flops, and there is one story that is too good not to tell; we had put on a special morning per-formance, but it had not been advertised and only two ladies turned up; how-ever, the show went on, and when in the middle of the first act I heard the sound of chairs scraping I concluded that the audience had been increased, and redoubled the energy with which I was delivering the lines; it was *The Miller*, and Grindoff snarled, Claudine twittered, and Kelmar quavered as they had never done before. It was not until the interval that I discovered that the scraping of chairs had been the ladies making their escape, and that I had been declaiming to an empty house! However, this really was exceptional, and for most of the time our difficulty was to cope with the crowds; children and adults both came, and their response was wonderfully encouraging.

This 'Bumpus revival' was great fun while it lasted. It proved, I think, that practical toy theatre performances were perfectly feasible; it brought some prosperity to the last years of Pollock and Webb; and it introduced the Juvenile Drama into a social milieu that had never heard of it before. Her Majesty Queen Mary honoured us with her patronage, and quite a trickle of well-known personages sat among the children at the performances. But its permanent results were inconclusive. The plays were neither available nor sold in large enough numbers to constitute a real revival in popularity; both Webb and Pollock died during the run of these performances; it was not the beginning of a new toy theatre era, it was the last dramatic gesture of the old.

The Juvenile Drama is dead; and yet there is something in these sheets that defies death. Toy theatre plays can never again be economically produced by hand-colouring, and twentieth-century children will not settle down to the laborious business of colouring and cutting out perhaps twenty or more sheets to a play; but must toy theatres therefore disappear from English homes? The modern commercial attempts to produce toy theatre plays have lacked all grace and style. Can the old Juvenile Drama be presented in an acceptable contemporary form?

Alan Keen, whom we have already met as the purchaser and preserver of Pollock's, was determined to make the attempt. As I was deeply involved in this venture, too, I must continue with a further chapter of autobiography, for I was engaged by Keen as the manager of the enterprise that now became Benjamin Pollock Ltd.

Smart premises were taken at John Adam Street in the Adelphi, stages were manufactured with plastic fronts for the traditional designs to be pasted on, colour-printed versions of some of the old plays were produced, a new play, *The High Toby*, was written by J. B. Priestley and designed by Doris Zinkeisen (which was well in the tradition of the Juvenile Drama by looking splendid but proving almost unperformable), and generally speaking a good deal of money was spent. It made quite a splash, Sir Ralph Richardson and Robert Donat joined the Board, publicity was good—the journalists always have loved the toy theatre for a good story—but the financial return was not enough. The shop itself did fairly well, and many new young enthusiasts were introduced to the toy theatre, but sales to the toy trade, upon which much depended, were poor. Various smooth characters calling themselves by fancy titles passed across the scene, taking good salaries as they went but contributing little in return, and after three years it was clear that sail must be trimmed. We moved to humbler, though pleasant enough, premises in Little Russell Street, near the British Museum; but by this time a load of debts was on our back, my salary, always uncertain, became more and more overdue, and after five years I had to call it a day. The firm staggered on from one crisis to another for another year or so, but in the end the debenture holder put a receiver in and the business closed down.

The credit for what was achieved and the blame for the failure must both be laid upon Alan Keen. In appearance he was stout, red-faced, cigar-smoking, more like a bookmaker than a bookseller; his background was in advertising; his manner was warm, jocular, and bustling; some people were amused by him and called him a card; others were irritated by him and called him a cad; he was always full of wonderful schemes; he was clever at getting people to put up money for them; but they usually lost their money; some people thought he was a crook. I would like to say here that I liked and admired him —though he drove me mad with worry; he was enormously enthusiastic, and tremendously generous; he loved giving presents; he had vision; and he loved the toy theatre. That was enough. His house of cards collapsed around him before the end and he died, poor, in 1960. In the long roll-call of toy theatre publishers let the name of Alan Keen be honoured.

The sequel was even more fantastic. The story that I am going to tell now is true—or nearly so. When Pollock's shut up shop a lot of regular customers were disappointed; in particular, lots of people wanted the wire slides that are essential for pushing the characters to and fro on the stage. These cost twopence each at that time. But when people wrote up for a dozen slides their orders were returned unfulfilled, and they were obliged to abandon their performances in disappointment. All except an indomitable Frenchwoman married to an Englishman, Marguerite Fawdry, whose son was an enthusiastic toy theatre performer. This lady bearded the accountant who represented the debenture holder and demanded why she could not buy a dozen slides. 'Are there no slides?' she asked. 'I believe there are a hundred thousand in the warehouse,' answered the weary accountant, 'but we have no staff to look them out for you. You can buy the lot if you like and look them out for yourself.' 'Very well,' answered Mrs Fawdry, 'I will.'

Having bought the entire business of Benjamin Pollock Ltd in order to obtain a dozen wire slides for her son, Mrs Fawdry then set about relaunching toy theatres. She took a house in Monmouth Street, furnished the upper floors as a Toy Museum, and extended the range of toy theatre plays with new productions, reprints of old sheets, and all sorts of ingenious developments. The shop became a mecca for parents in search of unusual toys and decorations; boutique owners in swinging Britain of the 'sixties flocked to Monmouth Street in search of 'with it' stock for their shelves; and they were followed by a stream of foreign visitors who regarded a visit to Monmouth Street as third only to Carnaby Street and Portobello Road in their London itinerary. A generation of boys and girls from Seven Dials has run up and down the narrow staircase of the Toy Museum, and some of them have come back in jeans or miniskirts to serve in the shop. Every time one revisits the shop a new set of helpers or home colourists seems to have sprung up to keep the wheels turning. Plans are being made to give the toy theatre and the Toy Museum a more permanent basis, and the Museum has now spread to new premises in Scala Street, in the shadow of the Post Office Tower. Once again the toy theatre has exerted its magic.

Any toy theatre revival must, I feel, satisfy two conditions. It must be in the *traditions* of the Juvenile Drama, which has proved itself so English and so true to toy theatre technique; and it must accept the limitations of time and trouble imposed by modern standards of life. If these conditions are fulfilled, surely toy theatres will continue to enliven our homes with their mimic dramas, and enrich our lives with the memory of their inspiration.

The Juvenile Drama is dead. Long live the Juvenile Drama!

Characters from *Der Freischutz* by Skelt

Caspar with Eagle　　*Zamiel*

16 The Influence of the Juvenile Drama

While the rain pattered against the window-panes, and the yellow fog rolled slowly down the street, from these long evenings, before a crackling fire, what visions were implanted and what influences remained in the mind? The toy theatre proscenium was a gateway to a new world of the imagination. What have we brought back from our travels in this unknown country?

To the boys of its time, the Juvenile Drama undoubtedly gave an intimate knowledge of the theatre, not only in a general way but in all the details of properties and stage management. How often this led to the uncertain pitfalls of an actor's life one can hardly say, but it must have exercised a considerable influence. J. B. Howe thus describes his first appearance upon the stage, when, as a boy of twelve, he watched with watering mouth the erection of Harmer's portable theatre in Somers Town, and was even allowed to help in sprinkling the sawdust across the stage. When this was done the show was ready to commence, and the proprietor asked the little boy if he had ever seen the drama of *Jack Sheppard*; 'I told him I had seen Skelt's characters and scenes,' J. B. Howe tells us; 'All right, that will do, I'll tell you what to say every time you come off,' answered the theatrical proprietor, and there and then the curtain went up with the boy in the character of Jack Sheppard, the idle apprentice.

Many great English actors from Ellen Terry to John Gielgud have recalled the toy theatres with which they played. Many more, neither great nor famous, first tasted in that enchanted fairyland the heady wine of theatrical achievement, and learned the rudiments of stage technique upon its lilliputian boards.

But the toy theatre was not only an introduction to a larger theatre, it was an introduction to life. There we found romance, bright colours, dreaming landscapes, stagy dramatic plots; we brought them back to enliven the darkness and the fog, and they are with us still. Stevenson is the supreme example of a man who lived his whole life in the world of the toy theatre; what is *Treasure Island* but one of the piratic dramas retold? It was this schooling in the Juvenile Drama that made his own attempts at play-writing so wooden and stilted; and the same might be said of the plays of Dickens; the toy theatre is not a good model for a realistic dramatist.

It was G. K. Chesterton, I think, who first pointed out the influence of the toy theatre upon all Stevenson's life, and Chesterton too is an example of its influence; he played with one as a child and as a man, and wrote often in its praise. To Chesterton the toy theatre was the real theatre; he saw all life in its bright colours and exaggerated shapes, and all philosophy in its clear division between the good and the bad.

And its high bombastic speeches, mouthed with relish to shake the gallery rafters—what remembered echoes are here? The play is *The Miller and his Men*, and in the final scene Grindoff, hotly pursued by Count Fribourg and his soldiery, takes a last refuge in the gallery of his mill. 'Surrender,' cries the Count. 'Surrender?' answers Grindoff with a terrible snarl. 'Surrender? Never! I have sworn never to descend from this spot alive!' Is there a memory here to link this proud defiant boast with the England of 1940?

'We shall fight on the beaches, we shall fight on the landing grounds, we shall fight in the fields and in the streets, we shall fight in the hills: we shall never surrender!' Can there be a remembered echo here?

Yes. Winston Churchill, too, had his toy theatre. He was a customer of Webb's, and for three or four boyhood years was an enthusiastic producer upon its boards. His most popular play was *The Miller and his Men*. The letter in which he describes his experiences with a model stage may be read in A. E. Wilson's book, to whom must go the credit for revealing this early influence in the life of England's future Prime Minister. Mr Webb well remembered those visits from the fourteen-year-old schoolboy: 'He was a jolly and impulsive lad,' he told Mr Wilson, 'and I shall never forget the way he would vault over my counter.'

And so, as a school of rhetoric, the toy theatre plays its part in English history, and in the hour of England's peril, its speeches, dimly remembered, give shape to a challenge that echoed round the world.

Stevenson, Chesterton, Churchill; three examples of men upon whose lives the influence of the Juvenile Drama can be discerned, and together representative of that romantic strain which runs through our sober northern blood and lifts us into genius. That is the gift of the Juvenile Drama to the nation that gave it birth; bright 'twopence coloured' images in the fog, exaggerated shadows like caricatures, a touch of drama, a brave and boyish romance, the breath of poetry.

Publishers of the Juvenile Drama

This list attempts to provide a complete record of every publisher of the Juvenile Drama and theatrical portraits. It gives his name, his address or addresses, and as far as possible the years between which he was in business; usually it is impossible to determine the dates with accuracy, and in these cases only one date is given, which may be regarded as an indication of the period when he worked. After this come a few notes on his career, and then a list of the plays published by him; where it is possible to date these plays from the evidence of the sheets this is given, but owing to the practice of redating every reprint these dates should be accepted with reservation. Many of the plays thus listed are in fact reprints from the plates of earlier publishers, but it has not normally been found feasible to distinguish these.

The publishers are placed in alphabetical order; boys' magazines, 'penny packets', toy theatre revivals, and American publishers are treated separately.

1822   J. Allen, 23 Princes Road, Kennington: Opposite the Asylum, Francis Road, West, minster

An early 'halfpenny' publisher. *Philip Quarl* of 1822 was published in 'halfpenny'-size sheets.

Philip Quarl 1822	*The Secret Mine*
The Miller and his Men 1822	*Aladdin*
Magna Charta	*Rob Roy*
Timour the Tartar	*The Forest of Bondy*
Blue Beard	*Guy Fawkes*
The Forty Thieves	

1815–25 G. Anderson

According to A. How Mathews this publisher was in partnership with Slee, 1815–1825, and published about ten plays in penny sheets; a year or so after the dissolution of the partnership he sold his stock to Straker, from whom it passed via Lloyd to Skelt. So far as I know, no sheets bearing the name of Anderson are in existence today, and it has not been possible to substantiate this story.

1830   J. Bailey and Co., 1 Clifford's Inn Passage: 13 Fetter Lane: 65 Gray's Inn Lane-Holborn: 2 Slade's Place, Little Suffolk St: 188 Fleet St

Some sheets bear the names of 'Bailey and Hunt' and 'Suzman and J. Bailey'.

Der Freischutz	*Blue Beard*
The Miller and his Men	*The Forty Thieves*
The Flying Dutchman	*The Exile*

c. 1830 H. Brown, 51 Bath St, City Road

Portraits.

c. 1830 T. J. Brown, 10 Great May's Buildings, St Martin's Lane: 21 Mercer St, Long Acre: 61 Water St, Manchester

Portraits and miscellaneous sheets; some taken over by Skelt. He described himself as an 'ornament maker', and probably manufactured tinsel ornaments.

1812   H. Burtenshaw, 130 St Martin's Lane
        Acted as an agent for I. K. Green.

Voorn the Tiger 1812	*Baghvan Ho* 1812
The Virgin of the Sun 1812	*The Golden Fish*

1821–4 W. Clarke, 265 High Holborn
        In some sort of partnership with DeBurson, who succeeded him.

Gil Blas 1821	*The Lady of the Lake* 1821
Kaloc 1821	*Mother Bunch* 1822
Korastikan 1821	*Blue Beard* 1822
Rob Roy 1821	*The Forty Thieves* 1824
Henry IV 1821	*The Black Prince*
Ivanhoe 1821	*The Blind Boy*

        William Cole (*see* Hodgson & Co)

c. 1850 Crawford, 3 Dean St, Holborn
        Portraits, Redington acted as his agent.

1818   G. Creed, 31 Exeter Street, Strand
        Mainly portraits and combats.

Lucretia 1818	*The Forty Thieves*
Undine	

c. 1819 Thos. Cristoe, 34 Drury Lane
        Portraits.

1826   D'Ash, 27 Fetter Lane
        Portraits.

1821   B. M. DeBurson, 10 Wilson St, Gray's Inn Road
        (*See* W. Clarke)

The Hunted Tailor   1817 (? misprint for 1827)
The Forty Thieves   1827

c. 1910 Walter Dunlo, Stoke Newington

Cinderella

1827–31 Dyer, 13 Dorset Crescent, Hoxton New Town: 55/33 Bath St, City Road: Featherstone Buildings, City Road: 109 Aldersgate St
        A family concern. The sheets are variously lettered 'J. Dyer', 'I. J. Dyer and Co., 'Dyer Senior', 'Dyer Junior', and simply 'Dyer'. A number of Hodgson and Co.'s plays, including some of the extra large 3*d.* scenes, were taken over by this firm.

The Flying Dutchman 1827	*The Silver Palace*
The Pilot 1828	*Pizarro*
The Bottle Imp 1828	*Tom Thumb*
The Castle Spectre 1828	*The Warlock of the Glen*
The Forest of Bondy 1828	*Blue Beard*
The Mountaineers 1829	*The Brigand*
The Red Rover 1829	*Der Freischutz*
Black Eyed Susan 1829	*The Forty Thieves*
The Bear Hunters	*Jonathan Bradford*
The Blind Boy	*The Miller and his Men*
Douglas	*The Old Oak Chest*
Guy Fawkes	*Valentine and Orson*
Mary, the Maid of the Inn	*The Woodman's Hut*
Paul Jones	

1824–8 F. Edwards, 49 Leman St, Goodman's Fields
Possibly some connection with Dyer.

Pizarro 1824	*The Floating Beacon* 1826
The Miller and his Men 1824	*The Woodman's Hut* 1826
The Innkeeper's Daughter 1825	

1828   J. Fairburn, 106–110 Minories and 40 Fetter Lane: 44 Barbican and Featherstone St, City Road
Portraits. This publisher, or his father, was issuing books and pamphlets as early as 1797. (*See* S. Fairburn)

1837   S. Fairburn, 44 Barbican
Portraits. Probably the successor of J. Fairburn.

1827   R. Forse, 57 St John's Square
Portraits.

c. 1880 W. S. Fortey, Monmouth Court, Bloomsbury
Portraits.

1823   R. Franey and Co., 53 East St, Marylebone
Portraits.

c. 1840 T. Frost, 40 Dudley St, Soho
Agent for Green.

c. 1880 J. Goodwin, Pentonville
Blue Beard

1830   J. Goulding (or Golding) (*see* A. Park)

1811–14 I. K. Green ? Clement's Inn Passage, Clare Market
(*See* J. K. Green)

The Secret Mine 1812	*The Seven Wonders of the World* 1812
(sold by Burtenshaw)	(sold by Perkins and Burtenshaw)
Valentine and Orson 1812	*The Tiger Horde* 1814
(sold by Burtenshaw)	(published by Green and Slee,
	5 Artillery Lane, Bishopsgate)

1832–60 John Kirby Green, 3 George St. Walworth (1834–6): 33 Salisbury Place, Walworth (1837–8): 34 Lambeth Square, New Cut (1839–43): 16 Park Place, Walworth (1843–5): 9 Thurlow Place, Walworth (1846–57)
Born 1790. Died 1860. Claimed to be the 'original inventor and publisher of Juvenile Theatrical Prints, established 1808'. Presumably this is the same man as I. K. Green. His son George J. Green published a few sheets from 9 Thurlow Place and some combats from 6 Chatham Place, Walworth.

The Miller and his Men (large) 1834	*The Brigand* 1836
Jonathan Bradford 1834	*Harlequin and Guy Fawkes* 1836
Douglas 1834	*State Secrets* 1837
The Miller and his Men (small) 1835	*The Lord Mayor's Fool* 1837
Robert Macaire 1836	*The Wreck Ashore* 1837
The Forty Thieves 1836	*Blue Beard* 1837
The Red Rover 1836	*Wapping Old Stairs* 1838

Lord Darnley 1839

Jack Sheppard 1839

Black Eyed Susan 1840

The Children in the Wood 1840

Rookwood 1840

The Waterman (reversed from Skelt) 1840

Aladdin (from O. Hodgson) 1841

The Maid and the Magpie 1841

Harlequin and the Giant Helmet 1841

The Silver Palace 1841

The Woodman's Hut (incomplete) 1841

Blue Jackets 1842

The Battle of Waterloo 1842

Harlequin Riddle-me-ree 1842

Harlequin Robin Hood 1843

Therese 1845

The Forest of Bondy 1846

The Flying Dutchman 1847

Harlequin St George 1847

Timour the Tartar (reversed from Skelt) 1849

Cinderella 1849

The Sleeping Beauty 1850

Belphegor the Conjuror 1851

Black Beard the Pirate 1851

Richard III 1851

Mary, the Maid of the Inn 1852

Harlequin Oliver Cromwell 1852

Whittington and his Cat 1853

Harlequin Uncle Tom's Cabin 1853

Jack the Giant Killer 1854

The Battle of Alma 1854

The Corsican Brothers 1854

The Life of a Soldier 1854

Tom Thumb 1854

Rob Roy 1855

The Battle of Balaclava 1855

Dred 1856

Sixteen String Jack 1857

The Daughter of the Regiment 1857

Goody Goose

The Miller and his Men (alternative small edition)

c. 1840 W. Hancock, 2 Falcon Place, Bethnal Green

Agent for Green.

1892 Sir Augustus Harris, Drury Lane

Published a booklet of plain scenes and characters, to be coloured and submitted with a toy theatre acting version for a prize of £20 and a toy theatre.

Little Bo-peep, Little Red Riding Hood, and Hop o'my Thumb

c. 1840 G. Harriss, 60 Bell St, Edgware Road

Agent for Green.

c. 1830 W. Harrison, 27 Long Alley, Finsbury

Portraits.

1823–40 W. Hawley and Co., 10 Henry St, Hampstead Rd: 5 Seymour Row: 27 Molineux St, Bryanstone Square

In his later years Park acted as his agent.

Aladdin 1823

Guy Mannering (from Hodgson and Co.) 1824

1811–14 Mrs M. Hebberd, 2 Upper Charlton Street, Fitzroy Square, Marylebone

One of the only two lady publishers. She was the proprietress of a circulating library in a good residential neighbourhood. West appears to have taken over some of her plays. Years later she, or her successor, is said to have acted as agent for Skelt.

The Forty Thieves 1811

The Fairy of the Oak 1811

The Battle of the Bridges 1811

Cinderella 1811

Valentine and Orson 1811

The Virgin of the Sun 1811

Harlequin Colossus 1812

Doctor Hocus Pocus 1814

The Tempest

Aladdin

Julius Caesar

Midas

The Forest of Bondy

186

1822–30 Hodgson and Co., 43 Holywell St: 11–43 King St, Snow Hill: 10 Newgate St: 111 Fleet St: 10 Cloth Fair, West Smithfield

The partners in the firm would appear to be Howes, whose name appears with Hodgson on a few sheets from King St, and W. Cole and S. Maunder, who seem to have been printers in Newgate St; Cole was in business in 1821, publishing portraits, and seems to have continued independently for a few years after the break-up of the firm, with the old stock. H. Kenilworth, a printer at 43 King St, may also have had some connection with the business. Many of the sheets were not dated; those that are mostly bear the dates 1822–3–4. (*See* Langham.)

Aladdin 1822	*The Devil's Bride* (probably a misprint
Black Beard the Pirate 1822	for *Bridge*)
The Blind Boy 1822	*Don Giovanni*
Cherry and Fair Star 1822	*The Dutch Pirate*
Edward the Black Prince 1822	*The Falls of Clyde*
The Exile 1822	*Green in France*
Gilderoy, the Bonnie Boy 1822	*Guy Mannering*
Guy Fawkes 1822	*Hamlet*
The Maid and the Magpie 1822	*The Heart of Midlothian*
Mary, the Maid of the Inn 1822	*The Infernal Secret*
The Miller and his Men 1822	*Ivanhoe*
The Miller's Maid 1822	*Joan of Arc*
Montrose 1822	*Jonathan in England*
Richard III 1822	*Kenilworth*
The Secret Mine 1822	*The Law of Java*
Cortez 1823	*Life in London*
The Forest of Bondy 1823	*Life in Paris*
Macbeth 1823	*The Mountaineers* (probably not put
Magna Charta 1823	on sale)
Othello 1823	*Napoleon Bonaparte*
Pizarro 1823	*Nelson*
Romeo and Juliet 1823	*The Old Oak Chest*
The Tempest 1823	*Quentin Durward*
Maid Marian 1824	*Raymond and Agnes*
Tekeli 1824	*Rob Roy MacGregor*
Timour the Tartar 1824	*Robinson Crusoe*
Zoroaster 1824	*Rugantino, the Bravo of Venice*
Two Gentlemen of Verona 1827	*The Sleeping Beauty*
Ali Baba	*The Temple of Death*
Ali Pacha	*Tippoo Saib*
The Battle of Waterloo	*Thalaba, the Destroyer*
Black Eyed Susan	*Valentine and Orson*
The Blood Red Knight	*The Vampire*
Blue Beard	*The Vision of the Sun*
The Cataract of the Ganges	*Wallace, the Hero of Scotland*
The Devil and Dr Faustus	*The Woodman's Hut*

1830   Bernard Hodgson and Co., 5 Cloth Fair
Portraits.

1831–43 Orlando Hodgson, 10 Cloth Fair, West Smithfield: 22 Macclesfield St: 111, 118, and 132 Fleet St

Probably a survivor from the dissolution of Hodgson and Co. He continued to publish books and pamphlets until the 'forties, when he had a printing works at Isleworth.

Black Eyed Susan 1831	
The Maid and the Magpie 1832	*Aladdin* 1832
Chevy Chase 1832	*The Siege of Troy* 1833
The Miller and his Men 1832	*Ali Baba*

187

1822 W. Hodgson

According to A. How Mathews there was also a Hodgson with this initial. He suggests that this man may have been the founder of Hodgson and Co, and that Orlando Hodgson was a completely different enterprise. The identity of the two Hodgsons is open to dispute, but the main evidence in favour of a connection between the two firms is provided by a few Portraits published in July 1830 by Hodgson and Co., 10 Cloth Fair. These must have been the last prints issued by Hodgson and Co., and the next year we find Orlando Hodgson in business at the same address. There is evidence that Cole had taken over the Hodgson and Co plays and was selling them from Newgate Street in 1825, and it seems difficult to draw an absolutely clear cut distinction between Orlando and 'the Co'.

1820 C. Hook, 33 Windmill St, Tottenham Court Road

Listed by John Ashton. All trace of this publisher now seems to have disappeared.

1822 Howes (*see* Hodgson and Co.)

1830 Hunt (*see* J. Bailey)

c. 1845 Moss Hyams, 15 Mint St, Borough

Agent for Green.

c. 1850 I. James, 13 Luke's Court, Bow St

Portraits.

1811–27 J. H. Jameson, 13 Dukes Court, Bow St

A prolific publisher of 'souvenir sheets'.

Tom Thumb 1811	*The Tiger Horde* 1814
Robinson Crusoe 1811	*Blue Beard* 1814
Sadac and Kalasrade 1811	*Red Hands* 1815
The Americans 1811	*Zembucca* 1815
Valentine and Orson 1811	*Harlequin and the Valley of Diamonds* 1815
Don Juan 1811	
One O'Clock 1811	*Comus* 1815
The Devil's Bridge 1812	*Wallace the Hero of Scotland* 1815
Harlequin Fancy 1812	*The Hero of Switzerland* 1815
The Hag of the Lake 1812	*Charles the Bold* 1815
The Illuminated Lake 1812	*The Miller and his Men* 1815
The Poison Tree 1812	*Richard III* 1815
The White Cat 1812	*The Magpie* 1815
Timour the Tartar 1812	*The High Mettled Racer* 1815
The House of Morville 1812	*Bertram* 1816
Peter the Cruel 1813	*Slaves in Barbary* 1816
Kaloc 1813	*The Forty Thieves* 1816
The Miller and his Men 1813	*Harlequin Fortunio* 1816
Remorse 1813	*Guy Mannering* 1816
Illusion 1813	*A Midsummer Night's Dream* 1816
The Blood Red Knight 1813	*Philip and his Dog* 1816
The Mystic Coffer 1813	*Iwanowna* 1816
Lodoiska 1813	*The Libertine* 1817
Aladdin 1813	*The Innkeeper's Daughter* 1817
Antony and Cleopatra 1813	*The Old Oak Chest* 1817
The Corsair 1814	*The Falls of Clyde* 1817
The Forest of Bondy 1814	*Brutus* 1818
Harlequin and the Swans 1814	*Harlequin Gulliver* 1818
The Ninth Statue 1814	*Hamlet* 1818

El Hyder 1818	*Jack and the Beanstalk* 1820
Douglas 1818	*Ivanhoe* 1820
Harlequin's Vision 1818	*Undine* 1821
Rob Roy 1818	*The Exile* 1821
La Perouse 1818	*Charles II* 1824
The Knight of the Black Plume 1818	*The Invasion of Russia* 1825
The Gnome King 1819	*The Flying Dutchman* 1827
The Ruffian Boy 1819	*Peter Wilkins* 1827
The Silver Arrow 1819	*Pizarro*
The Vampire 1820	*The Heart of Midlothian*

c. 1835 W. S. Johnson, 60 St Martin's Lane
Portraits.

1822   H. Kenilworth (*see* Hodgson and Co.)

c. 1850 Jonathan King, Chapel St, Somers Town (1844): 56 Seymour St, Euston Square
(1872): Essex St, Islington (1872–1913)
Agent for Green. A family business of three generations. The second proprietor was
the famous collector.

c. 1830 T. Lane, 4 Great Quebec St, New Road
Portraits.

1828   Langham, Red Lion Street, Holborn
This name appears on a few of Hodgson and Co.'s sheets, either as an agent or some
kind of partner. He also published some horse combats and portraits independently.

1820   W. J. Layton, 10 Petty's Court, Hanway St
Portraits. Some of Hodgson's scenes were signed 'W.L.' and 'W. Layton'.

c. 1840 E. Lazarus, 75 Chamber St, Goodmansfields
Portraits and tinsel ornaments.

1828–33 Robert Lloyd, 40 Gibson St, opposite the Coburg
Possibly published plays for both Straker and Dyer, or took over their stock. At
one time he published playbooks for Skelt, who later took over most of his list.

The Dumb Savoyard 1828	*The Castle Spectre*
Black Eyed Susan 1829	*The Flying Dutchman*
One O'Clock 1830	*Valentine and Orson*
Mary, the Maid of the Inn 1830	*The Murdered Guest*
Richard III 1830	*The Red Rover*
Mazeppa 1831	*Tekeli*
The Floating Beacon 1833	*The Bottle Imp*
The Pilot	*Pizarro*
Therese	*The Old Oak Chest*
The Miller and his Men	*The Innkeeper of Abbeville*
The Forty Thieves	*Der Freischutz*
The Woodman's Hut	*The Maid and the Magpie*
The Blind Boy	*The Maid of Genoa*
Blue Beard	*The Children in the Wood*
Aladdin	

189

1812–24 W. Love, 81 Bunhill Row, near Finsbury Square

Published in a similar style to West, from whose plates he republished all his plays, with the exception of *The Coronation*. At the beginning of his career he seems to have been a jobbing printer and engraver to the trade.

The Ruffian Boy 1819	*The Coronation* 1823
The Aethiop 1823	*Valentine and Orson* 1823
The Silver Arrow 1823	*The Land Storm* 1823
Julius Caesar 1823	*Knight of the Black Plume* 1824

c. 1820 J. Lumsden and Co., Glasgow

Portraits. He was publishing children's books in *c.* 1810.

c. 1880 R. March and Co., 18 St James' Walk, Clerkenwell

Black Eyed Susan	*William Tell*
The Haunted Tower	*The Red Rover*

1822–39 J. L. Marks, 17 Artillery St, Bishopsgate: 23 Russell Court, Drury Lane: 91 Long Lane, Smithfield: 6 Worship St, Finsbury Square

Timour the Tartar	*Blue Beard*
The Elephant of Siam	*Montrose*
The Exile	*Life in London*
Cherry and Fair Star	*The Pilot*

1822   H. Martin, Leigh St, Red Lion Square

Portraits.

1886–1906 A. How Mathews, Acton

Born 1856. Died 1940. Most of these plays were published first as normal reprints, and then in a 'penny packet' abbreviated form.

From Park:

The Red Rover   1903

Based on Skelt:

The Prisoner of Rochelle 1886	*Little King Pippin* 1887
Robinson Crusoe 1886	*Sailor George* (originally published as
The Floating Beacon 1887	*The Miller's Maid*) 1889

Based on Green:

Black Beard the Pirate 1895	*Jack O' Newbury or the Secret Despatches*
Robert Macaire 1898	*(State Secrets)*

Based on Webb:

Cheer, Boys, Cheer	*Three Fingered Jack* 1898
(The Rifle Volunteers) 1896	*The Brigand's Son*

Based on Pollock:

Cinderella 1887	*Blue Jackets*
The King of the Burning Mountains	
(The Silver Palace) 1902	

From various sources:

The Flying Dutchman (not completed) 1886	*Jack the Giant Killer* (not completed) 1891
The Miller and his Men 1888	*Tom Tug* (*The Waterman*) 1893
The Maid and the Magpie 1888	

1822　S. Maunder (*see* Hodgson and Co.)

c. 1840 C. Morrish, 12 Rose and Crown Court, Bloomfield St, Bishopsgate
Portraits.

c. 1850–*c.* 1900 Myers and Co.
This firm is found in two forms:

A. and S. Joseph, Myers and Co., 114 Leadenhall St *c.* 1850–75
A. N. Myers, 15 Berners St, Oxford St *c.* 1875–1900

They were educational agents, dealing in a large range of toys and pastimes, and acted as agents for Webb, Redington, Park, Skelt, and Trentsensky from Vienna and Winckelmann from Berlin.

The Winter's Tale　1856　　　　　*Henry VIII*　1856
(Both these Shakespearean adaptions were based on Charles Kean's productions at the Princess's Theatre and were printed by Trentsensky and apparently drawn by Trentsensky's artists.)

The Miller and his Men (this was apparently printed in Austria, but is not in the style of Trentsensky's publications)

1818–80 A. Park
A family concern. The succession was probably as follows:
Arthur Park, a free-lance artist and engraver, who worked for Hodgson and Co. and other publishers, died 1863. In partnership with J. Goulding, 6 Old St Rd: 6 Oakley St, Lambeth *c.* 1818–35
In *c.* 1835 Arthur Park went to America, and was succeeded by:
Archibald Alexander Park (probably his brother), to whom W. G. Webb was apprenticed, 47 Leonard St, Shoreditch *c.* 1835–63
Mrs Sarah Park (probably his wife) 47 Leonard St 1863–7
Alexander Park (probably their son) 1867–80
47 Leonard St: 40 Marshall St: 150 High St, Notting Hill (1867–8): 30 St John's Rd, Hoxton (1871–80)
Arthur was probably the publisher of most of the plays bearing their name; a few crude lithographed sheets were issued by Alexander.

Richard III	*The Old Oak Chest*
The Miller and his Men	*The Wood Daemon*
The Blind Boy	*The Woodman's Hut*
Der Freischutz	*The Children in the Wood*
The Red Rover	*Timour the Tartar*
The Maid and the Magpie	*Aladdin* (from Hodgson and Co.)

1812　B. Perkins, 40 Marshall St, Carnaby Market
Acted as agent for Green in 1812.

Aladdin　1813　　　　　*Julius Caesar*

c. 1840 J. Pitts, Great St Andrew's St, Seven Dials
A celebrated publisher of street ballads. Portraits.

1876–1937 Benjamin Pollock, 73 Hoxton St
Born 1856. Died 1937. Succeeded J. Redington, and republished the same list of plays. In addition he reissued the following, taken from Park:

The Woodman's Hut　　　　　*The Maid and the Magpie*
The Blind Boy

After his death the shop was carried on by his daughter, Louisa Pollock, 1937–44.

1946   Benjamin Pollock Ltd
        Succeeded Benjamin Pollock
        Directed by Alan Keen:
            1 John Adam St, Adelphi (1946–50): 16 Little Russell St (1950–2)
        Some hundreds of Green plates were reprinted to fill gaps in the Pollock plays; in
        addition the following plays were reprinted in their entirety:

    The Red Rover (Green and Park)   1946   *Therese* (Green)   1947

        The following old plays were reissued printed in colour (all except *The Silver Palace*
        in abbreviated versions and with new texts):

    The Silver Palace   1946   *Harlequinade*   1950
    Aladdin   1947   *Blackbeard the Pirate*   1950
    Cinderella   1947

        The following new plays were issued:

    The High Toby   1948   *The Bethlehem Story*   1950
    Hamlet (based on Laurence Olivier's
        film)   1948
        Directed by Marguerite Fawdry: 44 Monmouth St (1955–   )

        The following plays have been reprinted from the original plates:

    Richard III (Green)   1960   *Othello* (Skelt)   1964

        The following old plays have been reissued printed in colour, with large- and small-
        size scenes, in abbreviated versions and with new texts:

    Cinderella   1961   *Harlequinade*   1965
    Jack the Giant Killer   1961   *Blackbeard the Pirate*   1965
    Aladdin   1963   *The Children in the Wood*   1966

        The following new plays have been issued:

    The Massacre of Penny Plain   1956   *The Flying Saucerers*   1956

1821   H. Pyall, 6 Lambeth Walk
        Portraits.

c. 1870 J. Quick, 4 Dukes' Court, Blackfriars

    The Miller and his Men

1850–76 John Redington, 208 Hoxton Old Town, renamed 73 Hoxton St
        Born 1819. Died 1876. Agent for Green. Some of Green's sheets, dated as early as
        1836, carry Redington's name and address, but there is a suspicion that these may
        be later reprints, with the date unaltered; his name does not appear as an agent in
        Green's dated books of words (probably a more accurate guide) until 1851. Suc-
        ceeded by B. Pollock.
        Original publications:

    Don Quixote   *Charles II*
    Oliver Twist   *Baron Munchausen*
    The Mistletoe Bough   *King Henry*
    Paul Clifford

        Taken from Green:
    Douglas   *Timour the Tartar*
    The Miller and his Men   *Cinderella*
    The Forty Thieves   *The Corsican Brothers*
    The Brigand   *The Daughter of the Regiment*
    The Lord Mayor's Fool   *The Waterman* (with slight alterations)
    Lord Darnley   *The Sleeping Beauty*
    The Children in the Wood   *Whittington and his Cat*

Aladdin	*Jack the Giant Killer*
The Silver Palace	*Richard III* (not completed)
Blue Jackets	*The Red Rover* (not completed)
The Battle of Waterloo	*Black Beard* (not completed)

1818   J. Rippin, Theobald's Rd
Portraits.

c. 1890 G. T. Sanderson Barnes, Surrey
He published a small stage, with figures 1 inch high.

The Maid and the Magpie	*The Forty Thieves*

c. 1820 R. Scruton
The scene painter at the Coburg Theatre. He published lithographed reproductions of his stage masterpieces from West's Theatrical Print Warehouse.

c. 1880 Shorman, Great Poultney St

1835–72 Skelt, 11 (17) Swan St, Minories
A family business. According to A. How Mathews the succession was as follows (this differs slightly from the arrangement given by Ralph Thomas):
M. Skelt (Martin, the founder, a shoemaker) 1835–*c.* 1837
M. and M. Skelt (Martin and Matthew, his brother) *c.* 1837–40
    in 1840 Martin died
M. and B. Skelt (Matthew and his uncle Ben) 1840–50
    in 1850 Matthew died
B. Skelt 1850–62
    in 1862 Ben died in Stepney Workhouse
E. Skelt (Ebenezer, son of Ben. Died 1913) 1862–72
Plays in penny sheets:

The Miller and his Men	*Richard III*
Richard Turpin	*The Children in the Wood*
The Woodman's Hut	*The Miller's Maid*
Timour the Tartar	

Plays in penny sheets, taken from Lloyd:

The Miller and his Men	*Richard III*
Mazeppa	*Mary, the Maid of the Inn*
One O'Clock	*Black Eyed Susan*
The Maid of Genoa	*The Floating Beacon*
The Dumb Savoyard	*The Blind Boy*
The Pilot	*The Maid and the Magpie*
Therese	

Plays in halfpenny sheets:

The Miller and his Men (3 versions)	*The Inchcape Bell*
The Maid and the Magpie	*The Prisoner of Rochelle*
Captain Ross	*Tom Cringle*
Jonathan Bradford	*Walter Brand*
Mazeppa	*Lodoiska*
The Silver Palace	*My Poll and my Partner Joe*
The Echo of Westminster Bridge	*The Floating Beacon*
Harlequin Little King Pippin	*The Old Oak Chest*
Jacob Faithful	*The Woodman's Hut*
Therese	*The Blind Boy*
The Travellers Benighted	*Richard Turpin*
The Forty Thieves	*Harlequin Guy Fawkes*
The Miller's Maid	*Harlequin Cock-a-doodle-do*

The Pilot	Harlequin and Old Dame Trot
Robinson Crusoe	Harlequin Little Tom Tucker
Blue Beard	George Barnwell
The Rover's Bride	The Red Rover
The Waterman	Der Freischutz
The Falls of Clyde	Pizarro
Othello	Aladdin
Harlequin Jack Sheppard	The Brigand
The Battle of Waterloo	Douglas (probably not completed)
The Forest of Bondy	Ivanhoe (probably not completed)
Valentine and Orson	The Mountaineers (large scenes, ex
The Charcoal Burner	Dyer ex Hodgson, only)
The Wood Daemon	

c. 1899–1956 G. Skelt, 24 Clairview St, Saint Helier, Jersey

The imprint adopted by George Conetta (George Wood). Born 1881. Died 1956. His publications consisted almost entirely of copies from earlier publishers. After his death the stock was acquired by Benjamin Pollock Ltd.

From West:

The Council of Ten	The Old Oak Chest
The Land Storm	

From Jameson:

The Miller and his Men

From Love:

The Silver Arrow

From Lloyd:

Black-Eyed Susan	Mary the Maid of the Inn

From Skelt:

Der Freischutz	Harlequin Little King Pippin
Richard Turpin	The Miller's Maid
The Waterman	Robinson Crusoe
The Wood Daemon	The Children in the Wood
The Falls of Clyde	Harlequin Little Tom Tucker
Lodoiska	Harlequin Jack Sheppard
Pizarro	Harlequin Old Dame Trot

From Park:

The Miller and his Men	The Red Rover

From Webb:

Guy Fawkes	The Smuggler
Richard I	

From Green:

Douglas	The Flying Dutchman

Original:

Bombastes Furioso

1814   G. Slee, 5 Artillery Lane, Bishopsgate

In partnership with Green in 1814. According to A. How Mathews Slee was in partnership with Anderson from 1815 to about 1825, and then went in business on his own until about 1835, publishing about twenty plays in halfpenny sheets. These were eventually sold to Skelt, and constituted the bulk of his halfpenny stock; none, however, of those that are found today are known to carry the name of Slee.

1821   J. Smart, 35 Rathbone Place, Oxford St
       Mainly a publisher of portraits.

     The Miller and his Men   1822   *The Exile*   1822

c. 1835 W. Smith, 20 Paul St, Finsbury
       Portraits.

1818   J. Spencer, 65 East St, Manchester Square
       Mainly a publisher of portraits.

     Red Riding Hood   1818   *The Lady of the Lake*

1832   Sarah Stokes, 57 Wych St
       This lady is said to have been West's housekeeper, who republished some of his plays when he was too ill to carry on the business. She died at Wych St in 1844, aged fifty-four.

     The Olympic Revels   1831   *Ivanhoe*   1832

1825–30 D. Straker, 21 Aldersgate St
       He is believed to have had a fire *c.* 1830 and ceased publishing. His plates were acquired by Dyer and Lloyd, and later passed to Park and Skelt.

The Dumb Savoyard 1828	*Pizarro*
The Pilot 1828	*The Woodman's Hut*
Therese 1829	*The Flying Dutchman*
One O'Clock	*The Bottle Imp*
Guy Mannering	*The Blind Boy*
The Blood Red Knight	*The Castle Spectre*
Aladdin	*Der Freischutz*
Tekeli	*Valentine and Orson*
Blue Beard	*Richard III*
The Miller and his Men	*The Children in the Wood*
The Forty Thieves	

1830   Suzman (*see* J. Bailey)

1826   J. S. Thomas, 2 York St, Covent Garden
       Portraits.

1824   J. Thornton, 4 New Turnstile, Holborn
       Portraits.

     The Miller and his Men

c. 1820 H. Torond, 4 West St, Soho: 49 Gun St, Bishopsgate
       Portraits.

c. 1830 J. Webb, 75 Brick Lane, St Lukes: Central St, St Lukes
       A retail agent, and manufacturer of tinsel ornaments. The uncle of W. Webb.

1844–90 W. Webb, Ripley, Surrey: Cloth Fair: Bermondsey St: 49–104–124–146 Old St, St Luke's
       Born 1820. Died 1890.
       Apprenticed to Archibald Park, 1835–42, and then worked as a commercial traveller in theatrical portraits before setting up on his own. His sheets are inscribed W. Webb, W. G. Webb, and W. C. Webb. Succeeded by H. J. Webb.

The Forest of Bondy 1847	*Little Red Riding Hood* 1858
Union Jack 1848	*The Rifle Volunteers* 1861
Three Fingered Jack *c.* 1850	*The Brigand's Son* 1861
Uncle Tom's Cabin 1852	*Jack and the Beanstalk* 1861
Robin Hood 1852	*The Miller and his Men* 1861
The Battle of Alma 1854	*The Smuggler* 1861
Guy Fawkes 1854	*The Hunter of the Alps*
Dred 1854	*Blue Beard* (characters from Green,
Harlequin Dame Crump 1854	scenes from West and Hodgson)
The Battle of Balaclava 1855	*The Maid and the Magpie* (from Skelt)
Paul Clifford *c.* 1856	*Aladdin* (from Skelt)
Richard I *c.* 1857	*Timour the Tartar* (reversed from Skelt)

For the dates of the plays I am indebted to Dr Francis Eagle. The fact that Webb published over three different styles of initials may appear strange, and A. How Mathews maintained a theory to explain this and believed he had discovered the existence of another and previous Webb altogether; this was:

W. G. Webb (William George), familiarly known as 'Long Bill Webb' Long Lane, Smithfield (1827–52): 19 Cloth Fair, Smithfield; 206–234 Bermondsey St (1852–56). This man was responsible for the publication of the first ten of the Webb plays.

During this time W. Webb, the apprentice of Park, was still travelling the country; it is not clear if he was any relation, or merely a namesake of 'Long Bill'. In 1856 'Long Bill' died, and W. Webb bought the business, endeavouring to make it appear as if it were continuing without interruption; to this end he christened himself William Charles, and altered the W. G. to W. C. on all the plates he could lay hands on; later when issuing new plays he used the form W. Webb. A. How Mathews maintained that there was a distinct change in style after 1856, but I should prefer to reserve my opinion on this point. Although there was nothing shady in the transaction Mr Mathews suggests that W. Webb, and his son after him, did everything they could to remove every trace and deny all knowledge of 'Long Bill Webb', the originator of the firm.

I print this theory for what it is worth, but feel bound to point out that it was not borne out by the members of the family. I was assured that Mr Webb's own initials were W.G., but there is no obvious theory to explain why this sometimes appeared as W.C., except that the engraver omitted the cross stroke.

1890–1933 H. J. Webb, 146–124 Old St, St Luke's
Born 1852. Died 1933.
Son and successor of W. Webb, whose list of plays he republished.

  The Red Rover (from Skelt; not completed)

His son, H. J. Webb ('Young Harry') 1933–*c.* 1939.

  Richard Turpin (from Skelt; not completed)

1811–54 William West, 13 Exeter St, Strand (1811–23): 57 Wych St, Strand (1823–54)
Born 1783. Died 1854. The belief that West conducted his business simultaneously from both addresses would appear to have been based upon a misinterpretation of certain early sheets which were reprinted with the address but not the original date altered. The following list includes single 'souvenir' sheets, which at this period are not easily distinguished from complete plays; undated plays placed at the end of certain years' publications have been assigned to these years by Mr Seaton Reid on the strength of the style of drawing and other relevant considerations.

The Peasant Boy 1811	*The Tyrant Saracan* 1811
Blue Beard 1811	*Aladdin* 1811
Harlequin and Asmodeus 1811	*The Council of Ten* 1811
Tom Thumb 1811	*Dulce Domum* 1811
Timour the Tartar 1811	*Macbeth* 1811

The Mandarin 1811
Harlequin and Blue Beard 1811
Lady of the Lake 1811
Lodoiska 1811
One O'Clock 1811
The Fairy of the Oak 1811
The Iron Chest 1811
Raymond and Agnes 1811
Don Juan 1811
The Magic Pipe 1811
The Mountaineers 1811
The Beehive
The Americans
The Battle of the Bridges
The Death of Zanchir
The Siege of Belgrade
Tracy Castle
Harlequin Padmanaba 1812
The White Cat 1812
The Virgin of the Sun 1812
Bagvan-Ho 1812
The House of Morville 1812
The Brave Cossack 1812
Julius Caesar 1812
Old Belzebab 1812
The Secret Mine 1812
Valentine and Orson 1812
The Devil's Bridge 1812
Harlequin Colossus 1812
Jack and Jill 1812
Jonny Armstrong 1812
The Spanish Patriots 1812
The Aethiop 1812
The Hag of the Lake 1812
The Persian
The Prince
The Renegade
Mother Goose
Harlequin and Humpo 1813
Harlequin and the Red Dwarf 1813
Peter the Cruel 1813
The Battle of Krasnoi 1813
Ferdinand of Spain 1813
Llewellyn 1813
The Blood Red Knight 1813
The Temple of Concord and Pagoda
Harlequin Harper 1814
Harlequin and the Swans 1814
A Midsummer Night's Dream 1814
The Tiger Horde 1814
Illusion 1814
Richard III 1814
The Corsair
Sadac and Kalasrade
The Dog of Montargis
Harlequin Whittington 1815
Harlequin Sinbad 1815

Comus 1815
Coriolanus 1815
Henry IV 1815
The High Mettled Racer 1815
The Merry Wives of Windsor 1815
Harlequin Brilliant 1815
The Little Hunchback 1815
Red Hands 1815
The Ninth Statue 1815
Hamlet 1815
The Knight of the Black Plume 1815
Richard II 1815
The Miller and his Men 1815
Wallace 1815
Telemachus 1815
The Hunted Tailor 1815
The Maid and the Magpie 1815
Manfredi 1815
Romeo and Juliet 1815
Cymon 1815
The Forty Thieves
Harlequin Fortunio 1816
Harlequin and Fancy 1816
Guy Mannering 1816
Bertram 1816
The Broken Sword 1816
Jack Sprat 1817
The Old Oak Chest 1817
The Libertine 1817
The Innkeeper's Daughter
Black Beard the Pirate 1818
Harlequin Gulliver 1818
Lolonois 1818
Rob Roy 1818
The Falls of Clyde 1818
El Hyder 1818
Brutus 1819
The Casket of Gloriana 1819
The Ruffian Boy 1819
The Landstorm 1819
Pope Joan 1819
Jack the Giant Killer 1819
The Silver Arrow 1819
The Blind Boy 1819
Philip Quarl 1819
Robert the Bruce 1819
La Perouse 1819
Robinson Crusoe 1819
The Gnome King 1819
Beauty and the Beast 1819
The Dervise of Bagdad 1820
Horatii and Curiatii 1820
Ivanhoe 1820
The Red Witch of Moravia 1820
The Vampire 1820
The Abbot 1820
Frederick the Great 1821

Korastikan 1821	*Malvina* 1826
The Death of Christophe 1821	*Paul Pry* 1826
The Coronation of George IV 1821	*The Wild Boy* 1827
The Exile 1821	*Casco Bay* 1827
Tom and Jerry 1822	*The Pilot* 1828
The Temple of Death 1822	*The Bottle Imp* 1828
Montrose 1822	*The Red Rover* 1829
Edward the Black Prince 1822	*Black Eyed Susan* 1829
The Adventures of a Ventriloquist 1822	*The Elephant of Siam* 1829
The Battle of Waterloo 1824	*Olympic Revels* 1831
The Invasion of Russia 1825	*The Brigand* 1831

1835   H. Whaite, 4 Bridge St, Manchester
Portraits.

c. 1845 J. T. Wood, 33–41 Holywell St, Strand: 287 Strand: 17 Addle St, Aldermanbury
Agent for Green and Webb.

The Miller and his Men	*The Corsican Brothers*
The Waterman	*Uncle Tom's Cabin*

c. 1870 Young, Union St, Clarendon Square
An expert in painting the clouded backgrounds on the Bristol boards upon which
tinsel portraits were often mounted.

BOYS' MAGAZINES PUBLISHING TOY THEATRE PLAYS

c. 1880–c. 1890 Arthur Bailey
The Boy's Halfpenny Budget

The Miller and his Men	*Blue Jackets*
Timour the Tartar	*The Red Rover*
Little Tommy Tucker	

c. 1866–1880 Edwin J. Brett
The Boys of England

The Roadside Inn	*The Forty Thieves*
Jack Cade	*Blue Beard*
Alone in the Pirate's Lair	*The Miller and his Men*
Tom Daring	*Mazeppa*
The Giant of the Black Mountains	*Harkaway among the Brigands*
King Arthur	*Robinson Crusoe*
The Skeleton Horseman	

The Rovers of the Sea

Rolland the Pirate

The Boys' Budget (later The Young Gentleman's Budget)
    Turpin's Ride to York   *The Gunpowder Plot* (unfinished)

Our Boy's Journal
Portraits.

1873   Fred Farrah
The Wild Boys of London
This paper was banned by the authorities.
(A pantomime.)

c. 1870 Charles Fox
   The Boy's Standard

    Sweeny Todd

c. 1860 E. Head
   Turpin and Bess: a Romance of the Road
   Portraits and tinsel.

c. 1870 Henderson
   Jack Harkaway

    The Red Rover

c. 1870 Hogarth House
   Tyburn Dick

    Turpin's Ride to York

1866 Charles Stevens
   The original founder of The Boys of England (*see* Brett).

1865 Temple Publishing Co
   Black Eyed Susan

    The Red Rover

PUBLISHERS OF 'PENNY PACKETS'

1890 Andrews and Co., St Luke's
   'Champion Parlour Dramas', one penny. Mostly reprinted from Skelt.

George Barnwell	*Our Boys in Blue (Blue Jackets)*
The Dumb Boy and his Monkey	*Tommy Tucker*
Amy Robsart	*Robinson Crusoe*
Uncle Tom's Cabin	*Richard III*
Black Ey'd Susan	*The Tower of London* (sequel)
Captain Ross	*Walter Brand the Outlaw*
The Search for the North Pole (sequel)	*The Outlaw's Revenge* (sequel)
The Miller and his Men	*The Floating Beacon*
On the Stroke of One	

c. 1870 Bishop and Co., Houndsditch
   'The Theatre Royal.' Succeeded by S. Marks.

    Harlequin Mother Goose

1888 C. Clark, 53 Temple St, Manchester
   'Clark's Juvenile Drama', one penny.

The Brigand's Son	*Buffalo Bill's Wildwest*
The Smuggler	*Richard I*

   'Clark's Celebrated Halfpenny Plays.'

    Blue Jackets

1875–*c.* 1900 H. G. Clarke, 2 Garrick St, Covent Garden: 252 Strand
   Acted as agent for Webb, Pollock and Park, for whose plays he printed special
   books of words. Also issued a wide range of paper games, including penny plays; he
   may have bought up the stock of S. Marks, Murray, and Goode.

The Smuggler	*Jack the Giant Killer*
Bombastes Furioso	*Black Eyed Susan*
Cinderella	*Harlequin and Mother Goose*
Ali Baba	

c. 1880 J. Gage, Pembroke Place, Liverpool

Sweeny Todd	*Douglas*
Dick Turpin	*The Black Pirate*
The Miller and his Men	*Jack Sheppard*

c. 1900 Globe, Germany
'The Globe Drama', colour printed and stamped out on thin cardboard.

Uncle Tom's Cabin	*Aladdin*
Cinderella	*Black Eyed Susan*
The Beauty and the Beast	*The Brigand*
The Tower of London (*Richard III*)	*Blue Beard*
The Miller and his Men	

c. 1890 Goode Bros, Clerkenwell Green, Clerkenwell Road
'The King's Theatre.'

Little Red Riding Hood	*Black Eyed Susan*
Ali Baba	*Claude Duval*
Bluebeard	*Jack Sheppard*
Dick Turpin	

c. 1880 S. Marks and Sons, Houndsditch
Successor to Bishop.

Mother Goose	*St George*
Humpty Dumpty	

c. 1880 J. Murray, 54 Great Queen St
Possibly bought up by H. G. Clarke.

Bombastes Furioso

c. 1880 W. J. and A. Spark, 215 Globe Road, Mile End

The Roadside Inn

c. 1900 The Spear Series

c. 1880 Star, Gunthorpe Square
Portraits.

c. 1890 Yates and Co., Old Radford Works, Nottingham
'The Penny Theatre Royal (Coloured Twopence).'

The Colleen Bawn	*The Miller and his Men*
Blue Beard	*Black Eyed Susan*
The Red Rover	*The Corsican Brothers*
The Bottle	*Mazeppa*
The Green Bushes	*The Children in the Wood*

ARTISTIC REVIVALS

1901–04 Jack B. Yeats

James Flaunty, or the Terror of the Western Seas 1901	*Esmeralda Grande*
The Treasure of the Garden 1903	*James Dance, or the Fortunate Ship Boy*
The Scourge of the Gulf 1904	*The Mysterious Travellers, or the Game-*
(published by Elkin Mathews Ltd)	*some Princess and the Pursuing Policeman* (a Pantomime)
	(not published)

(*See* Ernest Marriott, *Jack B. Yeats: his Pictorial and Dramatic Art*, Elkin Mathews, 1911.)

1922–3 F. J. Harvey Darton, with drawings by Albert Rutherston

    The Good Fairy   1922   *The London Review*   1923 (published by Wells, Gardner and Darton Ltd)

AMERICAN TOY THEATRE PUBLISHERS

c. 1900 McLoughlin Bros, New York

    Little Red Riding Hood

c. 1870 Scott and Co., 146 Fulton St, New York City
    'Seltz's American Boys' Theatre.'

The Pirates of the Florida Keys	*Redheaded Jack, the Terror of London*
The Red Skeleton, or the Dead Avenger	*The Boy Sailor, or the Pirate's Doom*
Sir Lancelot and Guinevere	*The Fiend of the Rocky Mountain*
The Miller and his Men	(pantomime)

c. 1900 J. H. Singer, 31st St, New York

Jack the Giant Killer	*Beauty and the Beast*
Red Riding Hood	*Robinson Crusoe*
Cinderella	*Pocahontas*
Blue Beard	*The Young Soldier*

c. 1825 Turner and Fisher, New York and Philadelphia
    These names appear as agents on some of Hodgson and Co.'s sheets.

Plays Published for the Juvenile Drama

This is the complement to Appendix A, listing in alphabetical order, under broad subdivisions, the over 300 plays published for the English and American toy theatre. One has to draw a line somewhere, and new plays published after 1900 really belong to a different period and are not included. Similarly, German toy theatre plays printed in English are excluded.

The first column gives the full title; sometimes substantially the same play was issued by different publishers under differing names, and these have been grouped together, with the alternative titles separated by semicolons. There are cross references under the alternative titles, except for the pantomimes where the sub-titles run riot so confusingly that I have felt compelled to enter each subject only once. This is followed, where possible, by the name of the author of the original play upon which the earliest toy theatre version appears to have been based. Most plays of this period were derived from someone else, and where this can be traced, and appears of particular interest, the information is included.

The second column lists, in approximately chronological order, every publisher who issued the play. Some of these represent new original editions; many of them, piracies or reprints. It is not possible to differentiate these here. For the information in this column I am mainly dependent upon the listings of Mr M. W. Stone and of Mr D. Seaton Reid.

The third column details the theatre and year of the play's first performance. This was often, but by no means always, the production upon which the Juvenile Drama was based. A few of the later boys' magazines and American publications may not have had any previous stage originals. The information on stage productions and authorship is mainly taken from the invaluable handlists of plays in Allardyce Nicoll's histories of English drama.

PLAYS FROM SHAKESPEARE

Antony and Cleopatra	Jameson
Coriolanus	West
Hamlet	Jameson, West, Hodgson
Henry IV	West, W. Clarke
Henry VIII	Myers
Julius Caesar	West, Hebberd, Perkins, Love
Macbeth	West, Hodgson
The Merry Wives of Windsor	West
A Midsummer Night's Dream	Jameson, West
Othello	Hodgson, Skelt
Richard II	West
Richard III	Jameson, West, Hodgson, Park, Lloyd, Skelt 2 versions, Straker, Green, Andrews, Globe
Romeo and Juliet	West, Hodgson

The Tempest, or the Enchanted Island	Hebberd, Hodgson		
Two Gentlemen of Verona	Hodgson		
The Winter's Tale	Myers		

PLAYS FROM SIR WALTER SCOTT

The Abbot, or Mary Queen of Scots by H. R. Beverley	West	Tottenham Street Theatre	1820
Amy Robsart by A. Halliday	Andrews	Drury Lane	1870
Guy Mannering by D. Terry	West, Hodgson, Jameson, Straker, Hawley	Covent Garden	1816
The Heart of Midlothian by D. Terry	Hodgson, Jameson	Covent Garden	1819
Ivanhoe, or the Jew of York by T. J. Dibdin	West, Stokes, Jameson, Hodgson, W. Clarke, Skelt	Surrey	1820
Kenilworth by T. J. Dibdin	Hodgson	Covent Garden	1821
The Lady of the Lake by T. J. Dibdin	West, W. Clarke, Spencer	Surrey	1810
Montrose, or the Children of the Mist	West, Hodgson, J. L. Marks	Coburg	1819
Quentin Durward by J. T. Haines	Hodgson	Coburg	1823
Robert the Bruce, or the Battle of Bannockburn (from *The Lord of the Isles*)	West	Coburg	1819
Rob Roy Macgregor by Isaac Pocock	West, Jameson, Hodgson, W. Clarke, Allen, Green	Covent Garden	1818

DRAMAS, MELODRAMAS, TRAGEDIES, SPECTACLES

The Aethiop, or the Child of the Desert by W. Dimond	Love, West	Covent Garden	1812
Aladdin, or the Wonderful Lamp by Charles Farley	Hawley, Jameson, Hebberd, West, Perkins, Hodgson, Allen, O. Hodgson, Straker, Lloyd, Skelt, Webb, Green, Park, Redington, Pollock, Globe	Covent Garden	1813
Ali Baba (see *The Forty Thieves*)			
Ali Pacha, or the Signet Ring by J. Planché	Hodgson	Covent Garden	1822
Alone in the Pirate's Lair by C. Hazlewood	*Boys of England*	Britannia	1867
Baghvan Ho, or the Tartars Tartar'd	West, Burtenshaw	Pavilion	1812
The Battle of Alma	Green, Webb	Astley's	1854
The Battle of Balaclava and Inkerman	Green, Webb	Astley's	1855

The Battle of the Bridges, or Blood will have Blood by T. J. Dibdin	West, Hebberd	Surrey	1811
The Battle of Krasnoi	West		
The Battle of Waterloo by J. H. Amherst	West, Hodgson, Skelt, Green, Redington, Pollock	Astley's	1824
The Bear Hunters, or the Fatal Ravine by J. Buckstone	Dyer	Coburg	1825
Beauty and the Beast, or the Magic Rose	West, Globe	Coburg	1819
Belphegor the Conjuror, or the Mountebank and his Wife (from Marc Fournier's *Le Paillasse*)	Green	Surrey	1851
Bertram, or the Castle of St. Aldobrand by C. Maturin	West, Jameson	Drury Lane	1816
Black Beard the Pirate, or the Captive Princess by J. C. Cross	West, Hodgson, Green, Mathews, Gage	Royal Circus	1798
Black Eyed Susan, or All in the Downs by D. Jerrold	West, Hodgson, Dyer, Lloyd, Skelt, Green, Andrews, Goode, H. G. Clarke, Globe, Yates, March, G. Skelt, O. Hodgson	Surrey	1829
The Black Prince (see *Edward the Black Prince*)			
The Blind Boy by James Kenney	West, Hodgson, Straker, Lloyd, Dyer, Skelt 2, Park, Pollock, W. Clarke	Covent Garden	1807
The Blood Red Knight, or the Fatal Bridge by J. H. Amherst	West, Hodgson, Straker, Jameson	Astley's	1810
Blue Beard, or Female Curiosity by G. Colman, jun.	West, Jameson, Hodgson, W. Clarke, J. L. Marks, Allen, Bailey, Straker, Lloyd, Dyer, Skelt, Green, Webb, *Boys of England*, Goode, Yates, Globe, Singer, Goodwin	Drury Lane	1798
Bonaparte's Invasion of Russia (see *The Invasion of Russia*)			
The Bottle by T. P. Taylor (from G. Cruikshank)	Yates	City of London	1847
The Bottle Imp by R. B. Peake	West, Straker, Lloyd, Dyer	English Opera House 1828	
The Boy Sailor, or the Pirate's Doom	Seltz		
The Brave Cossack, or the Secret Enemy by J. Astley	West	Astley's	1807
The Brigand by J. Planché	West, Dyer, Skelt, Green, Redington, Pollock, Globe	Drury Lane	1829

The Brigand's Son by W. Oxberry (from Prosper Mérimée's *Mateo Falcone*)	Webb, Mathews, Clark	English Opera House 1836
The Broken Sword by W. Dimond	West	Covent Garden 1816
Brutus, or the Fall of Tarquin by J. H. Payne	Jameson, West	Drury Lane 1818
Buffalo Bill's Wildwest by Col. Stanley	Clark	Sanger's Circus 1887
Captain Ross, or the Hero of the Arctic Regions	Skelt, Andrews	Royal Pavilion 1833
Casco Bay, or the Mutineers of 1727 by W. Bernard	West	Olympic 1827
The Casket of Gloriana by H. R. Beverley	West	Regency 1819
The Castle Spectre by M. G. Lewis	Straker, Lloyd, Dyer	Drury Lane 1797
The Cataract of the Ganges, or the Rajah's Daughter by W. Moncrieff	Hodgson	Drury Lane 1823
The Charcoal Burner, or the Dropping Well of Knaresborough by G. Almar	Skelt	Surrey 1832
Charles the Bold, or the Siege of Nantz by S. J. Arnold (from Pixérécourt)	Jameson	Drury Lane 1815
Cherry and Fair Star, or the Children of Cyprus	Hodgson, J. L. Marks	Covent Garden 1822
Chevy Chase, or the Battle of Otterburn by C. A. Somerset	O. Hodgson	Astley's 1832
The Children in the Wood by T. Morton	Lloyd, Skelt, Green, Redington, Pollock, Goode, Yates, G. Skelt	Haymarket 1793
Claude Duval, or Love and Larceny by J. T. Haines	Goode	Surrey 1841
The Colleen Bawn, or the Brides of Garryowen by D. Boucicault (from G. Griffin's *The Collegians*)	Yates	Adelphi 1860
The Coronation (of George IV)	West, Love	Drury Lane 1821
The Corsair by C. Dibdin, jun.	Jameson, West	Sadler's Wells 1814
The Corsican Brothers by D. Boucicault (from Dumas)	Green, Redington, Pollock, Yates, Wood	Princess's 1852
Cortez, or the Conquest of Mexico by J. Planché	Hodgson	Covent Garden 1823
The Council of Ten, or the Lake of the Grotto by C. Dibdin, jun.	West, G. Skelt	Sadler's Wells 1811
Cymon by David Garrick (from Dryden)	West	Covent Garden 1767

The Daughter of the Regiment by E. Fitzball (Music by Donizetti)	Green, Redington, Pollock	Drury Lane 1843
The Death of Christophe, King of Hayti by J. Amherst	West	Coburg 1821
The Death of Zanchir	West	The Minor Theatre, Catherine St
The Devil and Doctor Faustus by G. Soane	Hodgson	Drury Lane 1825
The Devil's Bridge, or the Piedmontese Alps by S. J. Arnold	Jameson, West, Hodgson	Lyceum 1812
Dick Turpin (see *Richard Turpin*)		
The Dog of Montargis (see *The Forest of Bondy*)		
Don Quixote by G. Macfarren	Redington, Pollock	Drury Lane 1846
Douglas by John Home	Jameson, Dyer, Green, Skelt, Redington, Pollock, Gage, G. Skelt	Edinburgh 1756
Dred, or the Freeman of the Dismal Swamp by W. E. Suter (from Mrs Beecher Stowe)	Green, Webb	Queen's 1856
The Dumb Savoyard and his Monkey by C. P. Thompson	Straker, Lloyd, Skelt, Andrews	Coburg 1830
The Dutch Pirate, Charles de Voldeck by H. B. Girard	Hodgson, W. Clarke	Sadler's Wells 1822
The Echo of Westminster Bridge	Skelt	Victoria 1835
Edward the Black Prince, or the Glories of England in 1356 by G. Macfarren	West, Hodgson	Coburg 1822
The Elephant of Siam, or the Fire Fiend	West, J. L. Marks	Adelphi 1829
El Hyder, the Chief of the Ghaut Mountains by W. Barrymore	West, Jameson	Coburg 1818
The Exile of Siberia; The Exile, or the Coronation of Elizabeth by F. Reynolds	West, Jameson, Hodgson, J. L. Marks, Bailey, Smart	Covent Garden 1808
The Falls of Clyde by G. Soane	West, Jameson, Hodgson, Skelt, G. Skelt	Drury Lane 1817
Ferdinand of Spain, or Ancient Chivalry	West	Astley's 1813
The Floating Beacon, or the Norwegian Wreckers by E. Fitzball	Edwards, Lloyd, Skelt 2, Mathews, Andrews	Surrey 1824
The Flying Dutchman, or the Phantom Ship by E. Fitzball	Jameson, Bailey, Straker, Lloyd, Dyer, Green, G. Skelt	Adelphi 1827

The Forest of Bondy, or the Dog of Montargis by W. Barrymore (from Pixérécourt)	West, Jameson, Hodgson, Allen, Dyer, Skelt, Green, Webb, Hebberd	Covent Garden	1814
The Forty Thieves; *Ali Baba, or the Forty Thieves*	Hebberd, West, Jameson, DeBurson, W. Clarke, Hodgson, O. Hodgson, Allen, Bailey, Straker, Lloyd, Dyer, Skelt, Green, Redington, Pollock, *Boys of England*, Goode, H. G. Clarke, Sanderson, Creed	Surrey	1812
Frederick the Great and the Deserter, or the Assassins of the Forest	West	Coburg	1821
Der Freischutz by E. Fitzball (from Kind Music by Weber)	Bailey, Straker, Lloyd, Dyer, Skelt, Park, G. Skelt	Drury Lane	1824
George Barnwell, or the London Merchant by George Lillo	Skelt, Andrews	Drury Lane	1731
Gil Blas, or the Horse Banditti	W. Clarke	Astley's	1821
Gilderoy, the Bonnie Boy by W. Barrymore	Hodgson	Coburg	1822
The Gnome King, or the Giant Mountains	Jameson, West	Covent Garden	1819
The Green Bushes, or a Hundred Years Ago by J. Buckstone	Yates	Adelphi	1845
Guy Fawkes, or the Gunpowder Treason by G. Macfarren	Hodgson, Allen, Dyer, Webb, *Boy's Budget*, G. Skelt	Coburg	1822
The Hag of the Lake, or the Castle of Monte Falcon	Jameson, West	Royalty	1812
Harkaway among the Brigands	*Boys of England*		
The Haunted Tower	March		
The Hero of Switzerland, or the Helvetian's Freedom; William Tell	Jameson, March	Astley's	1802
The High Mettled Racer by T. J. Dibdin	West, Jameson	Astley's	1813
The Horatii and Curiatii by G. Macfarren	West	Coburg	1820
The House of Morville by John Lake	Jameson, West	Lyceum	1812
The Hunted Tailor	West, DeBurson	Astley's	1813
The Hunter of the Alps by W. Dimond	Webb	Haymarket	1804
The Illuminated Lake (see *The Prince*)			
Illusion, or the Trances of Nourjahad by S. J. Arnold	Jameson, West	Drury Lane	1813
The Inchcape Bell, or the Dumb Sailor Boy by E. Fitzball	Skelt	Surrey	1828

The Infernal Secret, or the Invulnerable by J. Amherst	Hodgson	Surrey	1822
The Innkeeper of Abbeville, or the Hostelry and Robbers by E. Fitzball	Lloyd	Surrey	1826
The Innkeeper's Daughter (see *Mary, the Maid of the Inn*)			
The Invasion of Russia; Bonaparte's Invasion of Russia by J. Amherst	West, Jameson	Astley's 1825	
The Iron Chest, or Murder Brought to Light by G. Colman, jun. (from Godwin's *Caleb Williams*)	West	Drury Lane	1796
Iwanowna, or the Maid of Moscow by C. Dibdin, jun.	Jameson	Sadler's Wells	1816
Jack Cade, the Rebel of London	*Boys of England*		
Jack Sheppard by J. Buckstone (from Harrison Ainsworth)	Green, Gage, Goode	Adelphi	1839
Jacob Faithful, the Lighter Boy, or A Tale of the Thames by J. T. Haines (from Marryat)	Skelt	Victoria	1834
Joan of Arc, or the Maid of Orleans	Hodgson	Olympic	1822
Jonathan Bradford; The Murdered Guest, or the Roadside Inn by E. Fitzball	Lloyd, Dyer, Skelt, Green	Surrey	1833
Jonnie Armstrong, or the Scottish Outlaw by C. Dibdin, jun.	West	Sadler's Wells	1812
Kaloc, or the Slave Pirate by C. Dibdin, jun.	Jameson, W. Clarke	Sadler's Wells	1813
King Arthur, or the Knights of the Round Table by W. Brough	*Boys of England*	Haymarket	1863
King Henry, or the Miller of Mansfield by Robert Dodsley	Redington, Pollock	Drury Lane	1736
The Knight of the Black Plume, or the Fisherman's Hut	West, Jameson, Love	Surrey	1814
Korastikan, Prince of Assassins, or the Dreaded Harem	West, W. Clarke	Coburg	1821
The Landstorm, or the Sledge-Driver and his Dogs	Love, West, G. Skelt	Coburg	1819
The Law of Java by G. Colman, jun.	Hodgson	Covent Garden	1822
The Libertine by Isaac Pocock (from Shadwell)	West, Jameson	Covent Garden	1817
The Life of a Soldier, or the Sailor's Daughter and the Soldier's Bride	Green	Britannia	1861
Lucretia	Creed		

Llewellyn, Prince of Wales, or Gellert the Faithful Dog by T. J. Dibdin	West	Surrey	1813
Lodoiska, or the Captive Princess by T. J. Dibdin	Jameson, West, Hodgson, Skelt, G. Skelt	Surrey	1811
Lolonois, or the Bucaniers of 1660 by O. Smith	West	Royal Circus	1818
Lord Darnley, or the Keeper of the Castle Hill by T. E. Wilks	Green, Redington, Pollock	Surrey	1837
The Lord Mayor's Fool, or the Grand Secret	Green, Redington, Pollock	Astley's	1837
Magna Charta, or the Eventful Reign of King John	Hodgson, Allen	Coburg	1823
The Maid and the Magpie; *The Magpie, or the Maid of Paliseau* by Isaac Pocock	West, Jameson, Hodgson, O. Hodgson, Lloyd, Skelt 2, Park, Green, Pollock, Webb, Mathews, Sanderson	Covent Garden	1815
Maid Marian, or the Huntress of Arlingford by J. Planché (from Peacock)	Hodgson	Covent Garden	1822
The Maid of Genoa, or the Bandit Merchant by J. Farrell	Lloyd, Skelt	Coburg	1820
Malvina by G. Macfarren (from Ossian)	West	Drury Lane	1826
Manfredi (performed as *Manfred, or the Castle of Otranto*)	West	Astley's	1803
Mary, the Maid of the Inn; *The Innkeeper's Daughter*; *The Roadside Inn* by G. Soane	West, Jameson, Edwards, Hodgson, Dyer, Lloyd, Skelt, Green, *Boys of England*, G. Skelt, Spark	Drury Lane	1817
Mazeppa, or the Wild Horse of Tartary by H. M. Milner (from Byron)	Lloyd, Skelt 2, *Boys of England*, Yates	Coburg	1823
The Miller and his Men by Isaac Pocock	West 2, Jameson 2, Smart, Hodgson, O. Hodgson, Allen, Bailey, Edwards, Straker, Lloyd, Dyer, Skelt 5, Park 3, Green 3, Redington, Pollock, Webb, Mathews, J. Wood, *Boys of England, Boys' Halfpenny Budget*, Andrews, Gage, Myers, Globe, Yates, Wood, Seltz, G. Skelt 2	Covent Garden	1813
The Miller's Maid by John Faucit	Hodgson, Skelt 2, Mathews, G. Skelt	English Opera	1821
The Mistletoe Bough, or the Fatal Chest by C. Somerset	Redington, Pollock	Garrick	1834
The Mountaineers by G. Colman, jun. (from *Don Quixote*)	West, Hodgson, Dyer, Skelt	Haymarket	1793

The Murdered Guest (see *Jonathan Bradford*)			
My Poll and my Partner Joe by J. T. Haines	Skelt	Surrey	1835
Napoleon Buonaparte, General, Consul, and Emperor	Hodgson	Coburg	1821
Nelson, or the Life of a Sailor by E. Fitzball	Hodgson	Adelphi	1827
The Ninth Statue, or the Irishman in Bagdad by T. J. Dibdin	Jameson, West	Drury Lane	1814
The Old Oak Chest, or the Smuggler's Sons and the Robber's Daughter by Miss Scott	West, Jameson, Hodgson, Lloyd, Dyer, Skelt, Park, G. Skelt	Sans Pareil	1816
Oliver Twist, or the Parish Boy's Progress by G. Almar (from Dickens)	Redington, Pollock	Surrey	1838
One O'Clock, or the Knight and the Wood Daemon; The Wood Daemon, or the Hour of One by M. G. Lewis	Jameson, West, Straker, Lloyd, Skelt 2, Park, Andrews, G. Skelt	Lyceum	1811
Paul Clifford by E. Fitzball (from Bulwer Lytton)	Redington, Pollock, Webb	Covent Garden	1835
Paul Jones, or the Solway Mariner by T. J. Dibdin	Dyer	Adelphi	1827
The Peasant Boy, or Innocence Protected by W. Dimond	West	Lyceum	1811
La Perouse, or the Desolate Island (from Kotzebue)	West, Jameson	English Opera	1818
The Persian	West		
Peter the Cruel, or the Maid of Castile	Jameson, West	Surrey	1813
Peter Wilkins, or the Flying Indians	Jameson	Covent Garden	1827
Philip and his Dog, or Where's the Child? by C. Dibdin, jun.	Jameson	Sadler's Wells	1816
The Pilot, or A Storm at Sea by E. Fitzball (from Fenimore Cooper)	West, Straker, J. L. Marks, Lloyd, Dyer, Skelt 2	Adelphi	1825
The Pirates of the Florida Keys	Seltz		
Pizarro, or the Spaniards in Peru by R. B. Sheridan (from Kotzebue)	Jameson, Hodgson, Edwards, Straker, Lloyd, Dyer, Skelt, G. Skelt	Drury Lane	1799
Pocahontas	Singer		
The Prince, or the Illuminated Lake by C. Dibdin, jun.	Jameson, West	Sadler's Wells	1812
The Prisoner of Rochelle	Skelt, Mathews	Strand	1856

Raymond and Agnes, or the Castle of Lindenburg; *Raymond and Agnes, or the Bleeding Nun*; *The Travellers Benighted, or the Forest of Rosenwald* by M. G. Lewis (from *The Monk*)	West, Hodgson, Skelt	Norwich 1809
Red Hands, or the Welch Chieftains by C. Dibdin, jun.	Jameson, West	Sadler's Wells 1805
The Red Rover, or the Mutiny of the Dolphin by E. Fitzball (from Fenimore Cooper)	West, Lloyd, Dyer, Skelt, Park, Green, Mathews, *Boys' Halfpenny Budget*, *Harkaway*, *Black Eyed Susan*, Yates, March, G. Skelt	Adelphi 1829
The Red Skeleton, or the Dead Avenger	Seltz	
The Red Witch of Moravia	West	Coburg 1820
Redheaded Jack, the Terror of London	Seltz	
Remorse by S. T. Coleridge	Jameson	Drury Lane 1813
The Renegade by F. Reynolds (from Dryden's *San Sebastian*)	West	Covent Garden 1812
Richard I, or Coeur de Lion by T. J. Dibdin	Webb, Clark, G. Skelt	Surrey 1819
Richard Turpin; *Rookwood*; *Turpin's Ride to York* by G. D. Pitt (from Harrison Ainsworth)	Skelt 2, Green, *Tyburn Dick*, Gage, Goode, *Boy's Budget*, G. Skelt	Sadler's Wells 1840
The Roadside Inn (see *Mary, the Maid of the Inn*)		
Robert Macaire by C. Selby	Green, Mathews	Adelphi 1835
Robin Hood by J. Planché	Webb	Adelphi 1821
Robinson Crusoe, or the Bold Bucaniers by Isaac Pocock (from Pixérécourt)	West, Jameson, Hodgson, Skelt, Mathews, Andrews, *Boys of England*, Singer, G. Skelt	Covent Garden 1817
Rolland the Pirate	*Rovers of the Sea*	
Rookwood (see *Richard Turpin*)		
The Rover's Bride, or the Bittern's Swamp; *The Wreck Ashore, or A Bridegroom from the Sea* by J. Buckstone	Skelt, Green	Adelphi 1830
The Ruffian Boy by T. J. Dibdin (from Mrs Opie)	Love, Jameson	Royal Circus 1819
Rugantino, the Bravo of Venice by M. G. Lewis (from Pixérécourt)	Hodgson	Covent Garden 1805
Sadac and Kalasrade, or the Waters of Oblivion by E. Stirling	Jameson, West	Covent Garden 1814

The Secret Mine by T. J. Dibdin	West, Green, Hodgson, Allen	Covent Garden	1812
The Siege of Troy, or the Giant Horse of Sinon	O. Hodgson	Astley's	1833
Sir Launcelot and Guinevere	Seltz		
Sixteen String Jack by T. E. Wilks	Green	Sadler's Wells	1842
The Skeleton Horseman, or the Shadow of Death by C. Hazlewood	*Boys of England*	Britannia	1868
Slaves in Barbary	Jameson		
The Sleeping Beauty by G. Skeffington	West, Hodgson	Drury Lane	1805
The Smuggler by C. Dibdin, jun.	Webb, H. G. Clarke, Clark, G. Skelt	Astley's	1822
The Spanish Patriots a Thousand Years Ago by H. B. Code	West	Lyceum	1812
Sweeny Todd, the Barber of Fleet Street by G. D. Pitt	*Boys' Standard*, Gage	Britannia	1847
Tekeli, or the Siege of Montgatz by T. E. Hook (from Pixérécourt)	Hodgson, Straker, Lloyd	Drury Lane	1806
Telemachus (from Fénélon)	West	Covent Garden	1815
The Temple of Death by H. M. Milner	West, Hodgson	Coburg	1821
Thalaba, the Destroyer (from Southey)	Hodgson	Coburg	1823
Therese, or the Orphan of Geneva by J. H. Payne	Straker, Lloyd, Skelt 2, Green	Drury Lane	1821
Three Fingered Jack, or the Terror of Jamaica	Webb, Mathews	Britannia	1860
The Tiger Horde	West, Green, Jameson	Royal Circus	1814
Timour the Tartar by M. G. Lewis	Jameson, West, Hodgson, J. L. Marks, Allen, Skelt, Park, Webb, Green, Redington, Pollock, *Boy's Halfpenny Budget*	Covent Garden	1811
Tippo Saib, or the Storming of Seringapatam by J. Amherst	Hodgson	Coburg	1823
Tom Cringle, or the Man with the Iron Hand by E. Fitzball	Skelt	Surrey	1834
Tom Daring, or Far from Home	*Boys of England*		
The Travellers Benighted (see *Raymond and Agnes*)			
Turpin's Ride to York (see *Richard Turpin*)			
The Tyrant Saracen and the Noble Moor	West 2	Astley's	1811

Uncle Tom's Cabin (from Mrs Beecher Stowe)	Webb, Andrews, Globe, Wood	Standard 1852
Undine, or the Spirit of the Waters (from La Motte-Fouqué)	Jameson, Creed	Covent Garden 1821
The Union Jack, or the Sailor and the Settler's Daughter by C. Somerset	Webb	Surrey 1842
Valentine and Orson by T. J. Dibdin	Love, Jameson, West, Hebberd, Green, Hodgson, Dyer, Straker, Lloyd, Skelt	Covent Garden 1804
The Vampire, or the Bride of the Isles by J. Planché	West, Jameson, Hodgson	English Opera 1820
The Virgin of the Sun by F. Reynolds (from Kotzebue)	Burtenshaw, West, Hebberd	Covent Garden 1812
The Vision of the Sun, or The Orphan of Peru	Hodgson	Covent Garden 1823
Voorn the Tiger, or the Horse Banditti	Burtenshaw	Astley's 1812
Wallace, the Hero of Scotland by W. Barrymore	Jameson, West, Hodgson	Astley's 1817
Walter Brand, or the Duel in the Mist by E. Fitzball	Skelt, Andrews	Surrey 1833
Wapping Old Stairs, or the Rover's Cruise by J. S. Faucit	Green	Haymarket 1837
The Warlock of the Glen by C. E. Walker	Dyer	Covent Garden 1820
The Wild Boy of Bohemia, or the Hermit of the Glen by J. Walker	West	Olympic 1827
William Tell (see *The Hero of Switzerland*)		
The Wood Daemon (see *One O'Clock*)		
The Woodman's Hut, or the Burning Forest by S. J. Arnold	Edwards, Hodgson, Straker, Lloyd, Dyer, Skelt 2, Park, Green, Pollock	Drury Lane 1814
The Wreck Ashore (see *The Rover's Bride*)		
The Young Soldier	Singer	
Zembucca, or the Net-Maker and his Wife by Isaac Pocock	Jameson	Covent Garden 1815
Zoroaster, or the Spirit of the Star by W. T. Moncrieff	Hodgson	Drury Lane 1824

COMEDIES, FARCES, BURLESQUES, EXTRAVAGANZAS

The Adventures of a Ventriloquist, or the Rogueries of Nicholas by W. T. Moncrieff	West	Adelphi 1822

The Americans by S. J. Arnold	Jameson	Lyceum	1811
The Beehive by J. G. Millingen	West	Lyceum	
Blue Jackets, or Her Majesty's Service by E. Stirling	Green, Redington, Pollock, Mathews, *Boy's Halfpenny Budget*, Andrews, Clark	Adelphi	1838
Bombastes Furioso by W. Rhodes	H. G. Clarke, G. Skelt	Haymarket	1810
Charles II, or the Merry Monarch by J. H. Payne	Jameson, Redington, Pollock	Covent Garden	1824
Cinderella by R. Lacy	Hebberd, Green, Redington, Pollock, Mathews, H. G. Clarke, Globe, Singer	Covent Garden	1830
Don Giovanni, or a Spectre on Horseback	Hodgson	Covent Garden	1819
Green in France, or Tom and Jerry's Tour by W. T. Moncrieff	Hodgson	Adelphi	1823
Jonathan in England by R. B. Peake	Hodgson	English Opera	1824
Life in Paris, or the Halibut Family	Hodgson	Coburg	1822
Life in London (see *Tom and Jerry*)			
The Little Hunchback, or a Frolic in Bagdad by John O'Keefe	West	Covent Garden	1789
Midas by Kane O'Hara	Hebberd	Dublin	1762
The Olympic Revels, or Prometheus and Pandora by J. Planché	West, Stokes	Olympic	1831
Paul Pry by John Poole	West	Haymarket	1825
The Rifle Volunteers by E. Stirling	Webb, Mathews	Adelphi	1859
The Siege of Belgrade by James Cobb	West	Drury Lane	1791
State Secrets, or the Tailor of Tamworth by T. E. Wilks	Green, Mathews	Surrey	1836
Tom and Jerry, or Life in London by W. T. Moncrieff (from Pierce Egan)	West, Hodgson, J. L. Marks	Adelphi	1821
Tom Thumb by Kane O'Hara (from Henry Fielding)	Jameson, West, Dyer, Green	Covent Garden	1780
The Waterman, or the First of August by Charles Dibdin	Skelt, Green, Redington, Pollock, Mathews, Wood, G. Skelt	Haymarket	1774

PANTOMIMES

Beauty and the Beast	West, Globe, Singer		
The Dervise of Bagdad, or Harlequin Prince of Persia (performed as *The Enchanted Horn*)	West	Astley's	1818
Doctor Hocus Pocus, or Harlequin Washed White by G. Colman, jun.	Hebberd	Haymarket	1814
Dulce Domum, or England the Land of Freedom by C. Dibdin, jun.	West	Sadler's Wells	1811
The Fairy of the Oak, or Harlequin's Regatta	Hebberd, West	Astley's	1811
The Fiend of the Rocky Mountain	Seltz		
The Giant of the Black Mountains, or Jack and his Eleven Brothers	Boys of England		
Goody Goose by C. Hazlewood	Green	Marylebone	1858
Harlequin and Asmodeus, or Cupid on Crutches	West	Covent Garden	1810
Harlequin and Blue Beard by C. Dibdin, jun.	West	Sadler's Wells	1811
Harlequin and Fancy, or the Poet's Last Shilling by T. J. Dibdin	Jameson, West	Drury Lane	1815
Harlequin and the Giant Helmet, or the Castle of Otranto by J. Planché	Green	Covent Garden	1840
Harlequin and Humpo, or Columbine by Candlelight by T. J. Dibdin	West	Drury Lane	1812
Harlequin and Old Dame Trot, or the Fairy and the Comical Cat	Skelt, G. Skelt	Surrey	1837
Harlequin and the Red Dwarf, or the Adamant Rock	West	Covent Garden	1812
Harlequin and the Swans, or the Path of Beauty	Jameson, West	Covent Garden	1813
Harlequin and the Valley of Diamonds, or Harlequin Sinbad by T. J. Dibdin	Jameson, West	Drury Lane	1814
Harlequin Baron Munchausen, and his Comical Cream Cob Cruiser, or the Queen of the Fairy Steed's Haunt	Redington, Pollock	Victoria	1839
Harlequin Brilliant, or the Clown's Capers by C. Dibdin, jun.	West	Sadler's Wells	1815
Harlequin Cock-a-Doodle-doo by C. Millward	Skelt	Sadler's Wells	1865

Harlequin Colossus, or the Seven Wonders of the World by T. J. Dibdin	Hebberd, West, Green	Surrey 1812
Harlequin Dame Crump, or the Pig won't get over the Stile To-night	Webb	Standard 1854
Harlequin Fortunio, or Shing-moo and Thun-ton	Jameson, West	Covent Garden 1815
Harlequin Gulliver, or the Flying Island	West, Jameson	Covent Garden 1817
Harlequin Guy Fawkes, or the Fifth of November	Skelt, Green	Covent Garden 1835
Harlequin Harper, or a Jump from Japan by T. J. Dibdin	West	Drury Lane 1813
Harlequin Jack and Jill, or the Clown's Disasters	West	Lyceum 1812
Harlequin Jack Sheppard, or the Blossom of Tyburn Tree	Skelt, G. Skelt	Drury Lane 1839
Harlequin Little King Pippin, or the Golden Crown and Goblin of the Apple	Skelt, Mathews, G. Skelt	Surrey 1834
Harlequin Little Tom Tucker	Skelt, Andrews, *Boy's Halfpenny Budget*, G. Skelt	Queen's 1845
Harlequin Oliver Cromwell	Green	City of London 1851
Harlequin Padmanaba, or the Golden Fish	Burtenshaw, West	Covent Garden 1811
Harlequin Riddle-me-ree, or You can't Guess What This May Be	Green	Olympic 1841
Harlequin Robin Hood	Green	Sadler's Wells 1844
Harlequin St George and the Dragon	Green, Marks	Drury Lane 1846
Harlequin Uncle Tom's Cabin by F. Neale	Green	Pavilion 1852
Harlequin Whittington, Lord Mayor of London; Whittington and his Cat, or Harlequin Lord Mayor of London	West, Green, Redington, Pollock	Covent Garden 1814
Harlequin's Vision by Lethbridge (founded on *Don Juan*)	Jameson	Drury Lane 1817
Humpty Dumpty	Marks	
Jack the Giant Killer; Jack and the Beanstalk	West, Jameson, Green, Redington, Pollock, Webb, H. G. Clarke, Singer	Lyceum 1810
Jack Sprat and his Cat	West	
Little Bo-Peep, Little Red Riding Hood, and Hop o' my Thumb by Augustus Harris and Wilton Jones	Augustus Harris	Drury Lane 1892

Little Red Riding Hood	Spencer, Webb, Goode, Singer, McLoughlin		
The Magic Pipe, or Dancing Mad	West	Sans Pareil	1810
The Mandarin, or Harlequin in China	West	Astley's	1811
Harlequin and Mother Bunch, or the Yellow Dwarf	W. Clarke	Covent Garden	1821
Mother Goose by T. J. Dibdin	West, Bishop, Marks, H. G. Clarke	Covent Garden	1806
The Mystic Coffer, or Harlequin the Swan Queen	Jameson	Royalty	1812
Old Belzebub and Harlequin, or Taffy in Holland	West	Astley's	1812
The Poison Tree, or Harlequin in Java	Jameson	Sans Pareil	1811
Pope Joan, or Harlequin on Card Island	West	Coburg	1819
The Silver Arrow, or Harlequin and the Fairy Pari Banon	Jameson, Love, West, G. Skelt	Drury Lane	1819
The Sleeping Beauty in the Wood, or Harlequin and the Magic Horn by C. Stanfield James	Green, Redington, Pollock	Queen's	1849
The White Cat, or Harlequin in the Fairy Wood	Jameson, West	Lyceum	1811
Whittington and his Cat (see *Harlequin Whittington*)			

MASQUES, BALLETS, ENTERTAINMENTS

Comus by George Colman (from Milton)	Jameson, West	Covent Garden	1773
Don Juan, or the Libertine Destroyed (a pantomime ballet based on Shadwell's *The Libertine*)	Jameson, West	Drury Lane	1790
Grumpy	West		
Philip Quarl, or the English Hermit by C. Dibdin, jun.	West, Allen	Sadler's Wells	1803
The Silver Palace by G. Almar (a masque from *The Cedar Chest*)	Dyer, Skelt, Green, Redington, Pollock, Mathews	Sadler's Wells	1834
The Temple of Concord and Pagoda	West		
Tracey Castle, or Love and Jealousy	West	Astley's	1811

Public Collections of the Juvenile Drama

LONDON

The British Museum (Print Room)
The Ralph Thomas Collection
There are also a number of items in the library, catalogued under the names of publishers.

The London Museum
The Jonathan King Collection

The Victoria and Albert Museum (Enthoven Theatre Collection)
The M. W. Stone Collection. A Pollock toy theatre is also displayed.

OXFORD

The Hinkins Collection
Application to examine this should be made to Mr Herbert Hinkins, Lantern House, 2 Blenheim Drive.

BIRMINGHAM

The Public Library
The Leslie Bennett Bequest of Nineteenth Century Theatricalia contains a number of early Juvenile Drama sheets.

EDINBURGH

The Public Library
A small collection, principally of Skelt sheets.

The Robert Louis Stevenson Birthplace and Museum, Howard Place
A Pollock stage and a few Skelt sheets are on view.

UNITED STATES OF AMERICA

New York Public Library
A considerable collection of toy theatres, model circuses, etc., from many countries. The Hiram Stead Theatrical Collection contains a large number of Juvenile Drama sheets filed under the names of plays, actors, etc.

Museum of the City of New York
The Alfred Lunt Collection of toy theatres.

Brander Matthews Dramatic Museum, Columbia University, New York
A small collection, principally of the later publishers.

Harvard College Library, Theatre Collection, Cambridge, Mass.
A large collection in which many publishers are represented containing unique early sheets.

University of Texas, Hoblitzelle Theatre Arts Library, Austin, Texas
A small collection of the later publishers.

The University collections are not normally open to the general public, but permission to examine them can usually be obtained by bona fide students and researchers.

Bibliography of the Juvenile Drama

The following articles or books are devoted exclusively to the appreciation or history of the Juvenile Drama. No attempt has been made to detail the innumerable newspaper and magazine articles of the last fifty years, except where they clearly possess more than a passing journalistic interest.

Every Little Boy's Book	Articles on 'The Model Stage' and 'Tinselling'. Routledge, 1866.
Edward Draper	'Characters and Scenes' in *The Savage Club Papers*, 1868.
John Oxenford	'The Toy Theatre' in *The Era Almanack*, 1871.
Samuel Highley	'Our Model Theatre' in Routledge's *Every Boy's Annual*, 1874.
R. L. Stevenson	'A Penny Plain and Twopence Coloured' in *The Magazine of Art*, April 1884. Reprinted in *Memories and Portraits*, 1887.
Godfrey Turner	'A Penny Plain; Twopence Coloured' in *The Theatre*, 1886.
E. L. Blanchard	An article by this author, who wrote for *The Era* and similar papers, is referred to by William Archer. It has not yet been rediscovered.
William Archer	'The Drama in Pasteboard' in *The Art Journal*, April and May, 1887.
Theo Arthur	'The Toy Theatre' in *The Era Almanack*, 1891.
John Ashton	'Childhood's Drama' in *Varia*, 1894.
Francis Eagle	'The Webb Juvenile Drama' in *The Mask*, April 1913.
Francis Eagle	*The Glamour of a Toy Shop*, published by the author, 1919.
A. E. Wilson	*Penny Plain Two Pence Coloured. A History of the Juvenile Drama*, 1932.

PERIODICALS CONTAINING ARTICLES ON THE JUVENILE DRAMA

Notes and Queries
Numerous letters from Ralph Thomas were contributed between 1867 and 1920. Correspondence on the Juvenile Drama has continued at intervals ever since; in 1931 the Webb–Stevenson controversy was thoroughly ventilated; during 1944 and 1945 a series of articles on the later toy theatre publishers appeared from the pen of C. D. Williams. F. Algar's researches were published in 1949.

The Collector's Miscellany, originally *Vanity Fair*
Articles from Frank Jay, M. W. Stone, George Speaight, Gerald Morice, C. D. Williams, and others appeared at intervals: 1917–39.

The Times Literary Supplement
Among various articles of permanent value, the issues of January 1st, 1931, September 8th, 1932, and February 26th, 1944 containing 'The Century of Juvenile Drama' by M. Willson Disher, should be especially noted.

Collectors' Items
An occasional miscellany published in Edinburgh, 1953–6.

The Puppet Master
The journal of the British Puppet and Model Theatre Guild. The *Wartime Bulletin* of the Guild, 11th (1941) and 15th (1944) issues, contained important material.

Theatre Notebook
This journal has included several articles, including those by H. D. Spencer (vol. 4), D. Seaton Reid (vols. 5 and 6), Sybil Rosenfeld (vol. 15) and Martin Holmes (vol. 17) 1945–

The following books contain interesting incidental references to the Juvenile Drama:
The Parent's Poetical Present . . . Poems for Juvenile Minds, 2 vols. William Cole, [1829]. (Contains 'The British Stage in Miniature')

John Leech	*Young Troublesome, or Master Jacky's Holidays*, 1845.
William Thackeray	*Vanity Fair*, 1847.
Albert Smith	*The Struggles and Adventures of Christopher Tadpole*, 1848.
Charles Dickens	'A Christmas Tree' in *Household Words*, December 21st, 1850. Reprinted in *Reprinted Pieces*, 1868.
J. Forster	*The Life of Charles Dickens*, 1872.
Anon.	'Looking In at Shop Windows' in *All the Year Round*, June 12th, 1869.
Henry S. Leigh	*Gillott and Goosequill*, 1871. (Contains 'Coloured and Plain'.)
Richard Doyle	*A Journal kept in the Year 1840*, 1885.
[J. F. Wilson]	*A Few Personal Recollections, by an Old Printer*, 1896.
J. B. Howe	*A Cosmopolitan Actor*, 1888.
Percy Fitzgerald	'The Model Theatre' in *The Bachelor's Dilemma and other Stories*, c. 1900.
Ralph Thomas	*Serjeant Thomas and Sir J. E. Millais*, 1901.
Captain R. J. H. Douglas	*The Works of George Cruikshank, Classified and Arranged with Reference to Reid's Catalogue*, 1903.
Brander Matthews	*A Book about the Theater*, 1916.
G. K. Chesterton	*Autobiography*, 1936. *Robert Louis Stevenson*, 1927. See also the biographies by Maisie Ward and Mrs Cecil Chesterton.
D. L. Murray	*Trumpeter Sound*, 1933.
Horace Horsnell	*The Horoscope. A Biographical Poem*, 1934.

(*Penny Plain* by O. Douglas and *Twopence Coloured* by Patrick Hamilton are two novels, having no direct connection with the Juvenile Drama.)

The following books and articles on the allied subjects dealt with in this work have been useful to me; to their authors I express my indebtedness and thanks. These lists are not intended to be complete bibliographies.

FOREIGN TOY THEATRES
Gosta M. Bergman	'Les Agences Théâtrales et l'Impression des mises en scène aux environs de 1800' in *Revue d'Histoire du Théâtre*, II–III, 1956.
Walter Röhler	*Grosse Liebe zu kleinen Theatern*, 1963.

EARLY NINETEENTH-CENTURY POPULAR PRINTS
F. D. Klingender	*Hogarth and English Caricature*, 1944.
Harold Child	'Theatrical Prints' in *The Print Collector's Quarterly*, Vol. XIV, No. 7.
Henry M. Hake	'Dighton Caricatures' in *The Print Collector's Quarterly*, February, October 1926.

Tools and Materials used in Etching and Engraving. A descriptive catalogue of an exhibition at the Victoria and Albert Museum, 1904.

EARLY NINETEENTH-CENTURY CHILDREN'S TOYS AND BOOKS

R. W. Chapman	'The Manners of the Age', in *The Collected Novels of Jane Austen*, 1923.
F. J. Harvey Darton	*Children's Books in England*, 1932.
Percy Muir	*English Children's Books 1600 to 1900*, 1954.
Antonia Fraser	*A History of Toys*, 1966.
F. R. B. Whitehouse	*Table Games of Georgian and Victorian Days*, 1951.
Linda Hannas	*Two Hundred Years of Jigsaw Puzzles*. Introduction to the catalogue of an exhibition at the London Museum, 1968.

THE EARLY NINETEENTH-CENTURY THEATRE

Allardyce Nicoll	*A History of Early Nineteenth Century Drama, 1800–1850*, revised edition 1955.
M. Willson Disher	*Blood and Thunder: mid-Victorian Melodrama and its Origins*, 1949.
M. Willson Disher	*Clowns and Pantomimes*, 1925.
Richard Findlater	*Grimaldi, King of Clowns*, 1955.
H. Barton Baker	*The London Stage*, 1889.
Errol Sherson	*London's Lost Theatres of the Nineteenth Century*, 1925.
Charles Dibdin the Younger	*Professional and Literary Memoirs*, edited by George Speaight, 1956.

Index